Debt, Investment, Slaves

T0307943

DEBT, INVESTMENT, SLAVES

Credit Relations in East Feliciana Parish, Louisiana

1825–1885

Richard Holcombe Kilbourne, Jr.
Foreword by Gavin Wright

The University of Alabama Press

Tuscaloosa

Hardcover edition published 1995.
Paperback edition published 2014.
eBook edition published 2014.

Cover illustration: Sample bank notes from the 1860s; courtesy of the author.

∞

The paper on which this book is printed meets the minimum requirements of
American National Standard for Information Science–Permanence of Paper
for Printed Library Materials, ANSI Z39.48-1984.

Paperback ISBN: 978-0-8173-5775-7
eBook ISBN: 978-0-8173-8755-6

A previous edition of this book has been catalogued by the Library of
Congress as follows:

Library of Congress Cataloging-in-Publication Data

Kilbourne, Richard Holcombe.
Debt, investment, slaves : credit relations in East Feliciana
Parish, Louisiana, 1825–1885 / Richard Holcombe Kilbourne, Jr., with a
foreword by Gavin Wright.
p. cm.
Includes bibliographical references (p.) and index.
ISBN 0-8173-0730-3 (alk. paper)
1. Credit—Louisiana—East Feliciana Parish—History—19th century.
2. Slavery—Louisiana—East Feliciana Parish—History—19th century.
3. Debt—Louisiana—East Feliciana Parish—History—19th century. I. Title.
HG3756.U54K55 1995
332.7'0976316—dc20
94-5785

British Library Cataloguing-in-Publication Data available

To the memory of my great-great-grandfather,
Judge James Gilliam Kilbourne
(Captain, A.Q.M., F & S 4th La. Infantry, C.S.A.)
(1828–1893)

Can you realize that the wealth
of this Parish alone in June, 1860,
was valued at $14,734,895 and *now* it is
reduced about *one seventh* part of that sum?
Our Negro population governs, completely
demoralized, with *1500* colored to 900 white voters.

—Henry Marston to Messrs. Snow, Coyle & Co.,
July 10, 1869

The late Secession war has reduced me very much
in pecuniary point of view (the loss of 60 fine Negroes
being one item, and which has caused me to be left considerably
in debt). If it were otherwise I would not probably think of
asking for a debt against which prescription has run for so
many years—Being old & feeling the effects of poverty,
you can decide whether I do not need it—

—Henry Marston to Mr. J. E. Paschal,
October 12, 1874

[T]he Planters of the South, by the operation of the 13th, 14th,
and 15th Amendments of the Constitution have experienced a
loss of *two thousand millions* of their *slave property* for which
not one dollar of *compensation* is expended . . .

—Henry Marston to President R. B. Hayes,
September 28, 1877

Contents

Foreword

To THE BEST of my knowledge, Richard Kilbourne's book is the first systematic study of the role of slave property in credit contracts. As such, it fills a gaping void in the existing literature on the economics of American slavery. This statement may seem surprising, because slavery has been the object of prodigious historical research, including several massive and well-known quantitative projects. Yet the financial aspects of slavery have been neglected. Even those historical economists who have given a prominent interpretive place to the implications of slave property as a form of wealth, such as Roger Ransom and Richard Sutch, have done so more on the basis of theory than on a detailed examination of portfolios and credit relationships.

With the publication of *Debt, Investment, Slaves*, these topics can no longer be ignored. Kilbourne shows unmistakably that the unique liquidity of slave assets served as the basis for a vast extension of collateralized credit in East Feliciana Parish, and the same store of wealth indirectly supported another huge volume of uncollateralized credit. As a basis for credit, land was distinctly inferior, being illiquid and immobile. In this respect, southern plantations constituted a more "advanced" and financially sophisticated form of agriculture than their family-farm counterparts in the free states. Although Kilbourne's research is concentrated in a single parish in a single southern state, it is difficult to believe (as he argues) that these market fundamentals were essentially different elsewhere in the antebellum South.

Quite possibly, however, the phenomena he describes were unique to the United States, where favorable demographic and economic conditions caused slave values to soar, creating an unprecedented focus on slave assets as an object of accumulation. This conjecture and others will undoubtedly come in for more rigorous scrutiny in comparative studies following on Kilbourne's lead. His research thus advances an important new trend in economic history, the increased interest in financial institutions and markets and their role in economic development.

Kilbourne is not an academic historian by profession, and as a result his presentation is often not closely keyed to the familiar longstanding debates in the literature. For some readers this feature may require an adjustment, but I see it as an advantage. Kilbourne brings to the subject a strong technical background in the law, including a facility with modern descendants of the financial instruments on which he reports in the book. His independence from established historical camps also allows him to transcend some scholarly arguments that have long since become stale. For example, the issue of whether southern planters displayed a "capitalist mentality" seems quite beside the point, when one contemplates the extreme levels of wealth held by even moderate slaveholders, and the fact that their wealth was held in a unique form unavailable to nonresidents of the region, however entrepreneurial they might have been.

Kilbourne's evidence is equally relevant for understanding the wrenching restructuring of economic relationships after the war. To be sure, the trauma of emancipation and reconstruction involved much more than the "implosion" of credit so vividly described in what follows: war, politics, violence, racial fears, and the full range of human ambitions and emotions. But Kilbourne shows that the financial adjustment would have been cataclysmic, even if none of these additional elements had been present, because the collateral underpinning the entire credit structure had been destroyed and could not be replaced. This is surely sufficient reason for students of American history to give this book their closest attention.

Gavin Wright
Stanford University

Acknowledgments

I HAVE RECEIVED invaluable assistance from two people in particular. Gavin Wright read and commented on an early draft and was especially helpful in suggesting revisions in the Introduction. Tony Freyer also read an early draft and made a number of useful suggestions.

Most of my research was in the judicial archives of East Feliciana Parish. The Honorable Debbie Hudnall, Clerk of the Twentieth Judicial District, afforded me every convenience during the two years spent in research. Deputy Clerks Amanda Smith and Mandy Hall patiently retrieved ancient suit records from storage.

The staff of the Louisiana and Lower Mississippi Valley Collections at Louisiana State University was always helpful and considerate. The many who have assisted me over the years include Bob Martin, Director of Special Collections, the late Stone Miller, Judy Bolton, Faye Phillips, Luana Henderson, Sally Power, Steve Collins, Louise Martin, Anne Edwards, Merna Ford, Linda Schneider, and Jo Jackson. Colin Hamer and Wayne Everard of the Louisiana Division of the New Orleans Public Library always went beyond the call of duty during my visits to that institution.

The Louisiana State University History Department sponsored a colloquium for graduate students on my research, which I found very valuable. Special thanks to Paul Paskoff, Tom Owen, and Edward Muir, Jr.

An early version of Chapter 3 was the subject of a paper that I read at the annual meeting of the American Society for Legal History in 1990. Panel participants Joseph W. McKnight, Judith K. Schafer, and James Viator all provided helpful comments.

Thanks also to the people at Your Extra Staff of Baton Rouge, who typed the numerous drafts of my manuscript.

Sherry L. Womble was responsible for the copy editing, and she did a superb job.

I am most grateful to the members of the staff of the University of Alabama Press for all of their many contributions to making my book more readable and accessible. Malcolm M. MacDonald, director of the Press, was very efficient in guiding the manuscript through the review process and has responded to all of my queries and concerns with great sensitivity.

The research and writing of this book would not have been possible without the generous financial support of my parents. I hope the fruits of my labors and their capital does them proud.

Glossary

accommodation endorser—One who endorses a note for the purpose of guaranteeing the payment of the note, thereby lending his credit to the borrower.

accommodation note—Usually a promissory note, but sometimes drawn in the form of a bill of exchange, draft, or check, that is collateralized by the endorsement of an accommodation endorser.

antichresis—A pledge of immovable property. A debtor gives income from the pledged property to his creditor in lieu of interest on the debt. In Louisiana income from property subject to an antichresis is applied to reducing the principal indebtedness as well.

bill of exchange—A credit instrument drawn by the maker in favor of a designated payee or order on funds in the hands of a third party. Bills of exchange may be payable at sight or after some stated period of time.

bill of lading—A written contract for the shipment of goods issued by a shipping concern. Such instruments were conspicuous in the shipment of staples from producers to consumers and served as collaterals for short-term credit arrangements.

cession for the benefit of creditors (cessio bonorum)—An insolvent debtor's assignment of all his property to a syndic or syndics for the benefit of his creditors. This is the Civil Law equivalent of bankruptcy.

collateral security note—A debt instrument that is secured by mortgage or pledge of collaterals; one of many tautologies for which the law is famous.

commercial paper—Bills of exchange, promissory notes, drafts, and other negotiable instruments that are governed by the law merchant.

community of acquets or gains—The legally imposed matrimonial regime in Louisiana. Formerly, the husband was the administrator of the community and could alienate assets acquired during the marriage.

discounting—The negotiation or sale of commercial paper, either with a deduction of accrued interest or for a sum less than the face of the instrument.

endorsement—The signature of a payee, drawee, accommodating party, or holder of a negotiable instrument on the back of the instrument for the purpose of negotiating it.

evidence of indebtedness—A promissory note or other instrument that on its face evidences a debt.

holder in due course—One who acquires any negotiable instrument in the ordinary course of business, taking it free of any equitable defenses any preceding party might have to payment of the debt shown on the face of the instrument.

immovable—Real property. In Louisiana slaves were classified as immovables.

mortgage—In Louisiana a right granted by a debtor to his creditor over real property of the debtor for the securing of a debt. The mortgage entitles the creditor to have such property seized and sold to satisfy his claim in the event the debtor defaults.

movable—A personal chattel such as a stock, bond, or debt or credit instrument and any property that is movable.

negotiable instrument—A promissory note, bill of exchange, draft, check, or letter of credit that invests any subsequent holder with legal title, whether by endorsement or delivery.

notarial paraph—The notary's recitation on an evidence of indebtedness for the purpose of identifying the instrument with a collateral instrument such as a mortgage.

paraphernal property—Extradotal property; that is, the wife's property, which forms no part of her dowry.

pledge—The physical delivery of collateral to a creditor by a debtor or a third party as security for a debt. Under Louisiana law a pledge can only be effected with movable collaterals (but see antichresis).

prescription—A manner of acquiring ownership of property, movable and immovable, or of discharging debts by the passage of time. Certain formal requisites must be met before prescription is deemed to have run.

privilege—A right of preference to be paid ahead of other creditors that arises by operation of law. The nature of the debt not only determines the ranking of creditors vis-à-vis each other but also which property of the debtor may be subject to a privilege.

promissory note—A written promise to pay a specific sum, at a future time or on demand, to a named individual or his order, or bearer. Such a note may be negotiable or nonnegotiable.

suretyship—A security device whereby one person, the surety, contracts to guarantee the obligation of another, the principal. Under Louisiana law an accommodation endorser is deemed to be a surety.

syndic—A trustee appointed to represent the creditors of the estate of an insolvent person.

testator—A person who dies leaving a valid will.

usufruct—The right of enjoyment of a thing belonging to another and drawing "from the same all the profit, utility and advantage which it may produce, provided it be without altering the substance of the thing" (Louisiana Civil Code, Article 533).

writ of fieri facias—A writ of execution commanding the sheriff to levy on property of a judgment debtor to satisfy that judgment.

Debt, Investment, Slaves

Introduction

THIS STUDY BEGAN as an attempt to quantify the role of slaves in credit transactions. Did slave owners collateralize their debts with slave property? Logically, this should have been the case because transactions on the slave market were made in cash. As research progressed it became apparent that a significant body of material in postbellum suit records regarding antebellum credit relations was beyond the pale of the Civil War. Indeed, the overall collapse of the credit economy during and after the war and the surge of collection proceedings in its wake yielded a voluminous amount of material that but for the war and the emancipation would never have been recorded.

Much of the literature on the antebellum southern economy has conjectured about the role of slaves in collateralized credit relations. According to Gavin Wright, "Abolition destroyed the basis for credit in the antebellum economy. The movability of slaves and the well-developed slave markets made them highly attractive as collateral for loans, even at long distance."[1] Roger L. Ransom notes that "antebellum planters had ample collateral to cover any shortfall that might arise from year to year, whereas tenant farmers after the war could offer no such financial buffer."[2] Gerald David Jaynes observes that the implications of emancipation for the credit system were not lost on contemporaries.[3] Harold D. Woodman's classic study of the nineteenth-century South's credit system, *King Cotton and His Retainers*, largely bypasses the whole subject of slave property in credit relations.[4]

Nowhere does there exist a comprehensive evaluation of the scope and magnitude of the credit resources in the southern economy before and after the emancipation. *Time on the Cross*, by Robert William Fogel and Stanley L. Engerman, approaches slavery as a labor system with particular attention to profitability and productivity. Fogel's *Without Consent or Contract* is concerned primarily with questions about the development of the southern economy, demographics, slave culture, and the ideological and political campaign that eventually overthrew slavery in the South. George D. Green's study of Louisiana banking and Larry Schweikart's book on antebellum southern banking both deal with chartered banking in the region. Much of the banking in the antebellum South was outside such regular channels, particularly in the financing of plantation agriculture. How slavery shaped the development of the South's financial system, along with planters' perceptions regarding property rights in human beings as financial assets, remains to be explored.[5]

Antebellum East Feliciana Parish was not altogether typical of the several hundred counties and parishes that made up the Cotton Belt. It was among the handful of relatively large population concentrations in Louisiana, outside of New Orleans, during the first five decades of the nineteenth century. Settlements in the parish preceded those in other areas of the state by decades. Many wealthy households had been resident in the parish for two and three generations, a pattern that appears to have been relatively rare in slavery's westward migration. By 1860 as many as one-quarter of all planter households had acquired land elsewhere in Louisiana and Texas—especially in the alluvial areas of central and southern Louisiana—and had established plantations in those regions. During the 1840s and 1850s, owners did transport slaves from the parish to the alluvial lands, but they and their families generally chose to continue to reside in the parish. Few landowners in the parish were absentees, but many residents did own property elsewhere.

Health considerations, no doubt, were critical in the determination of many to remain in the parish. Location was another. The parish was an easy day's journey from New Orleans. It was also above the fever line, and epidemics in the city generally did not spread to the locality, though the great yellow fever epidemic of 1853 occasioned much loss of life.

However distinctive the parish may have been in its geography and sociology, the market fundamentals surely were the same as those elsewhere in the cotton South. The slave market was regionwide, and prices in the locality only reinforce this truth. The land market, however, was localized across the region, and land was not a significant portion of most planter portfolios in the parish.

Most of Wright's findings regarding the region apply to East Feliciana Parish, particularly in the postbellum decades. An insular labor market, relative to the rest of the United States, led to a localized credit system, and Wright notes that "the isolation of the labor market was the basis for the isolation of the capital market" in the postbellum period.[6]

What about the antebellum credit system? To what extent was it uniquely southern? Whatever the consequences of labor market efficiencies in the antebellum South, slavery did create a regionwide class of property holders vitally interested in the institution of slavery.[7] Slavery, I argue, made for unique credit markets as well, or more precisely, a regionwide and unified credit market with perhaps two or three subregions. The New Orleans region encompassed most of the lower Mississippi Valley. Charleston and Richmond were the major credit centers for the Atlantic seaboard.

In the last decades of the antebellum period, the southern credit market appears to have undergone a rapid consolidation, especially at the three primary centers mentioned above. The interstate slave trade created a demand for long-distance financial services across the region. That trade gave a tremendous impetus to the consolidation of southern capital markets in the late antebellum period.

Michael Tadman and others have remarked on the cash nexus that drove the interstate slave trade.[8] Liquefying that trade was a need peculiar to the South, and it required Gargantuan exchange operations, by contemporary standards, to organize the flow of wealth back to the slave-exporting states on the eastern seaboard from the slave-importing states in the lower Mississippi Valley.

Chapter 1 concerns the early decades of the nineteenth century, the years before the consolidation of the credit system at New Orleans. In the years before 1845, the credit market was in many respects localized. That is not to say that planters in places such as East Feliciana did not obtain loans from afar, particularly from factors in New Orleans, but local lenders did predominate.

Slave mortgages, for example, often collateralized third-party endorsers (i.e., accommodation endorsers), not distant cotton factors in the city who might in fact be making such loans by accepting and discounting accommodation paper. A city lender relied on the creditworthiness of the endorser, not slaves pledged by the borrower, to secure the endorser against the potential of default. That pattern of contingent guaranties, which emerged in the early decades of the nineteenth century, was decisive in the evolution of the credit system and was repeated countless times as the economy of the region grew and credit markets consolidated in places such as New Orleans. While chartered banks were relatively less numerous in the antebellum South than in the North, they were on average much larger, a powerful indicator of consolidation across the region.

By 1860 the factorage system had evolved into a regionwide network of private investment banks. Such private banks rarely had more than one hundred clients but typically had upwards of one million dollars in assets invested in financing plantation agriculture.[9] Factors as financial agents or private bankers are the subject of Chapter 2.

Factors gained in stature as financial agents for plantation agriculture in the two decades before 1860. What role they played in making a secondary market for "plantation" debt securities is obscure. The forces that gave rise to the formation of this complex market in plantation debt, which may well have drawn participants from far beyond the borders of the slave states, are equally obscure.

The slave market was a cash market, but credit sales predominated in the market for acreage tracts. The buyer of a slave acquired a fairly predictable income stream, so the slave was fully priced. The seller of acreage on credit hoped to acquire an income stream by financing the sale with interest for a period of years, but whether such hopes were realized depended upon the industry and good fortune of the buyer. Some acreage did change hands for cash, but at substantial discounts. A seller of acreage on credit had an expectation that the purchaser would enhance his collateral with improvements on the land, but he had no way of guaranteeing that such improvements would be made. The claim against the purchaser on credit was highly contingent. Land was an insignificant factor in the development of the credit system.

How dependent was the South on northern credit markets? Woodman devotes a chapter in *King Cotton and His Retainers* to the subject of the dependent South, relying principally on the despair-filled declarations of southern commercial boosters and conventions.[10] In fact, most of the internal investment in the region was funded with savings that had been accumulated over several generations in numerous wealthy households throughout the Cotton Belt.

Credit facilities outside the region were required in the marketing of cotton. Short-term exchange transactions facilitated the movement of the staple from plantations to consumers in New England and Europe.

The typical cotton planter is represented as always being a year behind in meeting his obligations, incurring debts during the planting season in the winter and spring months and settling them when the cotton was sold in the fall.[11] Many planters in the lower Mississippi Valley settled with supply wholesalers in New Orleans and St. Louis monthly by drafting on their factors. A factorage firm covered such drafts either with an extension of credit to the drawer or with funds deposited by the drawer. If the firm ever needed to raise funds it generally did so by borrowing short term from a city bank or private investor. Such loans were collateralized with pledges of promissory notes drawn by firm clients. Such notes generally evidenced long-term loans by a firm to its clients. Most notes were never collateralized with mortgages on slaves or other real property. Factors also pledged accepted drafts (i.e., the drawee, or firm, guaranteed payment) to third parties to raise current funds to honor such drafts.

What is important is not whether planters were chronically in debt (short-term) to their factors, but the practical result of numerous factors providing short-term and long-term financing on secured and unsecured notes. Such facilities offset the absence of a futures market. The need for a futures market only became apparent when factors ceased being able to provide for their clients' credit needs after the war. Another aspect of a planter's credit relationship with his factor was the possibility that he also had substantial savings in cash equivalents in the hands of his factor, who acted as his financial agent. A planter might still require short-term loans and thus could be

both creditor and debtor of his commission merchant. Short-term borrowings, offset by long-term investments, would not be surprising.

The debt that planters contracted during the planting season on open
accounts should be excluded from calculations of overall debt levels, unless
settlement at the end of the season was with an unsecured promissory note.
Calculating the level of such debts is practically impossible. Most planters not
only settled such debts at the end of each year, but many also probably had
sufficient cash with their factors to carry them forward for some time to
come. Clinton, Louisiana, planter and businessman Henry Marston was chagrined when bad harvests in the 1870s left him in debt to his factor even a
few hundred dollars. No planter enjoyed losing money on a planting operation.

During the antebellum period, a planter might expect to obtain advances
from his merchant up to the value of his forthcoming crop. Such generous
short-term credit facilities were not to be had after the war, although, para-
doxically, the staple became central to the credit system in the three turbulent
years after 1865.

Long-term and most short-term financing were direct consequences of
substantial savings accumulations in the region. Whether those savings were
invested in slaves, debt instruments, railroad bonds, or bank stocks is beside
the point. Antebellum agriculture was substantially capitalized, and a huge
store of highly liquid savings vehicles stabilized the credit markets in the
region.

Slaves represented a huge store of highly liquid wealth that ensured the
financial stability and viability of planting operations even after a succession
of bad harvests, years of low prices, or both. Slave property clearly collateralized a variety of credit instruments and was by far the most liquid asset in
most planter portfolios, yet Woodman has argued that because numerous
slaveholders could not liquefy their slave holdings simultaneously without
causing a general price collapse, both the high value and liquidity of slave
property are somehow illusory. As repugnant as it may seem from our vantage point in the last decade of the twentieth century, an investment in slaves
was a rational choice, given the alternatives for storing savings in the middle
of the last century.[12]

Our own concept of "savings" is in large part shaped by the choices that
are available to us for storing wealth for future needs. No one who watched
the stock market collapse in 1987 can forget what happened to a modern
equities market when financial assets, which represented only a small percentage of market capitalization, were liquidated by numerous and panicky stockholders. Perhaps valuations quoted daily on the New York Stock Exchange are
illusory, and their true value will only be established after the entire market

capitalization is liquidated, whether into dollars, deutsche marks, or rubles. Valuations for slaves were realistic, and considering the available choices for investing savings, investing in slaves was an attractive option. Under the Woodman hypothesis, those with savings could only stash them in gold, cash, or cash equivalents.[13]

Perhaps the most difficult thing to appreciate about the Old South is just how wealthy many plantation households were. It is well known, for example, that two-thirds of the millionaires in the United States in 1860 lived in the South. Ten percent of the free families in East Feliciana Parish were multi-millionaires in today's dollars. As previously mentioned, much of their banking was conducted through factorage firms, not chartered commercial banks.

The fact that numerous slaveholders derived most of their income from capital is a socioeconomic paradox in American economic history. It was not just that there were rich people in the South or in East Feliciana Parish; rather, it was that they were so numerous and constituted a sizable minority. Managing and augmenting the capital of a rich clientele were functions well suited to private investment bankers, and here the factorage firms filled an obvious niche. However, such functions were largely anachronistic after emancipation.

It is my contention that the antebellum South was very much a society of rentiers, and the rentier psychology may well have been as pronounced among planters as it was among those who invested in planters' debt securities. This observation would be consistent with a population that derived the greater part of its income from capital (i.e., slaves). Such a population would likewise have been considerably more averse to risk than the entrepreneur usually associated with the development of America's manufacturing industries.

The rentier mentality is consistent with Wright's contention that planters had a loose association with the land, that they were "laborlords," not "landlords."[14] A survey of the land market during the 1850s showed that an acre of land was twenty times more likely to change hands than a slave. On average, 6 percent of all the land in the parish was sold every year, and the percentage of "improved" acreage sold was no doubt much higher. On average, .25 percent of the indigenous slave population probably changed hands yearly. The total dollars in the cash market for slaves, however, dwarfed that for acreage tracts by a ratio of four to one.

To say that a rentier mentality was pervasive in the Old South, however, should not be construed to mean that the slave economy was stagnant and that planters as a class were largely indifferent to or ignorant of their own economic self-interests. Preoccupation with income streams simply reflected the realities common to most pre-twentieth-century agricultural societies. Profits from agriculture, after all, financed the first industrial revolution. The key to understanding the rentier mentality is to recognize that profits from growing staples were highly contingent; the successful planter at some point had to choose whether winning gambles should be reinvested in expanding production or invested in relatively riskless, heavily collateralized income streams generated by third parties.

Aftermath

Rentiers disappeared with the war, along with slavery, plantation agriculture, factors, and long-term loans to agriculture. In less than a decade, the credit system retraced decades of consolidation, growth, and expanding sophistication. Like the units of production in postwar agriculture, credit fragmented, attenuated, and became largely localized.

Roger Ransom and Richard Sutch have argued in *One Kind of Freedom* that the loss of slave capital occasioned by the emancipation was more apparent than real because ownership passed from the slaveholder to the former slave. Their proposition has not gone unchallenged by other economic historians. In this study I argue that slave wealth was integral to a complex financial system that supported a debt load across the region that may have been in the hundreds of millions of dollars. Once the underlying security (i.e., the assets that produced the income streams) was stripped away, the value of such obligations plummeted to nothing.[15]

In the South's financial centers, especially New Orleans, the implications of the emancipation for long-standing financial relationships were apparent years before the war had ended. Discounting of short-term paper ceased. A speculation in mortgage debt ensued, driven, not by certainty in the future value of such bonds, but by the eroding value of Confederate notes and bonds. In the aftermath most of the mortgage-backed paper proved to be wholly worthless. Ninety percent of the city's factorage firms failed, either during the war or within the succeeding decade. The impoverishment of the South's propertied class is a unique event in American economic history.

We are accustomed to viewing massive economic contractions in modern western history as troughs in which economies reform themselves, revive, and emerge to prosper on sounder footing. This did not happen in consequence of the credit implosion occasioned by the Civil War. What happened in the South is without parallels. The inflation that decimated post–World War I Germany invites comparisons, but those at the top of the economic pyramid were able to shield their capital from the worst effects of the financial disaster. The bankrupting of the southern propertied classes was considerably more generalized.

A more apt comparison might be Russia after the 1917 revolution. The Communists simply outlawed private property. The long-term consequences of the destruction of private property rights in Russia after 1917 will someday be evaluated, no doubt.

Slaves were the major component in the wealth structure of the Old South. The Thirteenth Amendment to the United States Constitution "outlawed" property rights in human beings, and no politician outside the South ever contemplated a system for compensating owners. Jaynes estimated that slave capital represented 45.8 percent of the total wealth of the cotton-producing states and observed that "the uncompensated loss of such a significant fraction of the region's real wealth dealt the financial system a severe blow. . . . this loss of social wealth created serious inefficiencies in southern credit markets which permeated the entire economic system."[16]

It is little wonder that Wright concluded that emancipation was an economic revolution that decidedly overthrew all that had gone before. About the old planter class itself he wrote: "If, after the Revolution, the members of a class rigorously pursue goals they staunchly opposed before, in what economic sense has that class survived?"[17] There are, then, ample and good reasons for scrupulously avoiding parallels and contrasts between the two eras.

Wright indicates that much of the postbellum malaise can be traced to the credit system—its localization, the transfer of "financial" risks to tenants and sharecroppers, and, implicitly, the disintegration of the old factorage system.[18] The regional system of private banks did collapse with the emancipation, at least at the financial Mecca of the lower Mississippi Valley—New Orleans. Credit was indeed localized and short-term after the war.

But to explain how the postbellum agricultural system finally evolved, it is necessary to make a clearer correlation between planting arrangements and credit arrangements. In *Branches Without Roots* Jaynes writes that the "forces which altered the credit system cannot be separated from the broader questions concerned with the evolution of the tenancy system."[19] My study certainly supports his conclusion. It is my contention that furnishing merchants only became a presence in the local credit market after landlords lost the options of furnishing their laborers and purchasing their supplies wholesale.

What Ransom and Sutch attribute to the furnishing merchant's seeming territorial monopoly I contend was a loss of capacity in the system to spread planting risks throughout the region and perhaps beyond. "Debt peonage," rather than being an instrument of exploitation, simply reflected the end result of a process that was under way even before the war had ended. The postbellum South, despite the efforts of lawmakers and judges to repudiate antebellum debts, began heavily in debt. Debt distress characterized the first postwar decade, and what had been largely confined to the upper rungs of the economic ladder simply "trickled" down to the lowest. Large-scale planters had been able to finance their operations far more efficiently and with far fewer risks of default than was to be the case with the family-size unit of production that became standard after the war.

It may seem to beg the obvious, but the extent of the debt problem in the immediate aftermath of the war seems to have gone largely unappreciated by historians of postbellum agriculture. Jaynes underscores an obvious truth when he writes that the emancipation had ramifications far beyond a transfer of ownership of legal personality from masters to slaves.[20]

War and emancipation did not mark a clean break with the past. The New South began in an economy dominated by debt, in part a legacy of the Old South's imploded credit structure and in part a consequence of the war and the abrupt interruption of income streams from plantation agriculture. The temptation to relieve pressed debtors was too much, even for a legislature dominated by radical Republicans and a state supreme court composed of antisecessionist politicians. The task of debt repudiation ultimately devolved on the state supreme court. The justices accomplished their work in a series of important decisions rendered in the years from 1866 to 1868.

Land redistribution was the last thing on anyone's mind, at least in Louisiana. The supreme court's largely unenunciated policy was to preserve the plantation as the basic unit of production in the hands of its prewar owner. This meant that those who had purchased slaves before the war on credit were no longer liable for payment to their vendors or innocent third parties who had purchased such debts in the ordinary course of business. Those many unfortunates who had contracted obligations in Confederate currency were determined to be bound no longer to those who had lent them money or conferred other valuable considerations on them. Finally, the court concluded that not even war and the consequent closure of most courts of law in Louisiana for a period of years interrupted the running of prescription. Many creditors lost simply because their claims had prescribed. A careful reading of more than one hundred cases from this period leaves the impression that law is an illusion. Most of the jurisprudence from this period ought to be ignored because many of the doctrines set forth therein were at least indirectly repudiated by the United States Supreme Court in the 1870s.

Despite the state supreme court's best efforts, the debt legacy remained a serious drag on the economy for more than a decade. The amount of new debt contracted in subsequent decades was scant by antebellum standards, but it seemed many times more burdensome, and was. Much of that burden was a consequence of rising interest rates in a period of rapid asset deflation. In East Feliciana, the crisis year appears to have been 1874, when a poor harvest, combined with low staple prices, resulted in the failure of most furnishing merchants in the area, the theft of cotton from the fields by starving tenants, and an upsurge of political violence. The black sheriff was wounded in an attempted assassination, and the black legislative representative was murdered.

Much of the literature on the postwar South focuses on three things: changes in units of production in agriculture, whether antebellum planter elites survived war and the Reconstruction and recovered their economic and political status in subsequent decades, and whether newly emancipated blacks were saddled with a new kind of servitude. An analysis of the credit system usually begins with an examination of the much-maligned crop lien, or privilege, as it is called in Louisiana, and how furnishing merchants used this instrumentality to force tenant farmers to overproduce cotton at the expense of self-sufficiency in food crops.[21]

One important point about the crop lien or privilege seems to have been overlooked. The privilege simply established a security or collateral interest in the standing crop, and in Louisiana the legislation set forth the order in which classes of creditors would have their claims enforced. Most furnishers of supplies, whether those supplies were barrels of flour, pork, or other provisions, extended credit during the planting season, and most of the borrowers had no collateral; therefore, the furnishers were in fact unsecured creditors. A crop of cotton was always at risk until it was harvested, baled, and shipped. The *collateral* was always contingent upon the making of a crop. A furnishing merchant who sold on credit to poor sharecroppers and tenants assumed greater risks than those usually associated with secured creditors. He was more akin to a passive investor or limited partner.

Estimating default rates is difficult. Some borrowers probably defaulted but were able to settle such claims at a subsequent time. Other defaulters were never sued; either they died or left the area. Privileges filed in the mortgage records in the parish by furnishing merchants during the decade of the 1870s and collection suits prosecuted by those same merchants indicate that a 25 percent default rate was not uncommon. Were it possible to factor in uncollectible claims and claims ultimately settled, default rates might well be higher.

The furnishing merchant could only spread such losses to his other credit customers. Consolidation of the credit system and wealth levels in antebellum agriculture had spread such risks across the entire region. The localization of credit was an inevitable result of the disintegration of plantation agriculture. Crop privileges and exorbitant interest rates were only symptomatic of the loss of wealth in the region and a radically changed configuration for producing staples for distant markets.

Possible Implications

In a recent article, Ransom and Sutch argue that a growing slave population and rising prices retarded economic growth in the South because they depressed savings rates, a possibility Wright raises in *Old South, New South*.

The following discussion does not propose a contrary thesis but merely reports some findings about the local debt market and wealth levels in the parish that may have some import for the Ransom and Sutch thesis.[22]

Rising prices and growth in the slave population may well have depressed savings rates across the region, as Ransom and Sutch contend, but there is evidence of some diversification into financial assets among the wealthiest households—those with wealth levels above fifty thousand dollars. No doubt much of that diversification only found its way back into slave agriculture in the form of loans collateralized with mortgages. Still, total debt levels do not appear to have risen above a small percentage of gross assets. Much of the debt accumulated by planters in the parish during the 1850s might well be explained by the expense of bringing more acreage into cultivation to meet the growing demand for staples.

In the 1850s it was the middle-tier planters who mortgaged their slaves and plantations. The major exceptions were found among the half-dozen sugar planters in the parish, whose households were among the twenty richest in the parish. Sugar plantations, as a rule, seem to have had a more leveraged capital structure than was the case with cotton plantations. Such operations demanded heavy investments in processing facilities and equipment. Sugar plantations were uniformly large—a few hundred operations spread across the state's southern parishes accounted for the bulk of the production and processing.

Had there been consistent productivity gains on cotton plantations, one would expect to find much higher collateralized debt levels as a percentage of gross wealth, not only among middle-tier planters but among the richest as well. One would also expect to find passive investors in plantations who took no part in the management but owned shares in such enterprises. There is some evidence of this in the organization of factorage firms (i.e., commercial partnerships with limited partners who contributed capital and remained passive investors).

The wealthiest planters had surplus income to invest but encountered inhibitory risk-reward ratios if they chose to invest in and expand their own planting operations. Optimal plantation size may well have fallen into the range of what is described as middle-size, as Wright suggests.[23] Wealthy planters had good cause to seek stable income streams beyond their own plantations and thus to diversify the risks inherent in growing cotton or other staples.

An awareness of risk-reward ratios may well have been characteristic of middle-tier planters as well in the arrangement of their portfolios. The reliability of the census reports is questionable as to the extent or degree that they accurately reflect wealth held in debt securities or other such investments.

The growth of debt was constrained, not only by the expectation of growth in income streams, but also by an accompanying risk aversion psychology characteristic of wealthy rentiers who sought to preserve their capital and income streams first, rather than growing their fortunes into greater fortunes. If southern plantation agriculture at this juncture was incapable of regular sustained productivity gains, the possibility for income growth was likewise constrained unless more acreage was brought into production. However, expanding production was not an option unless the demand for cotton continued to grow. The 1850s witnessed an expansion in acreage planted in staples that was consistent with the growth in demand, but long-term debt levels remained fairly stable as a percentage of gross wealth. As previously mentioned, the growth of long-term debt during the decade of the 1850s can be largely explained as a response to the growth in demand for cotton.

A rough measure of long-term (five years) debt levels among planters with middle-size holdings (the usual customers for collateralized loans) was between 10 and 20 percent of gross wealth. Since planters in this group were wealthy, it is not unlikely that they were themselves prudent borrowers. In East Feliciana, the majority never contracted a collateralized loan. Some of the growth in collateralized debt may also have been due to a demand for such investment opportunities from those with funds to lend (i.e., wealth in search of income-producing assets such as bonds on plantations).

Arguably, slave prices above replacement costs should be factored into any estimate of potential future income, but the debt market appears to have been intolerant of leveraging unrealized capital gains. Asset-based lending may well have occurred in the decade of the 1830s during the heyday of the property banks, but those years were something of an aberration in the history of both the state and the locality. Borrowers in the 1850s were not selling equity in their plantations—they were selling future income represented by bonds.

Long-term debt levels alone do not confirm a conclusion that asset inflation in the 1850s, especially the dollar value of slaves, was depressing savings rates in the South or that the typical planter was obsessed with windfalls from rising slave prices. The propertied class was very much interested in augmenting income streams, not just from slave agriculture but from any asset that offered the possibility of diversification and a regular stream of income.

Risk aversion would not be a unique response, given the imponderables of staple production and the limited possibilities of productivity gains. The long-term debt load of the typical planter with medium-size holdings was light enough to ensure that the average income stream from planting operations over a term of five to ten years would be sufficient to meet all demands on that income.

In summary, income streams appear to be the dominant factor influencing long-term debt levels. The growth, sophistication, and consolidation of southern debt markets was only possible because there was a large class of rentiers actively engaged in buying income streams from slave agriculture. Many, perhaps, owned no slaves, but like other nonslaveholders in the southern economy, they were vitally interested in that peculiar institution.

Research Methods

This study is based primarily on a comprehensive survey of parish mortgage records. Louisiana, like most states, had and has a system of public registration for both conveyances of real property and contracts that create security interests in real property in favor of particular creditors. In Louisiana a mortgage is a contract whereby a debtor grants to his creditor, as security for a debt, a right over real property, and such property can be seized and sold in default of payment. It is a contract that is ancillary to the principal obligation, which is to repay a loan. In some common law jurisdictions, a mortgage effects a conditional conveyance of the property to the creditor, and such a conveyance is voided when the performance of the act secured thereby is accomplished (i.e., repayment of a loan). To be valid against the claim of a third person, a mortgage must be recorded in a public registry, usually located at the county or parish courthouse. In Louisiana, at least, the mortgage records are the best indicator we are ever likely to have of long-term debt levels in a locality.

The recordation of a mortgage is effective for a period of ten years, and the instrument may be reinscribed thereafter for an additional ten years. If the loan is repaid, the mortgage usually is canceled by the clerk of court upon application of the debtor. The fact that antebellum mortgages were reinscribed after ten years is a persuasive indicator of long-term debt arrangements—arrangements that all but disappeared from the postbellum records.

The survey of antebellum mortgage records spans the following periods: 1825–1829, 1834–1839, 1841–1846, and 1853–1868. The transactions analyzed and abstracted totaled upwards of five thousand. Not all of the entries were mortgages, however; credit sales of land and slaves, credit sales of succession (estate) property, and judgments on collection suits were among the instruments recorded in the mortgage records.

Debtors in the 1850s collateralized in excess of $1 million in debts, most of which represented long-term commitments by creditors in the parish and at New Orleans. In 1860 it is doubtful that such debtors in fact owed the face value of all the debts collateralized during the previous ten years; some portion of that total would have been paid off. There is evidence elsewhere, in factorage firm liquidations and collection suit records, that not all long-term debt arrangements were collateralized.

Another source of long-term debt was credit sales of land. Much of the improved acreage in the parish was encumbered with sellers' privileges, also recorded in the mortgage records. On the basis of this survey, I estimate that long-term debt levels in the parish had reached $1.5 million by 1860—about 10 percent of the gross wealth reported by parish residents in the 1860 census.

Short-term debt (i.e., annualized open accounts with local merchants and New Orleans factors) may have added another $1 million to the total debt load, but that figure is probably much too high. The furnisher of necessary supplies to a plantation or farm had a lien or privilege "on the product of the . . . [previous year's] crop and the crop at present in the ground."[24] The furnisher's loan was collateralized by operation of law; there was no provision for recording this kind of security in the mortgage records. A creditor might well have asked for and obtained a mortgage on slaves or other property in the event his claim was not satisfied out of the proceeds of the crop. Most debts contracted on open accounts were not, however, collateralized by the privilege. Cash advances and drafts accepted and charged to such accounts were not collateralized with a privilege until after the Civil War, when the privilege was extended to such charges.

Scholars of the postbellum economy owe a debt of gratitude to the party responsible for the 1868 constitution's requirement that all privileges on standing crops and other property had to be recorded in the mortgage records to be effective against third parties. Such recordings added to the transaction costs for poor sharecroppers, but they give fairly precise numbers for short-term (less than one year) credit facilities provided by landowners and furnishing merchants to sharecroppers and tenants. The years surveyed are 1870–1871, 1875–1876, 1879–1881, and 1885. I would have preferred to abstract every transaction recorded from 1868 through 1885, but the recordings for those years exceed all the recordings for the antebellum period. In 1879, for example, 633 supply privileges were recorded with a face value of just $84,812.94. Eighty-four creditors are represented, some with only one contract, and three others with a total of 253 contracts.

Local furnishing merchants probably did not formally collateralize all their open accounts with recordings of crop privileges or crop pledges (after 1874). Still, it is clear that if they collateralized only 50 percent of their accounts, the total amount of credit available on a year-to-year basis was no more than 20 to 30 percent of what had been available during the 1850s. As previously mentioned, long-term debt arrangements all but disappeared. I would suggest that credit facilities in the 1870s were about 40 percent of the anticipated value of the forthcoming cotton crop, and that such credit rarely extended beyond six months. I did an extensive examination of collection suit records to develop a crude estimate of default rates.

I also did a survey of land and slave sales for the decade of the 1850s. The years examined were 1847, 1850, 1853, 1856, and 1859. Nowhere is the value of slave property in the local economy more apparent than in the radical divergence of cash sale markets for slaves and land.

The reader may at times wish for more precise numbers where I have only dared estimates, and certitude about conclusions drawn from highly nuanced sources. Nevertheless, it is well to remember that there is no model that conveniently encompasses an unwieldy body of legal source materials. It is to be hoped that this study will provide some useful insights for other researchers in their exploration of the rich and vast body of source materials that remains locked away in courthouses across the South.

East Feliciana Parish in 1860

Plantation agriculture dominated the economy of East Feliciana Parish in the middle of the nineteenth century. Forty percent of the seven hundred free households were involved in planting. Two-thirds of all free households owned at least one slave. The free population numbered about four thousand, and the slave population exceeded ten thousand. From 50 to 60 percent of the free population lived in one of the three small towns in the parish—Clinton, Jackson, or Port Hudson. Most local businesses provided services for the plantations in the area.

The distribution of slaves among free households suggests that ownership of slaves may have been in the process of becoming more concentrated in the last two decades of the antebellum period. In 1860 25 percent of the free households engaged in planting owned at least 50 percent of the slaves. The 1860 census listed fifty-four households with wealth accumulations from $50,000 to $100,000. Eighteen households had wealth accumulations of $100,000 to $400,000, and two households had wealth exceeding $400,000. Some of the wealthiest people in the United States lived in the parish, and the typical ratio of slave wealth to land wealth was four to one in any of the households that owned a slave.

The free population of the parish was rich even by Louisiana standards. They constituted just 1.3 percent of the state's free population but owned 2.5 percent of the wealth. Per capita wealth was twice the state average and ten times the national average. Most households with wealth of fifty thousand dollars and above owned land elsewhere in Louisiana. Most of the richest households owned slave plantations in other Louisiana parishes.[25]

1

The Origins of the
Antebellum Credit System

The Accommodation Endorser

B ANKING IN THE antebellum South has received a rather thorough examination. Louisiana, in particular, was the subject of a monograph by George D. Green twenty years ago. Larry Schweikart's recent study of the region also includes in-depth treatment of Louisiana. Both studies, however, are concerned primarily with state-chartered banking institutions. Green's book is especially valuable for its analysis of the commercial banking philosophy as opposed to that of investment banking or of the mix of the two that came to predominate in Louisiana during the depression of the 1840s.[1]

Schweikart discusses the possibility that a great deal of southern banking was conducted outside chartered banking channels. He suggests that extrapolations about money supply, drawn mostly from the very incomplete archives of antebellum chartered banks, may represent only a partial accounting, a possibility raised by Fritz Redlich as long ago as 1977.[2]

This exploration of credit relations in East Feliciana Parish at least confirms what others have suspected about the complex composition of the money supply, especially the role of "private" paper in everyday commercial arrangements. A study of chartered banks and their impact in the parish would not be without interest, but it would be of limited importance in piecing together the credit history of the area. Excepting the years 1832 to 1839, state-chartered banks had no presence in the parish.

In the years before 1845, most financial arrangements in the parish involved a local lender, an accommodation endorser, or a New Orleans factor. Three property banks chartered in the 1830s by the state legislature were actively engaged in investment banking in the parish, making loans collateralized with mortgages on land and, to a lesser extent, with slaves. However, all three banks were in liquidation proceedings by 1844. The Union Bank and Citizens Bank were revived by the legislature in the 1850s, but as commercial banks, not investment banks.

Accommodation paper has a bad reputation in most of the literature.

Green suggests that it had inflationary consequences and should be considered beyond the pale of ordinary commercial banking activities.[3] Making a strict dichotomy between "real bills," which originate in commercial transactions, and accommodation paper provides a useful perspective for understanding exchange operations and short-term credits for moving processed staples from producers to consumers. It also provides a more-or-less-correct representation of the lending activities of New Orleans's commercial banks.

The distinction, however, is far less useful in grappling with the debt market for agriculture. The picture that emerges in the locality is complicated by a variety of credit instruments that were primarily distinguished by their relative liquidity (i.e., their convertibility into specie or a cash equivalent). Accommodation paper was not a necessary evil; rather, it was simply one more mechanism for collateralizing loans of money and loans of credit. Obviously, sterling exchange could not be purchased with such paper, but the paper passed freely as money in a variety of local and even regional contexts.

In his examination of financial fluctuations in the nineteenth century, Green explores three monetary theories: the "central banking" school, the Friedman school, and the "financial intermediary" school. The last of these theories appears to have the most relevance when attempting to explain the behavior of debt instruments, other than true bills, at any given time in the pre–Civil War period. It is the third financial variable mentioned by Green, "the ratio of 'ultimate liquidity' to aggregate income," that seems especially relevant for elucidating the relationship between the debt market and the monetary system. Private investors in plantation debt were willing to hold debt instruments for long periods of time provided the relative loss of liquidity was compensated for with various premiums. Land sales on credit, which were the norm, generally resulted in a rise of 25 to 50 percent in the acre price. Short-term loans denominated in specie-convertible bank notes carried a discount premium of 1 percent per month for less than six months. Long-term financing arrangements with factorage firms generally did not entitle the borrower to a fixed interest charge; rather, the borrower paid the financing costs borne by the firm, which varied with the short-term costs of money. Private investors, then, who held various debt instruments had fewer incentives to liquidate such paper at a sacrifice in periods of financial stringency. It must be remembered, too, that during a bank suspension of specie convertibility, bank notes continued to circulate, but at a deep discount. The whole debt market became relatively less liquid, but private paper of every description compensated for such inherent risks.[4]

The market for plantation debt was many times larger than the exchange and discounting operations of the handful of New Orleans commercial banks. New Orleans banks accounted for less than 5 percent of the mortgage-backed loans made in the parish during the 1850s. Clearly, someone was willing to lend on mortgage-backed securities and provide financing in a variety of other situations.

Accommodation Endorsers

Accommodation endorsers predominated in the locality's loan relationships in the decades prior to 1845. They lent their credit, not their financial capital, as security for loans from third parties. Just how they were compensated is not clear, but it is unlikely that most such suretyships were merely gratuitous. Only the proliferation of state-chartered banks with mortgage banking powers in the 1830s overshadowed accommodation endorsers, or at least further obscured their important role as primary lenders in the local economy.

A typical arrangement involved a promissory note made payable to the order of the endorser, who then endorsed the note, thus collateralizing it with his credit and good name; the maker subsequently negotiated it to a willing third-party lender. A note made payable to "bearer" could be collateralized with a simple endorsement. A party might also make an accommodation by drawing a note in favor of the debtor.

Bills of exchange did not arise often in commercial transactions; a bill of exchange was in fact a form of accommodation paper that was sometimes substituted for a promissory note. The face of such an instrument simply showed an order to pay a stated sum, usually at thirty, sixty, or ninety days, to a named party. The borrower would get an acceptance from the drawee, the accommodating party, and then would negotiate the paper to a lender.

The names of the wealthiest households in East Feliciana Parish rarely appear as borrowers in the mortgage records. They do appear as mortgagees, however, with their accommodation endorsements or suretyships serving as considerations for such mortgages. Some speculated in cotton and probably used their credit resources to guarantee a regular and sure supply of the commodity by guaranteeing credit arrangements for small growers in return for their consignments. Others may have received a percentage of the loan proceeds. In lawsuits on notes, a few accommodation endorsers asserted as a defense in collection proceedings that they had received no portion of the loans. The defense was without legal merit, but it evidences an understanding that compensation for lending one's credit was customary.[5]

During the worst years of the depression that began in 1839, those who valued their reputations continued to redeem their liabilities, primary and contingent, in specie or its equivalent in depreciated paper. Certain guaranties could be negotiated at or near par, something that could not be done with any of the note issues of city banks.

A few names predominate in the mortgage office books as accommodation endorsers in the years from 1825 to 1840. That of William Silliman, a scion of an old Connecticut family and brother of Benjamin Silliman, was one. His connection with the area predated statehood, and like several other successful planters in the parish, he eventually established a factorage business in New Orleans. By the 1840s he had amassed a valuable portfolio of commercial properties in the city's financial district and owned hundreds of thousands of dollars of bank and insurance company stocks.[6]

Others included Benjamin Kendrick, Elias Norwood, Thomas Scott, Albert G. Carter, A. D. Palmer, and David Pipes. All had interests besides planting and were well connected in the financial world of the city. Some operated factorage businesses at various times, both in the locality and at New Orleans. Others were simply private lenders who underwrote financial arrangements that had no connection with their own planting operations. Silliman and Norwood made direct loans of cash, most of which were collateralized with mortgages on slaves.[7]

It should be pointed out, however, that many endorsements, and probably the majority, never were formally collateralized. Consequently, there is no record whatsoever of such transactions unless the paper ended up in lawsuits.

Many others besides the individuals enumerated above lent their names as endorsers. This was especially so in the decade of the 1830s, when discounts from newly chartered banks were readily available for the asking.[8] In many an instance it is likely that the accommodation endorser was relatively naive about his potential liability in the event of a default. The much-maligned property banks owed many of their collection woes to defaults on accommodation paper, not to mortgage-backed stock subscriptions.

Loans on accommodation paper reached a zenith during the heyday of the property banks. Families in the parish subscribed to more than $200,000 in stock in the Union Bank and almost as much in the Citizens Bank.

In the ten years before the legislature ordered the Union Bank's liquidation in 1843, the bank experienced a 1-percent default rate annually on its mortgage-backed stock subscriptions in the parish.[9] Most who gave mortgages to secure stock in the institution apparently did so in part to diversify their assets and, at least indirectly, to tap the lucrative loan market and obtain cash income from dividends. Some had paid off their stock subscriptions in full within four or five years of the initial subscription offer. Others clearly intended to borrow against their stock. However, subscribing to the stock to gain access to a loan was not especially efficient or safe. A subscriber was liable for the full amount of the subscription but could only borrow fifty cents on every dollar subscribed.[10]

Most of the Union Bank's difficulties in the parish stemmed from accommodation paper discounted at its Clinton branch. It would be a mistake, however, to assume that such paper was totally worthless, although it usually was necessary to institute suit to make a recovery. When Darius L. Green borrowed $1,075 from the bank in 1835, the debt was evidenced and secured by a promissory note endorsed by Joseph Brown, Elias Boatner, and A. E. Brady.[11] Sixteen months later the bank sued Green and the three endorsers and obtained a judgment against Green and Brady. Boatner and Brown had not received timely notice when the note was protested, so they escaped liability. In 1841 Elias Norwood assumed to pay the judgment, which with interest was well over $1,400. He had a writ of fieri facias issued and seized fourteen slaves belonging to Brady. Seven of the slaves were adjudicated to him at sheriff's sale in satisfaction of the judgment. In two subsequent suits Boatner was himself sued as the primary obligor, along with his accommodation endorsers.[12]

In one especially egregious case, the bank discounted a bill of exchange for seven thousand dollars drawn by Frederick Taylor on a Natchez businessman named L. H. Besancon, who had accepted it, to the order of William M. Gwynn. The bank failed to have the bill timely protested and consequently discharged all the parties from legal liability. The bill clearly was accommodation paper, and Taylor used the proceeds of the loan to purchase slaves. Franklin Hardesty, president of the bank's Clinton branch, had apparently attempted unsuccessfully to negotiate a large sum of money in Mississippi bank notes that had accumulated at his branch. He even traveled to Natchez trying to exchange these notes for "such funds as would serve the Union Bank." The seven thousand dollars had "been received by the Cashier of the Branch in violation of the general usage of the Bank." Hardesty then discounted Taylor's bill and gave him the Mississippi bank notes. Taylor subsequently agreed to pay the debt even though he had been discharged but then reneged on his promise. Nevertheless, Taylor was held to be liable; under Louisiana law an unenforceable obligation is sufficient cause for a new obligation if the obligor acknowledges it and guarantees its performance. In the words of the district court judge, "He made the promise [to pay the debt] under the faith of his moral obligation."[13]

It appears from the record that Hardesty was himself indebted to Taylor, and he was sued on a writ of garnishment. During the worst of the speculation of the 1830s, it was not uncommon for individuals to make loans from banks on the security of accommodation endorsers and then split the loan proceeds with the endorsers. Gwynn, it appears, frequently endorsed accommodation paper for Besancon, who was a Mississippi state bank commissioner. Besancon had by virtue of his office obtained almost limitless discounts from the state-chartered banks in Mississippi, which he regulated. As one deponent testified in an unrelated collection proceeding, "He [Besancon] was determined to make use of his situation as commissioner to get as much money as he wanted from the . . . Banks—that the officers . . . knew all about the matter—as to his endorsers he said he was determined to use them, as he was on the road to fortune they could not suffer."[14]

The Clinton branch had other problems. The first cashier embezzled thirty thousand dollars and left the state. The sureties on his performance bond were all sued.[15]

In the instances where relationships between accommodation endorsers and the makers of the notes were formally collateralized, the endorsers almost always obtained mortgages on slaves from those whose debts they guaranteed. Of the forty-seven mortgages recorded from 1835 to 1839, however, twenty-one were solely mortgages on acreage and town lots. Almost all the accommodations collateralized with mortgages on real estate involved paper that was discounted at the Union Bank.[16] Most of the mortgages granted during that four-year period to secure antecedent debts, as apposed to contemporaneous loans, likewise probably involved accommodation paper secured with mortgages on real estate.

In soliciting a loan for his own account from the home office of the Union Bank at New Orleans, Henry Marston, then cashier of the Clinton branch, reminded the officers that he had mortgaged a considerable amount of property to the bank. He estimated the property to be worth fifteen thousand dollars, but the bank had lent him only six thousand dollars. He hoped the directors would "coincide with . . . [him that he had] a particular claim upon the Bank for the loan." He enclosed a note for three thousand dollars "endorsed by two respectable individuals. The number of months ha[d] . . . been left blank [and were] to be filled up" after the directors had reached a decision about his loan. He hoped that it would be for as long a period as the bank could indulge him, subject to annual renewals.[17]

The extent to which men like Marston used their credit resources to float their own paper, significantly augmenting their borrowing potential, can be gleaned from a series of letters involving a promissory note negotiated by Marston in renewal of a debt owed by him to an unrelated third party. He obtained a note from James Muse and Franklin Hardesty, drawn by them and endorsed by Thomas L. Andrews, payable at the Citizens Bank, and used it to renew a note then due to a Mrs. Laurence. Mrs. Laurence previously had discounted the note at the Citizens Bank, so the bank was Marston's primary obligee. He notified the cashier that the parties "wish[ed] . . . to have the renewal extended, if compatible with the rules . . . of [the] institution, to *six* months. As October [was] . . . a more convenient season to pay money than August."[18]

Marston also endorsed his share of paper during the halcyon days of the 1830s, and his correspondence for the subsequent decade contains numerous references to his defaulting friends whose notes he had so obligingly endorsed. He wrote the cashier of the Clinton and Port Hudson Rail Road Company, another of the state-chartered improvement companies with banking powers, that he was much distressed by having been served with a notice of suit commenced by the company against "Charles Black as Principal, and Mr. Norwood and [him]self as securities upon a note of $1,200—and which [was] . . . the first notification [he] . . . [had] received of the debt not having been arranged by Mr. Black." Marston explained that they had signed a note for Black "of $1,000 for renewal which . . . [they] thought had been accepted by . . . the bank."[19] A letter from Black led Marston to believe that "everything in regard to [the] . . . protested note of $1,200 was arranged with the exception of its withdrawal from the Courts." The branch bank's cashier, however, subsequently informed Marston that Black had not "paid the curtailments or interest." Marston notified Black that the cashier still had authority to receive these payments along with his renewal note of one thousand dollars. Marston obtained no satisfaction from Black, and within a year's time the bank sued Black, and Marston and Norwood had to compromise the debt by paying a portion of it themselves.[20]

The relative value of private paper was highly subjective, and debtors frequently settled their accounts with paper drawn and negotiated by unrelated third parties. In his capacity as cashier, Marston performed a variety of clearinghouse agencies for New Orleans factors and their clientele in the parish. He wrote to Horace Bean & Co. at New Orleans, enclosing two accepted drafts drawn by Louis Sturgis on P. A. Hardy personally for $1,000 and on P. A. Hardy & Co. for $718.70, both payable the following December. Sturgis had forwarded the drafts to Marston to pay a note of $1,648.75 then falling due. The name of the payee had been "left blank, to be filled up as [Horace Bean & Co.] . . . deem[ed] best."[21] The two acceptances were received by Horace Bean & Co. in satisfaction of the note, and the note was sent to Marston for delivery to Sturgis. The Bean firm then transferred the acceptances to A. Brand & Co.[22]

By the early 1840s, accommodation paper in general was much depreciated. Marston performed a number of collection agencies for New Orleans factors and New York and Philadelphia wholesalers. Most accounts were settled either with interest-bearing certificates of deposit issued by the Clinton branch of the Union Bank or drafts on factors, payable at sight or at some later date and accepted by the drawee.[23] In June 1841 Marston advised Grant & Barton of New York City that he had enclosed with his letter to them another certificate of deposit on the Union Bank at New Orleans for $181.71. Three other notes, which Grant & Barton had placed in his hands for collection, remained to be collected. Marston was of the opinion that those notes would not be paid until the next crop was gathered and sold.[24]

In March of the following year, he advised the New York firm that he had enclosed a certificate of deposit issued by the Union Bank in satisfaction of the Barfield notes. Kelly's note, he assured them, would "probably be paid out of the present crop."[25] Barfield and Kelly were both planters, and it is likely that they had given promissory notes to either local vendors or New Orleans wholesalers to liquidate open account balances. The transferees had in turn negotiated the paper as security to firms such as Grant & Barton. The firms then placed the paper in Marston's hands for collection.

Interregional settlements may have involved a great deal of local accommodation paper, although final liquidations of such obligations were necessarily negotiated with instruments such as bills of exchange or current bank notes.[26] Nevertheless, out-of-state creditors did take other accommodation paper or accepted drafts on factors in satisfaction of aging receivables. Marston wrote DeForest & Co. that he had compromised with A. Baily, agreeable to their instructions, a note of two thousand dollars for sixteen hundred dollars. Baily made the settlement with other notes with a face value of $1,807.33. The notes were "the very best [he] . . . could find in his [Baily's] possession—and although some of the parties m[ight] . . . be dilatory in making payment, [he thought] . . . they w[ould] . . . all be ultimately collected." Baily had endorsed only four of the notes, having refused to guarantee two notes that Marston considered most doubtful.[27] Baily still had contingent liabilities for the paper he had endorsed.

Marston collected numerous notes in satisfaction of delinquent accounts. He wrote another client that the paper he had remitted was "the best [he] . . . could procure—[the notes were] at [that] . . . time esteemed good and although there [might] . . . be some tardiness on the payments, [he thought] . . . that they would be all finally paid."[28] However, a few months later he had to report to DeForest that he was "extremely disappointed that [his] . . . exertions [had] . . . not been attended with more success and [he] . . . fear[ed] that some of those whose notes [had been taken in satisfaction of the Baily claim would] . . . not pay without suits." Moreover, he continued, "I wrote Mr. Barton a few weeks since and explained to him, one of the causes of my bad success was owing in some measure to an idea imposed upon the minds of the drawers of the notes that they were transferred to rich firms in New York who could well afford to be out of the use of the money."[29] Baily was a local merchant with numerous creditors in New Orleans and New York. Marston considered his condition "precarious, particularly on account of the danger of fire, to which from his location he [was] . . . more or less exposed and without insurance." It was impossible to determine "what m[ight] be, or m[ight] not be, his liabilities."[30]

The trough in the depression that had begun in 1839 probably was 1843. Marston observed to one creditor that he had "never before found it so difficult to make collections as at present."[31] In June he notified Smith, Henderson & Co. that he had not collected "one cent" on the claims taken from Baily in satisfaction of his debt to them. "Never since Louisiana ha[d] been a state . . . [had] collections been so difficult to make."[32] He was then holding claims by merchants in New York, received from Baily, amounting to four thousand dollars.

Accommodation paper, nevertheless, remained the primary instrument for funding loans, whether in the local or regional economies. To Gasquet & Co. Marston wrote that he had obtained two drafts from D. Thomas to pay Thomas's note of $750. Both were drawn on New Orleans firms at sight and were guaranteed by E. T. Merrick. Marston had also obtained Merrick's endorsement on the note, an additional security in the event that acceptances of the drafts were declined.[33] Merrick, a wealthy planter and lawyer in the parish, was lending his credit to fund a loan to Thomas, an in-law, by endorsing paper drawn on two New Orleans factorage firms. Merrick may have had credit relationships with the two firms, or else his endorsement was sufficient to permit a negotiation of the two drafts by the drawee firms. Marston had taken the additional precaution of obtaining Merrick's endorsement on the original note and his waiver of a notice of protest in the event the drafts, both drawn at sight, were not paid when presented by the holder.

Some of the paper transferred by Baily in satisfaction of his accounts payable, however, proved to be uncollectible. Marston advised one creditor that he was prepared to institute suit on a number of evidences of indebtedness at the meeting of the next parish court. One of the drawers, Thomas R. Chapman, "greatly to [Marston's] . . . surprise h[ad] taken the benefit of the Bankrupt law." He offered to get "Mr. Baily to change his note for other good paper."[34]

Most accommodation paper, however, had value even if it sometimes took years to liquidate. Marston, for example, purchased slaves in 1839 at a probate sale in Charleston, South Carolina, and took more than ten years to liquidate the indebtedness. Such an extended credit for slave purchases was unusual, however, and may be explained by the economic difficulties that characterized the 1840s. Marston's willingness to pay interest during all of those years on the unpaid balance also discouraged a foreclosure proceeding. In addition, he had removed the slaves to Louisiana, and reclaiming them would have been an inconvenience to the heirs, to say the least.

Private paper, like the note issues of the state-chartered banks, increased in value as the economy steadily improved in the second half of the 1840s.

Accommodation endorsers constituted the foundation on which all antebellum credit relationships rested. While formalized credit relationships between factors and planters became a conspicuous feature of financing arrangements in the last fifteen years of the antebellum period, such relationships, nevertheless, were grounded in endorsements (i.e., acceptances guaranteed by the drawee firms). In this context cross acceptances developed between factorage firms whereby firms afforded each other "mutual accommodations." The Louisiana supreme court rather naively observed that "[out] of this state of things, ha[d] arisen the notorious practice of the factor receiving from the planter his bill on the factor, which the latter accept[ed], and g[ot] discount[ed] in the market. . . . Acceptances to the amount of many hundreds of thousands of dollars, [were] thus . . . thrown into the New Orleans bill market annually."[35] The market was, however, considerably larger than any estimate of "many hundreds of thousands of dollars" put on it by the supreme court. The whole antebellum credit system was grounded in acceptances (i.e., accommodation paper).

Private paper as a monetary substitute, whether to facilitate short-term or long-term loans, was necessary and inevitable. While the relative safety and value of such paper may have been suspect at times when compared with a medium of exchange guaranteed by the national government, it was necessary if the economy was to grow. Such paper was the primary medium for allocating credit and capital. The marketplace determined the value of a particular endorsement. Slaves were the principal security when such relationships (i.e., mortgages by drawers to secure accommodation endorsers and commercial arrangements in general) were formally collateralized.

2

The Emergence of Factors as Investment Bankers

THE ROLE OF factorage firms in marketing the South's cotton is explored in great detail by Harold D. Woodman in *King Cotton and His Retainers*. Woodman's approach, however, emphasizes the financing and marketing of the cotton crop, and it is the cotton crop that shapes his analysis of the complex set of relationships that constituted most of the South's economy in the antebellum and postbellum periods. Focusing on the cotton crop is subject to many of the pitfalls inherent in trying to understand southern banking from the perspective of chartered banks. Woodman considers factors as financial intermediaries, but the subject is secondary to how cotton crops were financed and marketed. He seems to endorse the arguments of contemporary critics that accommodation paper was inherently inferior and risky compared to commercial paper, and he states that "wealthy factors . . . could not support the credit needs of their customers from their personal assets [but] . . . had to rely upon outside funds."[1]

Woodman's characterization does not comport with conditions as they existed in the financial world of antebellum New Orleans. In Louisiana, at least, each partner in a commercial firm had unlimited liability for the firm's obligations.[2] "Personal assets" were only beyond the reach of a class of creditors if a third party had been interposed as owner. It is likely that this was the case, not only throughout the South but throughout the nation as well; unincorporated "commercial firms" are not exceptional, even today. In this context no meaningful distinction exists between "firm" and "personal assets." The personal assets of each partner support the credit of the firm and its clients.

Most New Orleans factors came to the business by one of several routes. Some began as furnishing merchants in localities spread across the lower Mississippi Valley, others as wholesalers of plantation supplies in the city, and many more as planters.[3] Henry Marston's factor, Jacob U. Payne, had been a sugar planter and remained one throughout his career as a city factor. His commercial firm failed in 1874, but he was able to restructure it into a much smaller planting partnership in subsequent decades.[4] Postwar assignments for the benefit of creditors support a conclusion that many of the city's largest firms were involved directly in planting, with individual partners often listing plantations on their schedules of assets.

Richard Flower & Co. and its successor firms had a relationship with East Feliciana Parish that lasted into the twentieth century. Walter C. Flower reorganized his father's firm in the difficult years following the senior's death in 1878 and was elected mayor of New Orleans in 1896, a position he held until his death in 1900. Richard Flower had begun his career as a planter and furnishing merchant at Port Hudson. He married a daughter of the wealthy East Feliciana planter and lawyer, Judge Thomas Scott, and the couple moved to New Orleans in the 1850s; there Flower established his factorage business. His firm was a great favorite among East Feliciana planters.

A. Levi & Co., Bloom, Kahn & Co., Hawkins and Norwood, and Wright, Allen & Co. were all firms with strong East Feliciana connections. Abraham Levi and the several partners of Bloom, Kahn & Co. had all begun their careers in the parish as furnishing merchants and only left for New Orleans in the 1850s to open their factorage businesses.[5] The kinds of business they conducted in the locality before leaving for the city, particularly financing arrangements, were identical to the functions associated with factorage firms. Their local clients, of course, remained with them after they left the parish.

The banking and investment services afforded planters by their factors remains an obscure subject. A name other than "factor" might further clarify the picture. "Commercial agent," for example, embraces more of the particulars that characterized factorage firms' activities in this regard. A simple listing of services does not explain satisfactorily the relationship of factors to the financial and monetary systems and how that relationship shaped and defined their role. For purposes of this examination, factors were one tier in a hierarchy of liquidating agents.

The components of the monetary system within the locality and the region were a great deal more varied and complex than commercial paper originating in commodity sales or bank note issues redeemable in specie. The subjects of short-term versus long-term loans and debt levels in general are greatly obscured by relative levels of liquidity for various kinds of debt instruments. The kinds of paper that gravitated toward the New Orleans money market were varied enough to support numerous bill brokers. The volume and kinds of debt instruments brokered by these agents is completely unknown; nevertheless, their very presence in the money market points to the existence of a cosmopolitan paper market. Banking and factorage systems were ancillaries to this market.

Because so much debt was evidenced by nothing more than a promissory note, with no collateral security except an accommodation endorsement, speculation about debt levels and the relative burden of such debts is highly subjective. There is no paper trail that can be reconstructed from the mortgage records, the law suit records, or commercial archives, where such have survived.

Patterns of External Financing

It will be useful to explore some of the loan relationships between city factors, or commission merchants, and their clients in the locality. Open account statements from commission merchants to planter clients contained debit entries for drafts accepted and funds placed to the credit of such clients, as well as purchases of supplies charged to account and payments made on behalf of clients as requested. So long as the client had money on deposit with his factor, it is quite easy to see how the arrangement functioned smoothly. However, many clients frequently had unpaid balances with their factors for long periods of time, even years. How did the commission merchant support his debt load? Perhaps the firm had substantial capital, and the commission merchant lent these funds directly to the client. Such loan relationships, however, were relatively rare.

The commission merchant usually lent his credit, not his capital. He arranged financing for purchases far more significant than the supplies necessary to complete the next year's planting (i.e., whole plantations with slaves). The simplest arrangement involved the commission merchant's accepting the planter's drafts by endorsing them and making himself liable for their payment; he then discounted or sold them to a third party, a bank or private investor. With current funds in hand, the planter could then proceed to liquidate his obligations.

One source of long-term debt financing involved unpaid balances on open accounts that were liquidated with bills receivable or promissory notes. A planter might have an unpaid balance on his open account of several thousand dollars. His commission merchant or factor needed funds, so the commission merchant or factor obtained from the planter a promissory note that liquidated the unpaid balance or collateralized that balance. The promissory note could be sold or pledged to secure a totally unrelated debt to a third party.

When a factor took a note in satisfaction of the debt owed on the open account, the account was then liquidated, and the factor was free to sell or discount the note or pledge it to a third party. The note was his. The factor in effect made a direct loan to the planter.

Sometimes the planter gave the factor a note as "security" for the debt. Such notes were called collateral security notes. Typically, collateral security notes were mortgage notes and could be pledged by the factor to raise liquidity but not sold. The planter, then, retained some control over his paper, and the factor could borrow on it.

A brief digression on the subject of collateral security notes is appropriate and will help to establish a context for what was happening with mortgage notes in the paper market, a subject treated in considerably more detail in the next chapter. The practice of using promissory notes collateralized by mortgages on slaves and plantations as security for open accounts was relatively common in the 1840s and 1850s and probably originated at a much earlier time. The practice is difficult to visualize and was a long way from being free of pitfalls for contemporaries.

The seminal decision of the Louisiana Supreme Court on this subject was *Pickersgill & Co. v. Brown*, decided in 1852. The contest was between a judgment creditor and a mortgage creditor of the debtor; the defendant was a partner in the New York firm of Brown, Brothers & Co. Brown had claims aggregating to more than $700,000. The claims were secured by two mortgages on four plantations, one mortgage for $250,000 and one for $150,000. All of the loans had been made on an open account, and the mortgages had been given "not only as securities for existing advances, but such advances as might thereafter be made, so that [Brown] . . . should be covered in account current up to the amount and interest." The court held that the mortgages stood as security for all subsequent advances on the account as well as antecedent advances. The court was careful to distinguish the account current from the obligations given as security for debts owed on it, writing that "we must not confound the debt in account current, with the obligations taken as security for that debt." The court refused to give a strict construction to the arrangement, as contended for by the plaintiff, observing that a more limited construction "would be inadequate to all the practical purposes of business and the necessities of commerce."[6]

Pickersgill is not only a strong indication that substantial long-term loans were made by factors, but also that most such borrowing was funded on open accounts. Mortgage notes, then, in many instances were indeed collateral security notes (i.e., obligations that secured flexible loan arrangements that could be used by lenders to raise funds as the need arose).

The more usual situation was one in which the client owed the factor or a third party money and needed current funds to service that indebtedness. Perhaps the factor needed to liquefy his own encumbered lines of credit, so both the factor and the planter had to resort to external financing. In such a case, the planter gave his factor a promissory note, sometimes secured by a mortgage, which the factor as "agent" negotiated in the money market. Negotiation meant that the note (or multiple notes) was sold to a third party, usually with the factor's endorsement. The note might also be pledged. Whether a note was sold or pledged depended on the scope of the factor's agency with his principal, the planter. Loan relationships were not a one-way street. Planters lent money to their factors as well, sometimes simply by endorsing their notes.

Both planters and factors, as a rule, preferred agency loan placement. The factor preferred this arrangement because his liability was only contingent: he lent his credit, not his capital. A direct loan by the factor reduced his capacity to provide other clients with short-term credit facilities or accommodations. A direct loan was a long-term commitment of capital. The planter favored such an arrangement because he retained limited control over the note (or notes) that secured his debt.

It is likely that most "agency" paper in external financing arrangements was in fact pledged to third parties. A pledgee could not sell the note pledged to him, so the debtor prevented the negotiation of his paper to third parties who were relieved of all equities between the original parties to the loan as holders in due course. Debtors were not unconcerned about the hands into which their paper might fall.

Limitations on the power of pledgees to dispose of their pledges were waived where there was a default by the debtor and his surety, the factor. Agreements of forfeiture were and are contra bonos mores (against good morals) in Louisiana; nevertheless, there are pledge agreements from the antebellum period in suit records that contain forfeiture provisions, permitting the pledgee to sell the security at public or private sale and obtain a deficiency judgment against the debtor without recourse to judicially supervised collection proceedings. Commercial custom could override positive law.

A factor had to be especially careful, however, when he paid or took up the obligation of a defaulting client. If he had negotiated the paper as agent, he risked being reduced to the status of an unsecured creditor. As agent he was as one with the debtor; hence the debt was wiped out by confusion—a concurrence in the same person of debtor and creditor.[7]

What is important about all of these relationships, however, is that the factor was lending his credit, performing a service analogous in every way to the one performed by present-day investment houses that underwrite bond and stock issues. An individual did not, however, have to be a factor to lend his credit, to guarantee the debt of another party. Indeed, all antebellum credit arrangements can be subsumed under the heading of third-party guarantees. Borrowing on accommodation paper probably preceded formalized credit arrangements between factors and planters by decades; even formalized credit arrangements in the last two decades of the antebellum period retained their grounding in accommodation paper.

The role of factors in collateralized and uncollateralized credit transactions was certainly important: their accommodations permitted borrowers to gain access to the highly liquid note issues of the New Orleans commercial banks and the equally negotiable paper of merchant capitalists in the Atlantic trade. It must be remembered, however, that sales of southern cotton and sugar to Europe accounted for most of the nation's foreign exchange earnings prior to 1845; hence, southern planters a priori had a significant potential in their own right for tapping those same credit facilities directly.[8]

Ultimately, all long-term lending was tied directly to the store of savings in the local economy and, to a lesser extent, the regional one. Planters borrowed short term to finance plantings, slave purchases, and other acquisitions. The services furnished by their factors were those of ordinary commercial bankers. Purchases of slaves and expensive machinery might be financed on an open account; more often the planter would seek to roll the loan over into a long-term arrangement.

The exchange activities of New Orleans commercial banks were tangential to the process of securing debt in the local and regional economies.[9] The condition of the money supply ensured a conspicuous role for evidences of indebtedness. International exchange, particularly sterling exchange, was the highest quality paper in the marketplace, but its market was dwarfed by the huge debt market in local and regional paper accommodations that were grounded in the borrowing power of endorsers or guarantors.

Henry Marston's Liquidation
of the Union Bank's Clinton Branch Portfolio

In the case of East Feliciana Parish, one invaluable source has survived that more or less elucidates a small portion of the debt market in the parish. The Union Bank, one of the state-chartered property banks, went into liquidation in 1843, a proceeding that lasted more than a decade.[10] In 1851 the liquidators sold the portfolio of the Clinton branch to Henry Marston for $73,525. The face value of the mortgage notes and accommodation paper transferred to Marston was eighty-eight thousand dollars, with the liquidators allowing Marston a 20 percent discount for assuming to pay the indebtednesses.[11] Marston, of course, expected to make money, and he did very well for himself over the succeeding five years.

It is in the context of his collection activities that the various nuances and subtleties of the paper market and the debt instruments that functioned as a monetary substitute begin to emerge. Analyzing particular transactions to determine the composition of the money supply is important for a variety of reasons, but it is especially important when comparing and contrasting the antebellum and postbellum debt structures. The local economy supported an estimated long-term and short-term debt load of between two and three million dollars in the decade before the war.[12] In the two decades after 1865, the debt load contracted by about 90 percent. The antebellum debt load was at least twice the value of the annual sugar and cotton crops grown in the parish in the 1850s.[13] Clearly, many antebellum lenders had invested in the economy long term, expecting to recoup their principal and interest from improving income streams and capital appreciation. The debt structure imploded with emancipation, whether because a regular income stream from slaves could no longer be assured, or because most of the wealth underpinning the structure was gone. As will be seen in the next chapter, the financial system, and indirectly the monetary system as well, were grounded in slaves.

Marston tried to interest William Silliman, the richest man in the parish, in becoming his partner in the venture to acquire the branch portfolio, but Silliman declined, being "confident that a number of those debts due the Institution which [Marston had] . . . consider[ed] good w[ould] . . . not be paid in seven years." At the age of seventy-three, Silliman did not consider it prudent to undertake an investment in "monied engagements that will take years to mature."[14] Although many of the debts were already fifteen years old, they were still collectible nevertheless. This was not to be the case in the postbellum period with debts of ancient age.

It is clear from Marston's correspondence, however, just how such paper was used in commercial channels to settle other claims. To one Robert G. Beele he wrote that the Union Bank had transferred to him a judgment against Major Dunn, Beele's father-in-law, for nine thousand dollars. Dunn had written to Marston's friend, Mr. Hardesty, that the "debt had inured to his benefit, and [he] felt disposed to pay it, but it could be met only in driblets or small payments." Dunn held a claim against the estate of Marston's brother-in-law, so Marston proposed "to endorse an equal sum upon [his] . . . judgment against Dunn," if Dunn would release his claim against Dr. Caulfield's estate. "In fact," he added, "I should feel much gratified if several thousands could be realized on account of it—It is now over 15 years since the debt became due—If fair and equitable terms were offered in the way of compromise I should be disposed to meet them."[15] Obviously, Dunn's paper still had value, and Marston could have seized portions of Dunn's property.

In an unrelated proceeding involving the succession of Caulfield, Marston advised a succession creditor that he had decided to send him "the Gardiner note [for the credit portion of a probate sale of slaves] . . . [but] Mrs. Caulfield . . . concluded to exchange it with Maj. Graves."[16] Graves was then holding a claim against the Caulfield estate that had been transferred to him by a third party.

Marston often received third-party paper in satisfaction of his claims against a particular debtor. He wrote the maker of one such note that his note had "been transferred by Col. R. Fluker . . . [in satisfaction of Fluker's debt to the Union Bank, of whose assets Marston was the assignee] and consequently [the maker could not] set up any lawful reason why the same should *not* be paid." Marston observed that a "note given by Mr. Harrell to Mr. Hale and transferred at the same time and manner . . . was . . . sued upon, judgment obtained and paid."[17]

More often than not, Marston was pressing accommodation endorsers rather than primary obligors. To W. Marbury, whose paper Marston held in consequence of the Union Bank transfer, he wrote: "I have seen and conversed with Mr. S. W. Dunbar who is one of the endorsers on the note in question—He informed me that he had recently visited your place of residence—represents your situation and circumstances to be very prosperous—and consequently *amply able*—to meet this small demand."[18] He advised James W. Schenck that one of his endorsers, Mr. Tunnard, had inquired whether Schenck's note had been paid. When Marston answered him in the negative, the endorser "expressed a strong desire, that the note should be collected *as speedily as possible.*"[19]

Marston often had trouble with accommodation paper outside the context of his collection activities on the Union Bank portfolio. To J. A. Maryman of Jackson, Louisiana, he wrote: "I have just received a letter from Payne, Harrison [Marston's factors] informing me that your dft. of $193 favor C. M. Smith, on Miltenberger & Co. has not been paid. Upon receipt of this I hope you will lose no time in placing that house in funds to meet the payment of the draft. P.S. previous to Mr. Smith's departure for Kentucky I discounted the above named dft. for his accommodation."[20]

In another case, he wrote Payne, Harrison that he had drawn a small draft of four hundred dollars "favor of M. Bloom [for his accommodation]."[21] Bloom was a small merchant and cotton buyer in Clinton. Like other Clinton merchants, he maintained a relationship with a New Orleans commission merchant, for whose account he made the bulk of his cotton purchases. When the commission merchant failed in 1854, Marston was left holding two of Bloom's drafts on the commission merchant aggregating to something in excess of sixteen hundred dollars. Marston asked Payne, Harrison to provide every assistance to Bloom in reclaiming the cotton already consigned to the failed commission merchant. He noted that Bloom was good for the sixteen hundred dollars, and he had a "responsible endorser at least [for the $1600]."[22] Bloom subsequently transferred various bills receivable from his retail business to his endorser, who entrusted them to Marston for collateral security. Bloom had to bear the loss occasioned by the suspension of his New Orleans commission merchant, and Marston was adversely affected to the extent that he had to make collections on paper that was far less liquid than the drafts he had originally negotiated for Bloom. In consequence, Marston was late in making one of his installments to the Union Bank.

The Bloom drafts are especially interesting because they were apparently accepted for payment by another commission merchant. Marston cautioned George A. Freret, the cashier of the Union Bank, that he felt "anxious that the notices of protest on the acceptances of McRea Coffman & Co. [Bloom's factor] be *carefully made*, so as to be *certain to hold*, Misters Oakey & Hawkins, responsible—In a letter which I saw a short time from them, they are under the expectation of taking up the dft. after the 1/4 prox."[23] Marston was not a party to the underlying transaction that the dishonored paper evidenced; he had simply purchased the paper from Bloom in connection with an exchange operation he conducted for the Union Bank in 1854.

Marston's comments about his exchange operations for the bank provide yet another insight on the relative liquidity of bank notes and other debt instruments in antebellum credit relations. "The grand object [according to Marston] . . . was [to increase] the circulation of [the Bank's] . . . paper."[24] Before undertaking this agency for the bank, he expressed an opinion to the bank's president that "a safe business [in negotiating exchange could] . . . be transacted on one to two hundred thousand Dollars. . . . [The previous year] there [had been] . . . shipped on the [Clinton and Port Hudson] Rail Road [from Clinton] a few bales less than 19000."[25] All of Marston's discounting for the bank was restricted to thirty- , sixty- , and ninety-day paper drawn by just six Clinton commercial firms on New Orleans commission merchants. All such drafts clearly represented cotton purchases made for the accounts of New Orleans firms. However, as the Bloom case plainly indicates, Marston was secondarily liable if he exchanged bank notes for drafts that later turned out to be relatively worthless. When Marston purchased drafts from local merchants, he sent them to Payne, Harrison, who obtained acceptances from various drawees and then left the accepted paper with the bank as "collateral security" for Marston's drawing account. When the paper matured and was collected, the proceeds were placed to his credit in the same account. Marston was pleased with his conduct of the exchange business for the bank and observed to the cashier that the bank's notes were "preferred by *some* to those of other banks. . . . A few only of those sent to [him] . . . ha[d] found their way back to the Bank [at New Orleans]—A part of them [he was] . . . confident ha[d] been carried to the West."[26]

While Marston's exchange operations are of limited importance, they nevertheless underscore the highly subjective and personalized character of negotiable paper. By the 1850s most discounting of paper by Louisiana banks had been restricted by law to short-term self-liquidating commercial paper, at least in theory.[27] In fact, New Orleans banks discounted a considerable number of factors' acceptances that did not necessarily represent cotton in transit to the marketplace.[28]

Most of Marston's collections on the Union Bank portfolio came in the form of drafts drawn by five or six important local merchants on their New Orleans commission merchants. These Clinton merchants were the major buyers in the local cotton market, and at least four of them were at least as well capitalized as many New Orleans commission houses. Matthias Mills, Micajah Harris, Abraham Levi, and R. O. Draughon all had personal estates in excess of $100,000, and by the end of the antebellum period, all had established themselves as factors in New Orleans or contracted partnerships with city firms.[29]

Most of this paper, in fact, represented sales of cotton by Marston's debtors to local merchants who were buying primarily for the accounts of commission merchants in New Orleans. The localized character of the paper confirms one important fact about the activities of the Union Bank in the parish in the decade of the 1830s: much of the bank's difficulty stemmed from accommodation paper drawn by small planters. Few of Marston's debtors dealt directly with a New Orleans firm: all sold to local merchants and probably conducted most of their business through the same local firms.

It is also clear, however, that some of the debtors who had relationships with New Orleans factors were able to obtain loans from them to satisfy Marston's claims. Marston arranged for one of his debtors, Willis L. Hamilton, to draw on Payne, Harrison for one thousand dollars to facilitate a partial liquidation of his debt: "Enclosed I send you a dft. for $1000 drawn by Willis L. Hamilton Esq. . . . upon yourselves payable in 10 months. . . . Mr. H. is one of the most respectable planters in the West Parish and will be an acquisition to your list of consigners of cotton, and I trust it may lead to others."[30] To Richard Pritchard, another New Orleans factor, Marston wrote that if he allowed one Davis Gore to draw upon him for $130, Pritchard would "only run the ordinary risks . . . which all commercial houses [were] . . . obliged to encounter."[31]

The New Orleans factors who agreed to assume a portion of a particular debt owed to Marston in consequence of his purchase of the Clinton branch portfolio did so only after a thorough appraisal of the debtor's creditworthiness. Such loans were made by a debtor drawing on a designated factor for the specified sum, but payable in six or nine months. Marston often had Payne, Harrison obtain an acceptance from the drawee and then discount the accepted draft to a third party for bank notes with which to pay his installment to the bank.

Factors who had correspondence relationships with Clinton merchants relied on them to determine the creditworthiness of a debtor. Marston wrote to Matthias G. Mills, the senior partner in the Clinton firm of Mills and Cleveland, that he had been notified by Oakey, Hawkins, the Mills firm's New Orleans commission merchant, that Oakey, Hawkins would accept a draft drawn by V. H. Dunn for $475 to settle Marston's claim, provided the

Mills firm approved it. Because Mills was then in New Orleans, Marston had approached his junior partner in the Clinton office, who had declined the proposal. Marston said that his lawyer probably would recommend foreclosing on the mortgage, which he was "*much* adverse to unless *compelled*." He continued: "I have already pursued the course in one case,—this version of the case I did not present to Aleck—Otherwise he might have decided differently."[32] Marston wrote that he considered Dunn perfectly solvent, "but probably somewhat pushed at present." Oakey, Hawkins, he believed, would be "perfectly safe in the long run in giving their names upon his paper."[33] Marston himself was under great pressure to liquidate quickly as much of the portfolio as possible to meet his several installments to the bank; otherwise, it seems clear that he would have been prepared to wait on Dunn to make his collection. That factorage firms were his primary source of relief in disposing of the obligations of his debtors is fairly indicative of the process by which such firms contributed significantly to liquefying the debt market.

Marston occasionally solicited loans from his factors for third parties who, in return for such accommodations, would promise to ship a portion of their crop to the firm. In one especially interesting case, he solicited a loan from Payne, Harrison for Col. Preston Pond, a planter who had just inherited ten thousand dollars in property from his father-in-law and was seeking to raise a loan of five thousand dollars to be paid in two years. Pond had proposed giving a mortgage on twenty-one slaves as security for the loan and had promised to consign his cotton crop, which was in excess of one hundred bales. Marston had advised Pond that he "believe[d] it to be contrary to the custom of [the] . . . house to make advances beyond the proceeds of one crop—but notwithstanding" he had consented to make the proposal to the firm. He attached to his letter a list of the slaves.[34]

By the late 1840s, factorage firms were fast becoming the preeminent mortgage bankers in the parish economy. By the end of the 1850s, they had loaned or guaranteed for middle-tier planters long-term debts with a face value of $1 million. Mortgages on slaves were the primary collateral for such loans. In this instance the Payne firm did not loan Pond five thousand dollars on the twenty-one slaves; nevertheless, other firms did make such loans. It is clear, too, that the Payne firm did not as a rule advance money to any planter for sums in excess of the anticipated value of the year's forthcoming crop. Much of the accumulated debt with factorage firms, then, may well have been unsecured long-term debt. A planter who was going into debt year after year for planting expenses was not a good credit risk; hence it is likely that debts carried on open accounts and not collateralized in fact represented loans for capital improvements.

Factors were by no means the only ones making loans in the local economy. As previously noted, in the decades prior to the 1850s, the local accommodation endorser was the primary vehicle for making loans. Much of the surplus income in the local economy, however, increasingly was being left with various factorage firms, where it earned far higher returns than could be obtained on bank deposits. Leaving money on deposit with a factor was much less risky than lending directly without the factor as an intermediary.

Nevertheless, several wealthy men in the parish bought and sold debt instruments, not only helping to liquefy local paper, but providing a direct stimulus to local development as well. In a letter to a Thomas Lombard, for example, Marston wrote: "I submitted the proposition of our friend Judge Weems to Mr. Pipes—he appeared satisfied with the security, but thought the rate of discount (8 percent) too low—He was on the eve of leaving for the city where he expected to make investments at a better rate." Marston promised to continue attempting to place the loan and asked whether the judge would be willing to pay a higher discount.[35]

When pressing Schenck to pay up on his Union Bank debt, Marston suggested that he approach a Mr. Bond, who "had a large amount to loan at [10 percent] . . . interest." Marston thought such a loan would be less expensive than a twelve-month acceptance, which in addition to interest charges would incur discount costs of 8 to 10 percent: "An acceptance at 60 days will answer my purpose, or one of 12 months will suffice provided the money can be raised upon it, of which I have no doubt—The expenses, however, will be somewhat more than 10 percent interest which you offer."[36] Marston permitted his debtors to satisfy his claims with twelve-month paper, but they bore all discount charges for converting the paper to cash so that he could make his annual installment to the bank.

When collections became exceedingly difficult in 1855, Marston obtained permission from the Union Bank to pledge twelve-month acceptances as collateral securities for what was owed on the installment until such acceptances could be discounted and converted to cash. He advised one debtor that "good *acceptances* payable [the following fall would] answer . . . [his] purpose" if the debtor could not pay in cash.[37] In every instance where a debtor settled with a twelve-month acceptance, the debtor had to stand for the discount charges, which in times of credit stringency could run as high as 10 percent. In 1855 Marston told Freret that his "best exertions [would] . . . be required to close the payment of the last note . . . [because of] the tightness of the times."[38]

Discounting was integral to antebellum and postbellum credit relations, and the economic realities underlying the practice help to explain why credit sales of land for terms longer than twelve months on average were twice the value of cash sales. Even collateralized credit transactions provided for an annual renewal of the note, which could then be adjusted for changes in the costs of money, or for a pledge of the mortgage note to secure antecedent debts or future advances. In the latter instance, the lender could likewise make adjustments from time to time in response to the changing costs of money. Even long-term loans, then, contained mechanisms for adjusting interest rates and discount rates without affecting the collateral.

Clearly, it was more economical to settle a claim with a sight draft on a city factor; the draft could be charged to an open account at an interest rate of 8 percent. But paper payable in twelve months, even if accepted, was relatively less liquid, and anyone who discounted such paper for bank notes or other liquid paper expected an additional compensation. Rates of discount varied substantially even from year to year. In the fall of 1852, for example, Marston expected a 6-percent discount for converting three drafts into cash. His installment was due in March, so the discount rate probably was 1 percent a month. In March 1853 Marston wrote Payne, Harrison that one of his debtors had advised him that he had left an accepted draft for six hundred dollars on J. B. Byrne & Co. with the Payne firm for Marston's account. He instructed Payne, Harrison to do the following: "If not already done I will thank you to get the above named house to discount the same—on the most favorable terms—and if necessary you are hereby authorized to sign my name upon the back—If J. B. B. & Co. should decline I presume you will find no difficulty having it done elsewhere if you do not take it yourselves."[39] Accepted factors' paper may have traded more or less at par between factorage firms or with anyone else who would agree to take it at par. However, Marston needed bank notes, not the factor's paper, to settle his debt for the purchase of the portfolio; hence he had to convert the factor's paper into other more liquid paper and pay a discount charge for the conversion.

Discount charges could be quite onerous. Marston queried Payne, Harrison several times about such charges: "Your a/current I found correct with two exceptions—The dft of Wm. Dickey for $1000 drew 8 percent interest from date, which I think has been overlooked, judging by the net proceeds amounting to only $927.33—And the dft of Mills & Cleveland for $784.26 should have netted more than $724.16 unless it was negotiated at a heavy discount."[40] In another instance he wrote: "I wish these dfts to be discounted immediately and both the drawers are desirous of having them done on the best possible terms—Mr. C. thinks M. N. & Co. will do his at 8 percent—and Gen. Carter hopes that not exceeding 9 percent will be required of him. In both cases the brokerage is included."[41]

Discount charges, however, were rising, and the following year, in 1854, Marston advised Payne, Harrison that "I am disappointed in hearing that the dft forwarded in my letter of the 28 ulto will require a discount and brokerage of 10 1/2 percent to realize the money—I hoped such paper could be negotiated at *not exceeding* 9 percent exclusive of brokerage."[42] A few days after this communication to his factors, he openly expressed his fears that the drawers would be much disappointed "in the negotiation of their drafts—as the discounts f[ell] upon them." He suggested letting the *"acceptors* [the factorage firms on whom the paper was drawn] have an opportunity of buying their own paper before putting the same on the market."[43]

On ninety-day paper, banks generally charged a 6-percent discount. It is likely that borrowers could do better in the money market by selling evidences of indebtedness to private investors. There were of course professional note brokers, and Marston occasionally remitted paper to the Payne firm for collection that had been transferred to him by bill brokers. In one letter he enclosed a mortgage note drawn by William Hales that had been brokered by a New Orleans exchange dealer, Palfrey & Williams. Marston had received the note from one of his debtors in settlement of a claim but had taken it after its maturity date. He surmised that the note's maker had already deposited the money with the named depositary and requested Payne, Harrison to see to the collection.[44]

Clearly, there was a large paper market discounting mortgage notes, among other instruments of indebtedness, both long-term and short-term, that operated in many of the same channels as factors' paper but was only vaguely connected to the marketing of agricultural commodities. The dimensions of this market are hard to estimate, but it is plausible that paper evidencing transactions between planters and factors for financing each year's planting was only a small part of it. The aggregate value of the paper in the debt market may have been double the annual value of agricultural commodities produced in the lower Mississippi Valley. Such would be the case if planters collateralized their debts with even a small portion of the aggregate value of their slave property.

Slave property was the critical link in antebellum credit relations. Factors often were integral in the purchase and sale of slaves. In February 1855 Marston advised Payne, Harrison that he had purchased a slave, a blacksmith, from the Port Hudson firm of Badley & Slaughter & Co. In partial payment of the purchase price, he had drawn a draft on Payne, Harrison payable in eight months. The vendor had indicated that the draft probably would not be presented for acceptance "until near its maturity—but as there was no *positive* agreement to that effect, [he had] concluded to advise" Payne, Harrison that he had drawn on them. In the event the draft was presented, he urged the firm to charge their usual commission for accepting, because he had made seven to eight hundred dollars on the transaction.[45] Indeed, Marston had not only purchased the slave at a bargain price, but had also obtained financing for eight months for a part of the purchase price.

Before his death Dr. Caulfield, Marston's brother-in-law, purchased land in East Baton Rouge Parish that was encumbered with a mortgage to the Citizens Bank to secure a stock subscription of the bank. In the complicated business of transferring a portion of the stock subscription to Caulfield's heirs, Caulfield's widow mortgaged two of her slaves to satisfy the bank's request for additional security.[46] The two slaves were deemed to be of a value equivalent to the 640 acres already under mortgage.

Samuel Oakey & Co. and Successor Firms

One New Orleans factorage firm had an especially long and significant presence in the parish: Samuel Oakey & Co. and its successor firms, Oakey, Payne, and Hawkins; Oakey, Hawkins; Hawkins and Norwood; and Norwood and Richards. The presence in the parish of the Oakey firm and its successors spans most of the nineteenth century.

Gilbert S. Hawkins joined the firm of Samuel Oakey & Co. sometime in the 1830s. He remained a partner until the firm's dissolution in 1855 in consequence of Samuel Oakey's death.[47] Samuel Oakey & Co. and Oakey, Hawkins had a large clientele in East Feliciana Parish and subsequently obtained familial relations as well. Hawkins and Norwood succeeded Oakey, Hawkins, and the addition of Abel J. Norwood to the partnership solidified a connection with one of the wealthiest families in Louisiana. The presence of Norwood money in the new firm's capitalization was conspicuous.

It is impossible to reconstruct the activities of Oakey, Hawkins and its predecessors; none of the records have survived. Oakey's succession proceeding, however, contains valuable information on the firm's assets, debts, and capitalization at the time of his death.[48] A summary of the partnership property indicates that the firm was holding more than $1 million in assets at the time of Oakey's death. These were net good assets and included the following: balances due on open accounts, $906,815.42; bills receivable, $154,148.69; stock in the Bank of Louisiana, $12,907.57; stock in the Mechanics and Traders Bank, $10,006.74; and stock in the Union Bank, $5,000. The estimated total of bad debts was $47,793.79. In addition, the inventory counted $2,589.69 in stock dividends and $11,580 in insurance scrip, which the experts valued at fifty cents on the dollar. Liabilities consisted of $783,032.43 in bills payable and $140,290.45 in open account balances owed to clients. Much of the money owed to clients on open accounts drew 8 percent interest.

Before analyzing the profit and loss account, it is important to note that most of the payables probably were drafts drawn by planter clients to cover planting expenses during the annual growing season. Such drafts most likely were discounted at all three of the banks in which the firm owned stock. Some of the bills payable probably were for debts owed to wholesale vendors, but how much credit could be obtained from northern manufacturers, even short term, was likely relatively small. Most supply accounts were paid with either sight drafts or thirty-day drafts.[49] Many of the drafts discounted by the firm for planter clients probably went to pay interest and principal expenses on debts that were owed either to city banks, the factor, or a resident of East Feliciana Parish. Marston, for example, paid his annual installments to Henry Boyce for the purchase of Ashland Plantation by drafting on Payne, Harrison.

It is significant that the dollar amount of the bills receivable in the asset column practically matches the balance due on open accounts in the liabilities column. The amount of long-term financing (i.e., for more than 1 year) that factors could afford their clients probably was constrained by the size of the deposits maintained by the clients. Bills receivable generally evidenced debts that were older than the current planting year. They were a mechanism for closing out an old balance with a negotiable interest-bearing promissory note. Such notes were in some instances sold to third parties (i.e., banks, investors, and other firm clients).

Bills receivable did not necessarily represent old planting debts. The only justification for allowing a planter to contract debts with the firm for longer than twelve months was when he was expanding his planting operations. If the firm could accommodate him, so much the better. As Marston remarked in his letter to Payne, Harrison concerning a two-year loan on a mortgage for slaves, he believed it to be contrary to the "custom of the house . . . to make advances beyond the proceeds of one crop."[50] It should be noted that the Payne firm contracted few collateralized mortgages in East Feliciana Parish, and an instance where it did so in another parish involved the sale of slaves and a sugar plantation owned by the firm.[51] The firm of Oakey, Hawkins, likewise, was not a significant lender on mortgages, even in the decade of the 1850s.

The profit and loss account showed a credit balance of $291,416.10. After deducting Oakey's share of the partnership debts and dividing by two (he owned 50 percent of the partnership), a credit balance of $78,103.76 remained. The partnership had a capitalization equal to almost 20 percent of its total assets. Ninety percent of the $47,783.79 carried on the books as a loss was attributable to bad debts on open accounts. Losses from bills receivable were a mere $5,165.64. If a firm client could not meet the terms of his open account arrangement, he was not likely to be accorded the favor of having the term of his indebtedness extended with an interest-bearing note.[52]

This examination is crucial for a variety of reasons. Clearly, much of the banking of planters in the parish was conducted directly with factorage firms rather than banks. In many transactions bank notes never entered the picture; the primary medium of exchange for settling accounts between Clinton merchants and small local planters was the factor's acceptance. In 1854 Marston conducted an exchange operation for the Union Bank, but he found it so unprofitable that he did not engage to do it for another year.[53] New Orleans bank notes clearly enjoyed a wide circulation in the parish, but they were only one dimension of a complex monetary system. Many debts were simply paid with drafts on factors, the present-day equivalent of checks drawn on a checking account. Sometimes such drafts were converted into bank notes, but other times they were used to settle other accounts and might be redeemed ultimately by the drawee factor simply debiting or crediting his account with another factor.[54]

New Orleans factors apparently conducted an extensive operation in cross acceptances for mutual accommodation, which meant that much of their paper floated in commercial channels alongside bank note issues.[55] Making estimates of the antebellum money supply is a tricky business. So, too, is making generalizations about the credit system on the basis of total banking capitalization in the locality and region. Plainly, the New Orleans money market was many times larger than the $28 million of banking capital held by the state-chartered institutions resident there in 1860. Indeed, the reason per capita banking capital in the antebellum South lagged behind that of the North may in part be that much of the banking in places such as Louisiana was conducted through private channels.[56] The combined capitalization of the city's factorage firms at least equaled the capitalization of the state-chartered banks, and may have exceeded it.

Hawkins organized a new partnership with Norwood in 1855 and acquired most of the assets and liabilities of the Oakey, Hawkins firm. The claims of Oakey's heirs against the new firm had not been liquidated when the Civil War engulfed the country five years later, and in consequence they lost most of their inheritance. Hawkins died in 1863, and liquidation proceedings commenced in 1865. The firm was liquidated in Hawkins's succession proceeding, so a complete listing of the firm's accounts survives.[57]

Among the assets of the firm of Hawkins and Norwood were forty-one bills receivable with a face value of $92,346.53. The expert appraisers valued these notes and drafts at ten cents on the dollar. Book debts totaled $236,884 but were valued at $72,097.96. Of the $250,000 in partnership debts for bills payable and balances on open accounts, only $38,000 was owed to city banks, wholesalers, and other commission merchants. More than eighty thousand dollars was owed to just three East Feliciana families: the Norwoods, the Palmers, and the Kellers. The remaining $130,000 was owed to firm clients, many of whom were holding interest-bearing, but unsecured, promissory notes issued by the firm. One family was owed more than forty thousand dollars on an open account.[58]

One observation is especially pertinent. On average the firm's debtors were far more numerous than its general creditors and owed substantially less on each account than the firm owed its creditors. Just five planter families accounted for one-half of the debts owed by the firm. It is probable that wealthy planter families banked a substantial portion of their savings with their factors, rather than city banks, because the factors paid a higher rate of interest.

It is surprising, too, how small the total discounts of paper through city banks were when the firm suspended—just sixteen thousand dollars. This is not to say that banks would not have been important sources of discounts for short-term planting debts, but the war substantially curtailed plantings, and the city banks more or less stopped discounting as soon as Louisiana left the Union.[59] By the time Louisiana seceded, most of the discounts for 1860 through banking channels would have been liquidated, and the banks discounted very little thereafter. At least in the case of the Hawkins firm, whatever long-term loans it could afford its clients were the result of large sums of money left on deposit by a handful of wealthy planters. Whether this was the case with other factorage firms in New Orleans will probably never be known, but suffice it to say that the Hawkins firm had made only a few loans on mortgages in the 1850s. All of the debts were on open accounts or were evidenced by unsecured promissory notes.

Many of the book debts were valued at par or at fifty cents on the dollar. This was not the case with any of the bills receivable, which were valued at ten cents on the dollar, an indication, perhaps, that such debts were worthless in the aftermath of the Civil War.[60]

Hawkins and Norwood probably was as large as its predecessor, Oakey, Hawkins, although at the time of its liquidation in 1863 its assets and liabilities were only about one-third those of the Oakey firm. The wide discrepancy is most likely attributable to a substantial amount of debt owed from the 1860 planting year, which was liquidated by cotton sales in the fall of 1860.[61]

In the year-to-year operations of such firms, the liquidity provided by banks probably was significant. In a postbellum lawsuit that might best be described as the ancestor of the lender liability suit, a New Orleans factor who had operations in East Feliciana explained in detail how the banks lubricated the money market.[62]

William Fellows, Jr., was sued by the Citizens Bank for nonpayment of drafts accepted by him from a client, Mrs. Routh, and exchanged for the notes of the bank. His defense was that he had acted as the agent for the Citizens Bank in all the transactions named by the bank in its petition. In 1867 the bank, "in order to enable her [Routh] to cultivate her plantation and produce a large crop of cotton the ensuing year so as to enable her out of its proceeds to pay off all or a portion of her indebtedness to it," had furnished her directly with credits to purchase supplies. At some point in time, the bank's officers realized that this course of conduct violated the 1842 Bank Act, so they prevailed on Fellows to act as her factor for purposes of accepting. According to Fellows, "There was no risk to run" on his part, and "he was likely to get the selling of a large crop of cotton. . . . the Bank intended to advance the supplies to carry on Mrs. Routh's plantation but wanted a merchant to act for it in doing the business, who for his trouble would receive the commission for selling the crop."[63]

Fellows claimed that he had not warranted the drafts' payment when he accepted them. He had purchased supplies for Routh that were paid for monthly as was the custom. Routh drafted on Fellows, who accepted her drafts "at or about the first of the ensuing month, as directed by the President [of the bank]." The drafts "were handed over to the Bank and the net proceeds given to respondent [Fellows] with which to pay off the Bills for supplies theretofore made for said plantation and the same was so appropriated."[64]

According to Fellows, he had accepted or endorsed the drafts at the request of the president, who had assured him that the "acceptance was intended only as a matter of form, in order that the said drafts might appear regular on the Books of the Bank." If the proceeds of the crop were insufficient, the bank would absorb the loss without recourse to Fellows. When it became obvious that the crop yield would be disastrously small, the bank refused to discount any more of Routh's drafts. Afterward, Fellows made advances to Routh on his own account, but her crop yielded a meager fifty-one bales. He claimed that he divided the proceeds of the fifty-one bales pro rata between himself and the bank. The bank, however, had advanced fifteen thousand dollars to enable her to make a crop.[65]

It is not clear whether this case was ever prosecuted; very likely the bank relented in the light of Fellows's embarrassing revelations. The lawsuit, however, does raise the possibility that banks were directly involved in financing antebellum plantations to an extent not recognized heretofore. The relationship between Routh and the Citizens Bank indicates a willingness on the part of the bank to discount Routh's drafts, thereby affording her, rather than her factor, credit facilities so that she could make a crop. Of course, the Citizens Bank was one of the reconstituted property banks, and most of its stockholders were Louisiana planters. The bank could lend considerably more money to such clients through their factors than it could lend to them on mortgages. Such, at least, was the case with short-term loans.

Factors' Mortgages in the Last Years of the Antebellum Period

If Louisiana banks were circumscribed by the 1842 Bank Act in making direct investment loans to the plantation economy, such was not the case with factors, who had symbiotic relationships with such institutions. Woodman's account of relationships among banks, factors, and planters focuses largely on short-term loan facilities, contracted during the planting season, and the necessity of a factor's endorsement on a planter's draft before a bank would discount it. His analysis seems to accept the criticisms of southern commercial boosters that planters' paper was inherently inferior and that banks had to be highly circumspect when discounting even short-term notes with good endorsements. His examination does little to explain how commercial agents supported long-term debt arrangements.[66]

In the last decades of the antebellum period, the long-term debt market eclipsed the short-term market. The rising incidence of mortgage notes being pledged as security for debts on open accounts probably is indicative of an upsurge in long-term lending arrangements. What is not clear is whether the growing use of collateralized open accounts simply represented a relatively new mechanism for securing long-standing credit arrangements that heretofore had not been secured formally, whether it represented new lending, or whether it simply reflected the willingness of an increasingly affluent population of rentiers to hold such debt securities for long periods of time. Financiers lent on income streams, hence the continuing importance of the open account in most debt arrangements. What better way to collateralize open accounts than to secure them with pledges of the very assets that produced those income streams. Mortgage notes pledged to secure open accounts were eminently flexible—they could be repledged as collateral security to those who lent to factorage firms.

It is probable that most of the money lent by factors in the 1850s came from wealthy clients who were willing to leave funds on deposit in return for substantially better returns than could be had from bank deposits. Banks occasionally lent directly on mortgages to planters and received in pledge mortgage-backed paper from factors, thus providing a valuable source of liquidity.

Mortgage lending continued unabated to the very end of the antebellum period in East Feliciana Parish. Not even the 1857 panic slowed the growth of this market. In that year the aggregate value of such loan arrangements collateralized with mortgages was in excess of fifty thousand dollars. Twelve of the seventeen mortgages that year were exclusively on slaves, and seven of the twelve slave loans were made by lenders in the parish. Loans by factors usually encumbered whole plantations and were on average four times the size of loans on slaves alone, but in 1857 there were five loans by factors collateralized just with mortgages on slaves.

Mortgage financing clearly contemplated a long-term debt arrangement that would collateralize the lender over a period of years. Some of the smaller mortgages were intended to secure antecedent planting debts. Most of the mortgages in 1857 were contracted by planters in the middle tier with wealth from forty to seventy-five thousand dollars. The exception that year was Baily D. Chaney, who obtained a thirteen-thousand-dollar credit facility from the commission merchant, Joseph Sallande. For his part, Sallande would serve as Chaney's commission merchant during the three-year term of the agreement. During that time he would make to Chaney "all necessary advances, whether in money, supplies, and provisions, acceptances or otherwise in the ordinary course of business, provided the same . . . already made or incurred [t]here-after . . . s[hould] . . . not at any one time exceed" thirteen thousand dollars.[67] Chaney's worth in the 1860 census was estimated at almost $100,000, and he mortgaged to Sallande 1,420 acres and thirty-two slaves. So large a credit facility, collateralized with a mortgage on an entire plantation, clearly con-templated something more than annual planting expenses. Sallande had agreed to accept drafts up to thirteen thousand dollars, an amount at least four times Chaney's probable annual planting expenses, assuming such costs on average were about twenty-five hundred dollars a year.[68] Chaney, then, was free to purchase slaves, land, whatever, using his collateralized open ac-count arrangement.

It is far from clear whether even the mortgages securing much smaller debts in fact collateralized planting expenses. The slave mortgages, for ex-ample, frequently collateralized a single draft that was identified in the mort-gage instrument. The draft, then, may well have been an accommodation for an unidentified third party.

Sarah Sims, on the other hand, obviously was collateralizing a credit fa-cility with a New Orleans factor, Wright, Allen, through that firm's Clinton representative, R. O. Draughon & Co. The firm of Wright, Allen had ac-cepted her draft of $1,150, payable in eleven months, and she mortgaged to them five slaves.[69] According to the 1860 census, her wealth was less than twenty thousand dollars. She was required to ship her crop of cotton for that planting year to Wright, Allen and pay them their usual commission. Exclu-sive consignment arrangements were relatively rare in the antebellum period. The total credit facility afforded her by the firm was $3,000, inclusive of the $1,150 draft.

In 1858 factors and local lenders collateralized almost $100,000 in loans with mortgages on slaves and on slaves and land. Factors accounted for seven of the nineteen mortgages on slaves alone, but the dollar value of each trans-action was almost double that of loans funded by local sources. Two of the five plantation mortgages were each in excess of twenty thousand dollars and were actually funded by the Bank of Louisiana, but factors guaranteed both indebtednesses.[70] Virtually all of the loans secured by slave mortgages were to planters in the middle tier whose household wealth ranged from forty to seventy-five thousand dollars. Most loans went to households with forty to fifty thousand dollars in wealth, but the recipients of three loans had more modest accumulations of five to ten thousand dollars.

The two loans funded by the Bank of Louisiana on the guarantees of factorage firms were both clearly intended for large capital improvements. Both households had wealth in excess of $100,000, and the mortgaged prop-erties were both sugar plantations, which required heavy investments in pro-cessing plants.

In 1859 debts of sixty thousand dollars were collateralized with mortgages, and the sum included twelve thousand dollars in loans secured by mortgages on town lots. Loans exclusively on real estate had been relatively rare since the 1830s, and the fact that borrowers were able to collateralize that much on real estate loans is an indication that the economy was prospering. Most of the loans collateralized in 1859 were funded by lenders in the locality.

That mortgages were an important indication of long-term lending, as opposed to short-term credit arrangements secured by mortgages, receives support from one especially interesting reinscription in 1859. On May 30, 1848, John Livingston DeLee had negotiated a commercial arrangement with Oakey, Hawkins in which the firm agreed to accept his drafts and make advances to him "to an amount not exceeding in the aggregate the sum of $5,000 at any one time."[71] The arrangement was secured by a mortgage on six hundred acres, stock, cattle, horses, mules, utensils, and fifty-one slaves.

DeLee was heavily in debt, and the instrument identified each of the prior encumbrances, which included conventional and judicial mortgages. Many of his creditors had already sued him and reduced their claims to judgments. Among his judicial mortgagees were other factorage firms, local lenders, the Louisiana State Bank, and the Union Bank. His debts aggregated to something in excess of thirty thousand dollars. The property was also encumbered with mortgages to the Citizens and Union banks for stock subscriptions. Most of the claims were already ten years old in 1848.

DeLee's mortgage instrument also stated that he was granting this security to Oakey, Hawkins to raise money "to pay certain debts owing and due by him and particularly to pay to the Citizens Bank of Louisiana the sum of $847—to the Union Bank of Louisiana, $1,000—to the Police Jury, $1,000." He authorized Oakey, Hawkins to pay such drafts as he might draw to pay installments on his debts, and to that extent he agreed that the firm would "be subrogated and stand in the place of said Citizens Bank and said Union Bank and said Police Jury."[72] Because the mortgages of the Citizens and Union banks had priority, vis-à-vis other secured creditors, Oakey, Hawkins was succeeding to the banks' privileged position in consequence of having paid DeLee's indebtedness to them. The firm obtained the highest priority ranking among the twenty-three conventional and judicial mortgagees.

That this mortgage was reinscribed in 1859 is an indication that DeLee still was in debt to Oakey, Hawkins's successor firm.[73] Clearly, the loans from the firm had greatly assisted him in his liquidation of his obligations to the property banks. The whole arrangement partook of a debt restructuring agreement, a debt consolidation plan.

In the 1860 census, DeLee's gross worth was estimated at just fifty-five thousand dollars. That figure probably represented his net worth, or what was left after deducting all of his various debts. The case of DeLee and others discovered in the course of researching this study suggest that gross wealth in the parish may have been underestimated by as much as 20 percent in the 1860 census.

Loans by factors in the last two decades of the antebellum period were primarily financed from savings in the local and regional economies. There is simply no evidence of a foreign presence in this loan market.[74] Factors were financing a considerable amount of capital investment, not just making advances and accepting drafts to cover the expenses of the annual planting. As will be seen, slave property was conspicuous in all such arrangements.

The extent to which factors recycled savings from lenders to debtors probably will never be known, but a limited examination of postbellum lawsuits in the district courts of Orleans Parish suggests that other factorage firms besides Hawkins and Norwood had substantial amounts of money on deposit from a few wealthy clients that was re-lent in relatively small increments to numerous middle-tier planters.[75]

The biggest area of loan demand for capital improvements in the last two decades of the antebellum period clearly was that created by middle-tier planters. Much wealthier planters contracted mortgage loans in the 1850s, but they were a small percentage of all the households in the parish with more than $100,000 in wealth. Three of four such mortgages in the period from 1852 to 1860 involved sugar plantations, which required substantial capital investments besides slaves. Much wealthier households were more likely to have surplus savings to lend, particularly toward the end of the antebellum period when heavy investments in satellite plantations in the alluvial regions of the state had been completed, and such operations were generating hefty incomes for their owners.

The importance of commission income generated by debt arrangements brokered by factors among their clients should not be overlooked. Even if a debtor such as DeLee paid only his annual interest cost, he paid it in a draft on which he was charged a 2.5 percent commission when the draft was accepted and 2.5 percent when it was paid; if the draft had to be converted into bank notes, he paid a discount as well. Assuming factors collected 2.5 percent on all agricultural products shipped from the parish and sold at New Orleans in 1860, the total commission income would have been forty thousand dollars. Commission income for servicing debt arrangements might have been that much and more, and significantly more if payment of interest and principal charges were postponed even three months and incurred discount charges.[76] When such paper was discounted, factors often bought it for their own accounts, thus capturing the discount, which ranged from 6 to 12 percent.

3

Securing Antebellum Credit Transactions with Slaves

S LAVES ACCOUNTED FOR most of the collateral for both short-term and long-term credit arrangements in antebellum East Feliciana Parish. It could be argued that the lien, or privilege (which arose by operation of law and was not recorded), on standing crops for supplies furnished to a farm or plantation in fact was the primary form of credit for yearly financing arrangements. However, privileges did not extend to cash advances or credit facilities furnished on open accounts, by far the most important sources of debit entries in account current statements. The Civil Code was only amended after the war to extend the privilege to cash advanced on open accounts.[1] As mentioned in the Introduction, any privilege on standing crops was highly contingent, dependent on the making of a crop, a successful harvest, shipment, and sale. Sales of staples may have liquefied open account balances, but staples were not the collateral of the credit system—short-term or long-term.

Most of the literature has approached slavery as a labor system, an "organizational form or system of production," according to Gavin Wright, "as though that term represented a clearly defined, well understood economic arrangement, to be contrasted with 'free' or 'wage' labor." In a recent article Wright focused on slavery as a "set of property rights":

> The weight of the evidence suggests that the rise of modern slavery was not attributable to advantages in production or political organization, but to the third set of features . . . property rights. . . . owners could do things with slaves that they could not do with free persons. Slaves could be bought and sold; they could be transported to any location where slavery was legal; they could be assigned to any task with no legal right to refuse or resign.

Moreover, slave prices "were a basis for credit arrangements across long distances and thus affected settlement patterns throughout the South."[2]

A distinction, however, should be drawn between lending on slave prices (inclusive of unrealized capital gains, i.e., lending on asset values) and lending on prospective income streams from slave property. This study argues that lending practices were influenced primarily by income streams, not rising asset values. Income streams, of course, in large measure set slave prices, but when those prices contained a large speculative premium, which seems to have been the case in the 1850s, there was no corresponding increase in relative debt levels. Lenders collateralized with slave mortgages in the 1850s were by any modern measure oversecured. Income streams were improving in the decade before the war because of expanding cotton demand, and this improvement seems to have led to an overall increase in lending. However, the ratio of debts to assets for most borrowers was too regular to contemplate speculative lending on rising asset values.

The slave market did influence lending practices in one important way. The highly liquid condition of that market made loans collateralized with slave mortgages more or less risk-free. An examination of land and slave markets in the parish is therefore invaluable in establishing a context for understanding the role of slave collaterals in the local and regional debt markets.

External Financing Considered
in the Context of Land and Slave Markets

Recently, Michael Tadman pointed out the conspicuous role of the cash nexus in the intraregional slave trade, an observation that amplifies Laurence J. Kotlikoff's earlier findings regarding the New Orleans market in general.[3] The implication of this finding for credit relations, however, has yet to be appreciated. An asset that is readily convertible into cash clearly possesses an attribute that makes it especially desirable for collateralizing debt arrangements. If collateral is easily liquidated, the costs associated with default are minimized. Reducing the costs that inevitably flow from a default lowers transaction and interest costs.

What about land, the other asset in planter portfolios? A survey of slave and land sales in the parish during the decade of the 1850s yielded evidence of two parallel markets whose fortunes more or less mirrored those of the great staple, cotton; nevertheless, the liquidity evident in the slave market at all times dwarfed that of the land market. In three of four years sampled in the decade of the 1850s (1850, 1853, 1856, and 1859), the slave market accounted for almost 80 percent of the total cash market for both land and slaves.

In 1856 the slave market's share of the cash market did decline to 63 percent, but this was probably an aberration attributable to the unavailability of slaves from sources within the parish and the absence of out-of-state slave traders to meet the demand. In 1859 one slave-trading firm, Heckle and Wilson, of Richmond County, Georgia, accounted for 46 percent of the slaves sold for cash. The firm's share of the dollars in the cash market that year came to an impressive 55 percent.[4]

The average number of slaves sold for cash in the years making up the sample, with the exception of 1853, was one hundred. In 1853 146 slaves were sold for cash, the largest number for any year in the sample. Thereafter, prices rose precipitously, and the number of slaves sold dropped 33 percent. Parish planters depended on the importation of slaves from the eastern seaboard to meet their needs. The slave population of the parish rose 25 percent in the decade of the 1850s, and perhaps as much as one-third of the increase is attributable to slave imports.[5]

The survey of land and slave markets, however, excluded probate sales and sheriff's sales under writs of fieri facias. Also, there was no way to account for slaves bought and sold in other jurisdictions by parish residents. The particulars of Louisiana's law of public registry for immovable property, however, ensured that all transactions within the parish involving land and slaves were recorded, and such registers are in all likelihood the most complete compilations that are available, and certainly the most reliable.[6]

Owners were also removing slaves from the parish during the last two decades of the antebellum period. Henry Skipwith observed that before the emancipation, wealthy planters in the parish's Seventh Ward had transferred their young slaves to the alluvial lands across the Mississippi River. Although Skipwith did not publish his recollections until 1892, his accuracy respecting this particular need not be questioned. By 1860 fully one-quarter of all plantation households in the parish had established satellite planting operations in the rich alluvial lands of northern Louisiana and the Atchafalaya Basin and were generating substantial surplus income that more than serviced debts of every description. Besides the costs of relocating slaves to DeSoto, Caddo, and Morehouse Parishes, East Feliciana planters had borne huge improvement costs in bringing these lands into cultivation. Henry Marston, for example, estimated that he spent thirty dollars on every improved acre of his Red River plantation, in addition to the twelve dollars per acre he paid to acquire the land. The alluvial plantations required expensive levee systems, and the risk of overflow and ruined crops was substantial.[7]

While the slave market was far more liquid than the acreage market, the number of sales in the public registers during the 1850s seems to indicate that no more than 1 percent of the total slave population in the parish was in commerce in any single year. The percentage, in fact, was probably a fraction of 1 percent because so many of the slaves sold locally came from Georgia, Kentucky, and Missouri.

On average, 6 percent of the acreage in the parish changed hands every year during the decade. The percentage may have been considerably higher after accounting for the public lands; acreage in the towns of Clinton, Jackson, and Port Hudson; and acreage sold at probate and sheriff's sales. Less than 8 percent of the total acreage in the parish was planted in cotton. It is probably safe to conclude that more than half of the improved acreage in the parish changed hands at least once during the decade. All recorded sales of acreage reflected improvements on the property, such as houses, barns, fences, and clearings.

Although an acre of land was from six to ten times more likely than a slave to change hands during the decade, the size of the total land market in dollars, inclusive of cash sales and credit sales, on average was only 85 percent of the total dollar market for slaves.[8] Credit sales of slaves rarely had terms of longer than twelve months, whereas credit sales of land usually provided for extending payments over a period of two to five years. Credit sales of slaves, as a percentage of the total dollar market for slaves, ranged from a high of 37 percent in 1856 to a low of 14 percent in 1859. On average, credit sales accounted for about 20 percent of the total dollar market for slaves, whereas cash sales for land ranged from 21 percent of the total land market in dollars in 1850 to 34 percent in 1859. As the local economy prospered in the 1850s, the land market did become relatively more liquid.

The important point to be gained from the analysis presented thus far is that cash sales of acreage, as a percentage of the total cash sale market for land and slaves, on average were only 24 percent of the total market. The relative weight of slaves in the cash market may well have been greater, given the facts that slaves purchased at New Orleans for cash and brought to the parish would not be counted in these averages, and that credit terms for land sales were far more generous than those for slave sales. Slaves taken out of the parish and sold would not have been registered in the local conveyance records, but such slaves were almost certainly sold for cash.

The slave market, of course, encompassed the whole South. The land market, no doubt, varied considerably across the region, each locality immersed in its own peculiar nuances; nevertheless, the anecdotal evidence suggests that in the whole of Louisiana credit sales were predominant in the land market.

The dynamics of land and slave markets over a span of twelve years are shown in Table 1 on page 57. The cash price of a slave more than doubled, and the size of the market in dollars quintupled. The credit sale market for slaves rose 300 percent from the 1847 level in the first six years of the period, topped out at $36,187.62, then declined 45 percent from its 1856 high. It was not just that slave prices were rising over the decade of the 1850s; the size and liquidity of the market in dollars was expanding dramatically as well.

The land market was relatively sluggish, although the total dollar market did rise 65 percent from its 1847 level. A trend toward narrowing the differential between cash sale prices and credit sale prices may be observable, but on average the acre price rise and growth in the relative liquidity of the land market were far from spectacular.

Conditions peculiar to the land market have to be considered, however, when evaluating the liquidity of that market. Slave and land markets diverged in another significant way: the kinds of monetary instruments that were used to satisfy sale prices. Cash for slaves meant just that, ready money—a bill of exchange or sight draft drawn on a New Orleans factor that could be converted immediately to bank note issues redeemable in specie or bills and drafts drawn on other American cities. Discounts on such paper would have been about 6 percent. Cash meant ready money, negotiable paper that circulated freely in commerce. This is not to say, however, that a cash seller of slaves necessarily took instruments that could be immediately converted into specie. Buyer and seller might have agreed to satisfy the sale price with an interest-bearing instrument that had a highly valuable endorsement on it. Such paper passed for cash and was indeed a cash equivalent.

Paper, however, that was collateralized with a vendor's privilege on the property sold, and sometimes a mortgage as well, was in another category and was relatively less liquid than cash or its equivalent. Such paper, like the land in the underlying transaction, was localized and illiquid. Whether local paper could be negotiated or discounted for value close to par depended on whether it had good endorsements. Such evidences of indebtedness could be just as liquid as sight drafts on New Orleans factors, provided they had good endorsements. Assuming such paper had good endorsements, however, it would probably not have been used in a land sale; if it was, the sale price would have been substantially discounted in exchange for the liquid paper. A cash sale of land resulted in a hefty discount. Slaves, on the other hand, who sold for cash according to the tenor of the recitation in the conveyance instrument, were traded for drafts or promissory notes that were deemed to be cash by virtue of the endorsements on the paper.

Cash sales of land often contained nuances peculiar to the mediums of exchange in which such transactions were consummated. An example of one such sale was a transfer of 580 acres for four thousand dollars, wherein the consideration was twelve hundred dollars in cash (i.e., current bank notes or factor's paper) and the transfer of two hand notes for fourteen hundred dollars each that had originated in an unrelated transaction, executed by James G. Kilbourne and payable in 1857 and 1858, respectively.[9] Two-thirds of the consideration was valuable paper that would not mature for 12 and 24 months. The vendor of the 580 acres certainly should not have been still protected by the vendor's privilege and resolutory condition implied in credit sales of immovables, which would have given him a tacit mortgage on the property so long as the Kilbourne notes remained unpaid. It is certainly arguable that the vendor assumed all the risks for the paper he had accepted as cash.[10]

Paper evidencing the credit portion of credit sales of land often could not realistically be negotiated at any price. On November 21, 1856, Mary A. Noble sold 640 acres to Thomas M. Scott, the same tract she had purchased from

Scott twenty years before. The sale price was fifteen hundred dollars, which Scott paid "by the return to . . . [Mary A. Noble] of three notes of hand which she gave him when she purchased from him."[11] Scott had held Noble's paper for twenty-one years, perhaps collecting some interest on the debt during the good years. However, Noble had never been able to redeem even one of her notes for presentation to the clerk of the mortgage records for cancellation on the mortgage instrument. Nevertheless, the sale from Noble to Scott was denominated a cash sale of land.

A seller-financed sale of land meant that the seller exchanged his land for illiquid paper on a long-term credit arrangement of three, sometimes four, and even five years, and he exposed himself to substantial risks if he sold the paper, because no one would buy it without a large discount and his personal endorsement, and perhaps also the endorsement of a wealthy accommodation endorser. Many such land sales probably were in fact liquidated years after their terms had expired, and for something less than the prices recited in the instruments. Fifty percent of the average cash sale price was the risk premium that credit sales of land could command.

Considering, then, the markets for slaves and for land, it is clear that the market was substantially more liquid and fraught with far fewer risks for sellers of slaves and holders of paper collateralized with mortgages on slaves. Indeed, slaves were predominant in formally collateralized credit arrangements and were used not only in securing credit relationships between New Orleans factors and their planter clientele but in securing accommodation endorsers against potential defaults by primary obligors as well.

To secure to the seller a vendor's privilege on the property, either land or slaves, for the credit portion of the sale price, it was necessary that the deed evidencing the transaction be recorded in the mortgage books. Few vendors of slaves ever bothered to satisfy this portion of the registry requirement to secure the privilege for any unpaid portion of the sale price. Clearly, many of the so-called credit sales of slaves were in fact deemed by vendors to be cash sales. A few sales provided for terms of up to twenty-four months, but they were exceptional.

In the three decades preceding the Civil War, recordations of land sales in the mortgage records outnumbered recordations of slave sales six to one on average. This six-to-one ratio generally prevailed in the years from 1825 to 1837, then fell to a four-to-one ratio from 1838 to 1845. In 1846 the ratio was three to one. For obvious reasons the markets for land and slaves were sluggish, and debt liquidations were clearly having an impact on the relative likelihood of slaves being sold on credit rather than for cash.

By the beginning of the 1850s, the six-to-one ratio had been restored, even though slave prices were climbing more rapidly than acreage prices. Only eight of the thirteen purported credit sales of slaves in 1856 were recorded in the mortgage records. In 1859 only six of the nine purported credit sales of slaves were recorded in the mortgage records. Clearly, vendors felt secure enough in many cases and saw no need to incur a small additional charge for a recordation in the mortgage records.

Credit sales of slaves tended to be sales of multiple slaves; for example, in 1856 two-thirds of all such sales involved the transfer to two or more slaves. Two sales that year resulted in the transfer of twenty-one slaves in all. Virtually all credit sales of slaves in the years sampled involved local vendors. Slave traders sold for cash or cash equivalents. As Tadman discovered, most sales by traders were sales of single slaves in their teens or early twenties.[12] Local vendors dealt in a far more varied mix of age groups.

To some extent the patterns observed in the slave and land markets were repeated in the probate records, although many, if not most, probate sales were simply mechanisms for partitioning estate property among coheirs. The terms of such sales generally provided for a down payment of one-third of the purchase price; the remaining balance, evidenced by promissory notes, was to be liquidated in one and two years with legal interest on the unpaid principal. The financing arrangements were sufficient to attract unrelated third-party purchasers, and such sales offered a rare opportunity to purchase slaves on twelve months', and sometimes twenty-four months', credit.

In most years sampled in the decade of the 1850s, credit sellers of land substantially improved the sale price per acre by financing for a period of years. This premium was in addition to interest on the unpaid debt. If the paper representing the credit portion of the sale subsequently had to be sold at a steep discount to raise cash, the vendor-holder of such paper, or the transferee of such paper, could more easily bear a discount of even 50 percent. Credit financing of land sales, then, clearly improved an acre's sale price.

Buyers and sellers of land certainly were conscious of the advantages to be reaped from seller financing of such transactions. Marston advised one vendor that "the price of your plantation may be considerably low, but I think the cash terms are large in proportion to the price, and if I were to go into an operation of the kind, all the stock wagons, etc. should be included in the sale."[13] Marston obviously was not talking about purchasing a plantation with slaves. He was expecting to purchase land on a generous credit. Any improvements placed on the property by a vendee could only be to the vendor's advantage, and if the vendee subsequently defaulted, the vendor usually consented to a reconveyance of the acreage, taking all the improvements in satisfaction of the unpaid debt.

Liquidating obligations arising from land sales tended to extend over far longer periods than those stated in the written instruments. Vendors frequently were content to receive only interest, with no payments on principal, for several years, and vendees no doubt found better uses for their ready money than liquidating old land debts. The accumulated debt from land sales, whether by ordinary conveyance or probate sale, may have aggregated to $500,000 in 1860 and encumbered 40 to 50 percent of the acreage in the parish. This portion of the debt load represented only one-thirtieth of the gross wealth of parish residents, but it probably accounted for one-fifth of the pre-war value of acreage in the parish. In postwar decades it would prove to be burdensome.

Slave and land markets were incomparables. Land was a very poor second to slaves in overall market liquidity, and as will be seen, this fact may explain why slaves, and not land, made up the collateral of the credit economy. It may also explain why land was never a serious source of collateral for securing credit transactions in postwar decades. Land redistribution after the war would not, then, have been a panacea for the credit stringencies experienced by sharecroppers and tenants in postwar decades.[14] Revolutionary redistribution might well have produced an even more penurious credit environment, although it is hard to imagine a world in which all credit facilities had completely vanished.

The cash market for land in the antebellum period was small and restricted to the locality. It was never a viable source of collaterals for credit relations, either before or after emancipation. Even local lenders and accommodation endorsers rarely accepted land as security for a loan, preferring slave mortgages or pledges of negotiable instruments with good endorsements.

Securing Antebellum Credit Transactions with Slaves

Louisiana law classified slaves as immovable for purposes of conveyancing.[15] The creation of a valid security interest in a slave could only be accomplished with a mortgage instrument in notarial form. The instrument obtained its ranking vis-à-vis third parties according to time of filing in the parish mortgage office registry. Once recorded, the instrument preserved the creditor's security interest in the property described therein for a period of ten years, and it could be reinscribed for an additional ten-year period.

Excluding probate sales and sheriff's sales of foreclosed property, a recorded instrument would be used for the following kinds of transactions: a credit sale of land, a credit sale of slaves, and actual loans secured by mortgages either on slaves alone, land alone, or both land and slaves. In the case of credit sales, the most common practice was to record the sale in the conveyance records and encumber the property with a mortgage for the credit portion of the sale. Sometimes a single instrument conveyed title to the property and mortgaged the property back to the seller. Identical instruments were sometimes recorded in the conveyance and mortgage records wherein title was transferred to the buyer, the credit portion of the sale was acknowl-

Table 1
Dynamics of Land and Slave Markets, 1847–1859

	1847	1850	1853	1856	1859
Total cash sales—slaves	$20,685.00	$51,145.40	$105,704.00	$62,224.00	$122,435.00
Average cash cost per slave	$481.04	$574.67	$724.00	$665.49	$1,118.69
Total credit sales—slaves	$10,517.00	$14,803.00	$32,375.00	$36,187.62	$19,850.00
Average credit cost per slave	$375.60	$643.60	$789.00	$786.68	$827.08
Total cash sales—land	$7,225.00	$9,791.00	$26,687.00	$37,665.00	$34,450.00
Average cash cost per acre	$5.20	$3.34	$5.32	$4.23	$5.88
Total credit sales—land	$36,764.00	$37,213.16	$85,459.66	$86,046.55	$67,533.78
Average credit cost per acre	$5.17	$4.03	$8.00	$6.97	$6.52

Note: Table was compiled by the author from information in the Conveyance Books, East Feliciana Parish.

edged by the debtor, and the promissory notes evidencing the debt were fully described and paraphed, or identified, with the instrument by the notary. The seller was protected by the vendor's privilege. However, a mortgage incorporated into the act of sale was the preferred method for effecting credit sales.

Mortgages typically contained an acknowledgment of the debt by the debtor, a description of the notes evidencing the indebtedness (paraphed with the instrument by the notary for purposes of identification), a complete description of the property being mortgaged and whether the property had been purchased that day by the mortgagor from the mortgagee, a confession of judgment, and in the last decade of the antebellum period, liquidated damages in event of default.

A rarely used security device was the antichresis, or pledge of an immovable.[16] Instances in which it was used all involved slaves, but the fact that it was used at all is indicative of the importance of slave collaterals in credit relationships. A debtor generally combined an antichresis with a mortgage (i.e., a mortgagor acknowledged his debt to the mortgagee, described the slave securing the liquidation of the debt, and then acknowledged surrender of the slave to the mortgagee in pledge). The slave was to remain in possession of the mortgagee to be used by him to liquidate the debt. The necessity of combining a mortgage with a pledge of the slave was to protect the creditor's ranking vis-à-vis third parties.

Although credit sales, probate sales, and sheriff's sales were all important components of the credit system in East Feliciana Parish, they were tangential to the relationship between borrower and lender that was formally collateralized for contemporaneous loans and other purposes. They were one end of a spectrum of transactions: at the other end were the unsecured credit transactions that were a routine part of everyday life in antebellum East Feliciana. An unsecured credit transaction might be nothing more than an open account at a local store with a balance owing of a few dollars, or it might be a wealthy planter's account with his factor in New Orleans that ran into the thousands of dollars. Merchants in Clinton sold on credit and settled accounts when the cotton crop was sent to market. Discounts were given if payment for merchandise was made in cash. They also made cash advances for cotton consignments, and such arrangements were transacted on open accounts.

In April 1854 Andrew J. Brame mortgaged to Hull and Rodd of New Orleans his 463-acre China Grove estate, a portion of which was planted in sugar. The amount of the mortgage was thirty-two hundred dollars. The mortgage was "for advances made and to be made [for Brame] . . . and for acceptances made and to be made for his accommodations, as well as for supplies and provisions and other necessities for the use of said plantation."

A portion, if not all, of the thirty-two hundred dollars represented anteced-ent debts, but the mortgage was drawn with a provision that covered any future advances up to the limit of the mortgage. William Hull and Edwin Walters individually accepted the mortgage on behalf of the commission mer-chant firm of Hull, Rodd & Co. as "security for the payment of such balance as might be due by . . . Brame at any future final settlement that might be had and made between them, whether settlement . . . [was] made at the expiration of the present year or not," but any balance left at that time was due and payable unless the payment time was extended by Hull and Rodd.[17] The mortgage was not to be canceled until all indebtedness then existing or exist-ing at a future time was fully paid.

This mortgage is unique because it is the only one thus far discovered in which a partnership of commission merchants collateralized an ongoing credit arrangement with a mortgage on land alone. Brame's wife had slaves but had mortgaged them to local lenders, probably to finance that year's planting. He was, in other words, heavily leveraged, by the standards of the time.[18] Hull and Rodd, no doubt, needed to negotiate Brame's paper in the New Orleans money market to facilitate a liquidation of his account. They accepted a mortgage on land because it was better than no security and would allow time for Brame to reorganize his affairs. The arrangement might best be described as an open account secured by collateral security notes (i.e., mortgage notes). The parties obviously contemplated that the arrangement would last for a period of years, not just for one growing season.

The following classification practically exhausts the possibilities for col-lateralized credit transactions, omitting, of course, short-term loans on con-signments of cotton to a commission merchant and the drawing of a sixty- or ninety-day bill of exchange against the consignment. A collateralized credit transaction secured either an antecedent debt, a contemporaneous loan, a fu-ture advance, or an accommodation endorser. Unlike commercial credit in-struments (bills of exchange), such notes did not evidence short-term loans that were self-liquidating. They almost always were for sums in excess of five hundred dollars and often ran into the thousands of dollars. In any single year, such security interests were approximately 25 percent of all instruments recorded in the mortgage books.

The 1820s and 1830s

In the years 1825 through 1828, sixty secured transactions can be classified as cash loans or loans of credit between parties who were not directly in-volved with each other in the financing of a credit sale. During that same period there were 189 recorded transactions in the mortgage books. Sixty percent of the mortgages that secured actual loans of cash, antecedent cash advances, or loans of credit were on slaves alone. The bulk of these appear to have been actual loans of cash, but there are at least three mortgages given to secure accommodation endorsers on a primary evidence of indebtedness.

In the case of accommodation endorsers, it is well to point out that, while the endorsed note was identified in the mortgage instrument, the accommodation endorser did not himself receive a promissory note or other evidence of indebtedness paraphed to the mortgage instrument. The accommodation endorser often got a mortgage on property that was already mortgaged to a primary creditor.

Besides thirty-five mortgages on slaves, there were six mortgages on slaves and land. Mortgages on slaves and land generally involved large sums of money. On July 14, 1828, Frederick Williams gave Parsons Carter a mortgage on a tract containing five hundred arpents and the slaves Major, aged 35; Stephen, aged 18; Tom, aged 14; Betsey, aged 29; Sally, aged 24; Horace, aged 6; and Ovid, aged 4. Carter had endorsed a note for Williams at the Bank of Louisiana for six hundred dollars and had endorsed Williams's draft for twelve hundred dollars on Nathaniel Cox and Co. of New Orleans as an accommodation endorser. The mortgage was to indemnify Carter in the event that Williams defaulted and Carter was called upon to honor his debts.[19]

On September 14, 1825, Joseph Kirkland, to secure Frederick A. Browder, Andrew Collins, and Craven Cash on accommodation paper that totaled forty-nine hundred dollars, executed a mortgage to his endorsers on 640 acres and thirty-two slaves. The youngest slave was eighteen months old. Kirkland's endorsers no doubt had cause later on to be appreciative of his kind consideration: he began liquidation proceedings within a year's time.[20]

There were three antichreses of slaves in which the mortgagee was given physical possession of the mortgaged slave for as long as it took for the slave's labor to pay off the indebtedness. On April 9, 1827, Sampson Ball gave a mortgage and an antichresis to Robert Pool to secure a loan of four hundred dollars. The instrument specifies that "in case the said Negro Stephen . . . die before the payment of the said sum of money then he the said Sampson Ball [bound] himself to furnish another Negro in every respect as good as the said Negro Stephen and the said last delivered Negro to be subject to . . . [the] mortgage in the full manner in every respect as the said Negro Boy Stephen. Said Negroes, [were] to remain so mortgaged" until the debt was fully paid.[21]

Of the nineteen mortgages on land, nine encumbered lots in the towns of Clinton and Jackson. Two were plainly intended to indemnify sureties on judicial bonds, and three were mortgages to secure accommodation endorsers. The amounts of the debts acknowledged average about $350; debts secured by slaves average about twice that much. There were thirty-nine credit sales of land but only nine credit sales of slaves in the years from 1825 through 1828. There were thirteen bank loans secured by mortgage, three on land alone and ten on land and slaves.

The years 1835 through 1838 were important in the economic development of the area, but the data is skewed because of the lending activities of the three property banks. Thirty-two percent of all security transactions were either bank loans on land and slaves or loans on bank stock. During this four-year period, mortgages on land alone originating outside property banking channels almost equaled those on slaves. Mortgages on land need to be carefully scrutinized, however, and a closer look shows that most were made to secure accommodation endorsers on property in the towns of Clinton, Jackson, and Port Hudson. It is clear, too, that in most of these transactions mortgagors were actually borrowing from the property banks on the security of accommodation endorsements. When such transactions are excluded, a ratio of four slave mortgages to one land mortgage prevails. Roughly half the slave mortgages were executed to secure accommodation endorsers, and it is probable that some of this paper was discounted eventually at one of the property banks. The eventual lender in most of these transactions, however, does not appear to have been one of the property banks.

Even in the decade of the 1830s, slaves remained the preferred security for most lenders. However, the proliferation of loans on land mortgages was exceptional, a direct result of the state guaranteeing the bonds that financed the capitalization of the property banks and mandating that a portion of the loan portfolios be invested in real estate mortgages. The property banks disappeared in the early years of the depression that began in 1839, hence their exclusion, for purposes of this study, in quantifying the incidence of slave collaterals.

The following represents a typical loan on slaves: Adeline Johnson executed a mortgage to Edward Tooker on February 20, 1838, for two thousand dollars evidenced by three promissory notes paraphed by the notary to the act of mortgage. The instrument recited that the debt was predicated on a purchase of merchandise by Johnson from Tooker. She gave him a mortgage on Effy, aged 35. Johnson was binding herself for a community debt; Effy was her separate property, and the mortgage of the slave was given as additional security to Tooker.[22]

In another case that year, Joseph Nichols, who had just bought three lots in Jackson on credit, obtained a mortgage from his vendor on nine slaves to secure him in the event his vendor defaulted on a primary mortgage that still encumbered the lots. He had not assumed the existing mortgage as part of the sale price.[23]

Mortgages on slaves often resulted from unusually complex underlying transactions. In June 1836 Richard Cochrane and his wife, Adeline, gave A. &

J. Dennistoun & Co., exchange dealers, a mortgage on Harry, aged 25; Eliza, aged 24; John, aged 7; Margaret, aged 5; Martha, aged 24; Ned, aged 41; two lots in the suburb of Lafayette, Jefferson Parish; and two tracts of land in East Feliciana Parish, one equipped with a cotton gin mill. Dennistoun had given Adeline Cochrane, who was separate in property from her husband, "to help and aid her in the prosecution of her business and in the purchase of goods that she . . . [was] going to do in Europe, Letters of Credit on one or Different merchants in that continent to the amount of $6,600." The mortgagors promised and bound themselves insolido to reimburse A. & J. Dennistoun & Co. the full and entire payment at 10 percent interest.[24] The slaves, incidentally, were Richard Cochrane's separate property.

There were two antichreses of slaves during these years. John Bostwick mortgaged Humphrey, aged 16, to Thomas Chapman to secure a debt of four hundred dollars and put Chapman in possession of the slave with the stipulation that the slave was to remain in Chapman's possession until the interest on the indebtedness was paid. A few months later Bostwick found that he needed more money, so he executed a new note and mortgage on Humphrey for $615 with the same stipulation that "the work and services of said negro boy Humphrey [were] to be the compensation for the interest or use of said money until the same . . . [was] paid."[25]

From 1835 through 1838, seventeen mortgages on land and slaves originated outside the lending activities of the property banks. All were for debts in the thousands of dollars, with the average indebtedness being about three thousand dollars. All were to secure accommodation endorsers, antecedent debts, or both. Benjamin Kendrick's name appears as mortgagee on five of the instruments. Kendrick was one of the wealthiest men in the parish, a distinction passed on to his only child, Isabelle Fluker. On January 17, 1835, John G. Perry acknowledged his indebtedness to Kendrick for forty-five hundred dollars with 10 percent interest. Perry had "passed his note promissory . . . payable to the order of Kendrick . . . at the counting room of Butler, Shipp & Co., New Orleans." Kendrick had endorsed the note, allowing Perry to borrow on it.[26] Perry gave Kendrick a mortgage as indemnity in the event he failed to pay the accommodation note when it matured. Most of the mortgaged property consisted of slaves purchased from various slave traders, including Thomas McCargo of Monroe County, Alabama, and Richard Cooper of Selma, Alabama.[27]

In August 1835 Henry Marston, whose name would be prominent in business affairs for most of the rest of the century in East Feliciana Parish, acknowledged his indebtedness to Elias Norwood for fifteen hundred dollars, giving Norwood a promissory note secured by a mortgage on "Cuppy & Rose, Mary and a boy Sprightly."[28] The mortgage was canceled on January 1, 1836. Marston, a small planter and merchant and cashier of the Clinton branch of the Union Bank, largest of the property banks, understood well the role of wealthy accommodation lenders in his locality, and the names of Norwood, William Silliman, and Benjamin Kendrick often appear in connection with his business activities.[29]

Typical of the mortgages on slaves during the 1830s was one executed by Louis Martin to Norwood for $450, payable in six months. Martin mortgaged the following slaves: Betsey, aged 50; Darcy, aged 37; Angelina, aged 20; Milly, aged 17; Little Peter, aged 15; Matilda, aged 14; Claudia, aged 9; Hilda, aged 7; Henry and Harriett, both aged 3; and Joe, aged 11 months.[30] Norwood made direct loans of cash, as well as loans of his credit, by means of the accommodation endorsement.

Martin apparently needed more money, or credit, or needed to collateralize old debts, because she and her husband attempted two weeks later to collateralize their creditor with a pledge of their growing crops. In this case, Martin and her husband, to secure and indemnify their accommodation endorser, Isaac R. Caulfield, gave him a lien or privilege on their growing crop. They also tried to collateralize Caulfield with a privilege on their wagons and livestock. They promised to cultivate the crop and produce as much as possible and to deliver all their cotton and corn to Caulfield after the harvest. He was given authority "to dispose of the crop of cotton in the cotton market in New Orleans as he would if his own." The proceeds were to be applied first toward the liquidation of their indebtedness to Caulfield of fifteen hundred dollars. If the cotton crop was insufficient to discharge the note, Caulfield was to receive the corn at the price of the neighborhood.[31] The mortgage was never canceled.

The kind of security interest Martin and her husband attempted to confect for the benefit of Caulfield was unique among the thousands of instruments examined for the antebellum period. A furnisher of necessary supplies to a plantation or farm had a privilege on the crop by operation of law, and no recordation was necessary. That privilege did not include advances of money, and it could not be pledged to secure an accommodation endorser. The Martins could not mortgage the crop to Caulfield, and they could not grant him a lien or privilege on the crop.

The following year Martin gave Norwood a new mortgage on the slaves previously enumerated together with "the present corn and fodder also the crop of cotton that was growing on the plantation."[32] This mortgage, also, was never canceled.

During the years 1835 through 1838, there were numerous credit sales of land and slaves, with an average ratio of about five land sales to each slave sale. The ratio would be substantially higher for land sales were the trading activities of the Taylor brothers excluded from the slave sales on credit. The Taylors were slave traders from Virginia, and they sold for cash and on credit, usually for no longer than six or twelve months. Their trade accounted for more than half of all credit sales of slaves in this four-year period.[33] They purchased land in the parish, became permanent residents, and married into the old planter elite.[34]

The 1840s

From the onset of the depression in 1839, almost seven years passed before land and slave prices reached a bottom and began a modest recovery. The 1830s had been a period of credit expansion. In the 1840s there was a spectacular contraction precipitated initially by a collapse of cotton prices. The withdrawal of the property banks from lending and their subsequent liquidations was only one of many grim reminders of how vulnerable personal fortunes were at a time when central banking was nonexistent and a national monetary system, underwritten by the federal government, was a political impossibility. The first of the foreclosures and sheriff's sales appear in the mortgage records in 1839, but the magnitude of the collapse at the local level only becomes apparent in the years 1841 to 1847.

Of the thirteen credit sales of slaves in 1841, no less than nine were sales by syndics for insolvent debtors. These were the so-called voluntary surrenders of property for the benefit of creditors, or assignments for the benefit of creditors. Fourteen of the forty-eight credit sales of land were sales by syndics, and if such credit sales and probate sales, together with sheriff's returns, are subtracted from the total number of credit instruments recorded in 1841, credit transactions in the parish were about one-third of what they had been in 1836.

What activity there was involved mortgages on slaves, purchasers of slaves at syndic sales providing additional security by mortgaging other unencumbered slaves, and planters collateralizing credit relationships with New Orleans factors. On September 30, 1841, Thornton Lawson gave a mortgage to Samuel Lee, one of the wealthiest planters in the parish, to cover an advance that Lee had apparently taken up for Lawson when it became due and payable. Lawson had drawn a draft on James Conner, merchant, New Orleans, payable to the order of his two endorsers, John DeLee and Burnell Myers, and the draft had been accepted by Conner and presumably negotiated or discounted at New Orleans. Lawson obviously was not in a position to pay the draft when it was presented to him, and he had prevailed on Lee to negotiate the instrument for the benefit of the holder, either by endorsement or discount. The mortgage was to indemnify Lee in the event Lawson was unable to recompense him for taking up the paper drawn on Conner. Lawson mortgaged to Lee the following slaves: Jerry, aged 26; Milo, aged 26; Nancy, aged 25; Lucy, aged 26; her three children, Caroline, aged 12, Minna, aged 8, and Henry, aged 5; Dianna, aged 18; Elias, aged 11; and Patsey, aged 10.[35]

Sheriff's returns under writs of fieri facias peaked in 1843 with fifty-two

CLINTON, *March 18th* 183_

CASHIER OF THE OFFICE OF DISCOUNT AND DEPOSIT OF THE

UNION BANK OF LOUISIANA, AT CLINTON,

PAY TO *Myself* _____ OR BEARER,

Fifty four _____ DOLLARS. *fifty four* CENTS.

$ 54,34

J. Lawson

UNION BANK AT CLINTON

A draft by Thornton Lawson on the Union Bank of Louisiana, at Clinton.

seizures and sales of debtors' properties. There was one bank loan that year, compared to five in 1825, and it simply provided financing for a new owner of property bought at a sheriff's sale by the bank and resold on credit. The property banks' liquidators were kept busy during the 1840s reinscribing mortgages, security arrangements that had been contracted a decade before on which the underlying loans had not been paid. Mortgages contracted in the heyday of the property banks were still being reinscribed in the mortgage books of East Feliciana Parish on the eve of the Civil War. The debtors had achieved, at no small cost to themselves and the credit of the state of Louisiana, long-term loans of capital. The banks were aptly called property banks.

Sheriff's sales of debtors' property usually provided for a term of twelve months, so it was not unusual to find debtors buying their property back subject to all existing mortgages, contractual and judicial. How these debts were eventually disposed of is something of a mystery. Marston, for example, eventually bought the Clinton branch of the Union Bank and was able with strenuous exertions to collect on much of its defaulted portfolio.[36]

In 1845 there were eighty transactions recited in the mortgage records. Twelve were sheriff's returns under writs of fieri facias, thirteen were re-inscriptions of property bank mortgages, one was a bank loan on repossessed property, fourteen were credit sales of land, and four were credit sales of slaves. There were eleven mortgages on slaves, four on land and slaves, and five on land alone. There were eleven procès-verbaux of probate sales.

What credit there was came from New Orleans factors, and when collateral was required such loans were secured by mortgages on slaves. The usual case was a debtor providing additional collateral for antecedent debts. Margaret Morris and her husband, for example, executed a mortgage to secure an antecedent debt of $750 to Charles Lathrop of New Orleans, collateralizing eight "certain negroes and slaves to wit: Aisley, a yellow woman aged thirty-five (35) and her three children, Maria, a woman of yellow complexion age (19) years, Jim a boy fourteen (14) years and Eliza a girl of yellow complexion aged eleven (11) years—Caroline a woman of dark color aged twenty-five (25) years and her three children Mornha a girl of dark color seven (7) years, Mary a girl of dark color aged four (4) and Amelia a yellow girl (6) six months, all of which [were] slaves for life and the separate property of . . . Mrs. Johnson [Margaret Morris]."[37] This mortgage was canceled within a year's time. John Kernan executed a mortgage to Richards & Montgomery of New Orleans to secure what was obviously an antecedent debt of sixteen hundred dollars, collateralized with seven slaves. Lathrop took another mortgage that year on a slave family—Jim, aged 45; Mary, aged 35; and their five children—from William Reid and his wife to secure an indebtedness of seven hundred dollars.[38]

The year 1846 was characterized by the same low level of activity but with New Orleans commission merchants becoming increasingly more important as creditors in the collateralized credit transactions that were contracted. The commission merchants had their share of difficulties, however, as is evidenced by a deed of trust executed by William H. M. Magruder to Charles Lacoste, liquidator of William Nott and Company, New Orleans. Magruder probably was collateralizing an antecedent debt of $6,312.13. The instrument was in the form of a deed of trust that was intended to permit the creditor to sell the property (in this case, slaves) if the debtor-vendor defaulted on the loan without recourse to the courts and a formal foreclosure proceeding.[39] If contested, it is doubtful that the conditions of this instrument would have been enforceable.

On May 12 Stephen Johnson acknowledged his indebtedness to Bres, Frellsen & Co. of New Orleans for sixteen hundred dollars "current money of the United States, being [for] cash . . . [that] day advanced and loaned to him." A promissory note payable to the order of and endorsed by Bres, Frellsen & Co., payable December 1, 1846, with 8 percent interest after maturity, was paraphed by the notary with the act of mortgage on ten slaves. On December 16, 1846, Elizabeth M. Howell mortgaged twenty-eight slaves, her separate property, to Emile Johns of New Orleans to secure a debt of twelve thousand dollars, and Henry Knox executed a mortgage to Samuel Lee, the local planter previously mentioned, to secure various debts that totaled $1,320. Knox acknowledged a promissory note to Lee for $205, payable one day after date, a hand note for $400, payable on demand, and another hand note for $640, also payable on demand. He gave Lee a mortgage on two slaves to secure all three antecedent debts, which were two and three years old.[40] Mortgages to secure antecedent debts are a clear indication of how much paper circulated with only the name of a maker, and perhaps an accommodation endorser, as security for eventual payment.

There was one antichresis of a slave in the 1840s. On May 11, 1843, Penelope Edwards sold John Robertson "the services of a certain Negro boy named Sam, aged (?) years . . . which services [were] to be rendered until the return of the money borrowed in lieu of interest" on a debt acknowledged by her of $250.[41] She gave Robertson a mortgage and an antichresis to facilitate a liquidation of the debt.

The 1850s

The last decade of the antebellum period was one of sustained prosperity for the cotton South as a whole and a time of rising expectations, due in large part to a recovery of land prices to predepression levels and a doubling of slave prices above levels attained in the 1830s.[42] The particular species of planter-factor mortgage most commonly associated with the antebellum period, which secured both antecedent debts and future advances, only realized its complete evolution, both legally and economically, in the last two decades before the Civil War. Direct financing by banks was practically nonexistent, and much of the financing obtained from commission merchants was for capital investment (i.e., the purchase of slaves for cash). The overall prosperity lessened the need for formal collateralization of credit relationships, but when mortgages were contracted, slaves continued to provide the basic collateral. Moreover, slaves were being used to finance increasingly sophisticated transactions, such as the purchase on credit of a steam engine from a manufacturer in Cincinnati.

From May 1853 through December 1856, $286,287.86 in credits were formally collateralized to secure antecedent debts and future advances, accommodation endorsers, or loans of cash or credit. It is practically impossible to estimate the total amount of credit extended during this period from sources that required no security, but a rough estimate might be the gross value of staples shipped from the parish annually. Lending, after all, was predicated on cash flow. It is possible that credit facilities available to parish residents were considerably larger than any of the estimates thus far ventured. The value of slave property alone in 1860 approached $8 million.

From May 1853 through December 1856, there were twenty-two transactions in which debts to New Orleans factors were collateralized with mortgages on slaves. The average amount of each transaction was $2,244.92. Local lenders accounted for twenty-four mortgages on slaves, with an average value of $1,226.11 per transaction. There were fifteen transactions in which New Orleans factors took mortgages on land and slaves to collateralize debts, and these averaged ten thousand dollars per transaction. Debts secured by mortgages on land totaled $23,822.04. There were twenty-nine such transactions with an average value of $821.44. Mortgages on land alone accounted for 8 percent of the total value of all debts formally collateralized in this 3 1/2-year period. Most were small loans secured by mortgages on town lots and buildings in Clinton and Jackson. It seems clear that the true measure of wealth in this rural Louisiana parish was the number and quality of slaves in a particular household.

Mortgages on land and slaves to New Orleans factors to secure antecedent debts and future advances became the norm in the 1850s. Whether such relationships would have come to dominate the local credit economy, displacing local accommodation endorsers entirely, is a matter of speculation. Local credit sources were still important, even in the years immediately preceding the war.

Who held the upper hand in this relationship between commission merchant and rural planter is also a matter of speculation.[43] There appears to have been much competition in the 1850s for cotton consignments, whether in the locality or at New Orleans, and the economy was not heavily leveraged in the modern sense of the word. The biggest credits, formally collateralized, rarely represented more than 10 percent of a planter's wealth. Formally collateralizing drafts and acceptances permitted the commission merchant, or holder in due course, to negotiate such paper more easily and at a value close to par.

The first instance of a mortgage securing antecedent debts and advances to be made on an open account that closely resembled Louisiana's present-day collateral mortgage was recorded in East Feliciana Parish on February 20, 1856. George Purnell executed a mortgage to A. Miltenberger & Co. of New Orleans for eleven thousand dollars "for advances made and to be made for his own use and accommodation." He executed two promissory notes, paraphed by the notary, one for five thousand dollars and one for six thousand dollars, each payable twelve months afterward at the Bank of Louisiana with 8 percent interest. The mortgage encumbered three tracts of land, totaling about nine hundred acres, and twenty-four slaves. Purnell was a sugar planter, and the 1860 census placed a value of eighty-two thousand dollars on his real and personal estates. The mortgage was to remain "as a standing and permanent security in favor of the said A. Miltenberger & Co. to secure them the payment of all advances and acceptances and of all plantation supplies, the note . . . [to] remain in the possession of the said A. Miltenberger & Co." The parties waived the necessity "of making any further or additional mortgage at the maturity of said notes for the renewal or extension of the same, it being expressly understood that said notes secured by . . . [the] mortgage . . . [were] to be retained by . . . [A. Miltenberger & Co.] as security for all drafts which they . . . [might] hereafter accept for the accommodation of . . . G. W. Purnell . . . and which they [might] be compelled to pay without having been placed in funds to meet the same." This mortgage was canceled on March 25, 1859. A new mortgage was recorded that same day increasing the amount of the credit arrangement to $16,500.[44]

The instrument just described does not state that the mortgage notes are held in pledge by A. Miltenberger & Co., or that the mortgage has been accepted by the commission merchant for the benefit of future holders of the notes. It is doubtful, however, that A. Miltenberger & Co. ever negotiated the paper; probably they pledged the notes to one of the city's banks to secure the firm's own credit lines. Miltenberger could have sold the notes, but only as agent of the principal, Purnell.

The mortgage to Miltenberger is very different from the one executed by John McKneely on May 29, 1854, to J. W. Burbridge & Co. That instrument recites that Burbridge had agreed "to accept [McKneely's] drafts, endorse his notes, and make cash advances, from time to time, for his use and accommodation, with the understanding that the total amount of these liabilities for him and his indebtedness to them . . . [should] never exceed at any one time the sum of $18,500." The firm had already endorsed his note for ten thousand dollars. McKneely mortgaged his thousand-acre plantation and fifty slaves, each identified by name and age. There was no mortgage note for $18,500 paraphed by the notary with the act of mortgage.[45] The Miltenburger mortgage evidences a great deal more attention to legal particulars than the one that encumbered McKneely's property. However, McKneely was required to submit to the jurisdiction of a court in Orleans Parish in the event of default, thus obviating the problem of local justice, and he agreed to liquidated damages (for attorney's fees) in the event of default in the amount of 5 percent of the outstanding balance on the loan.

Both mortgages collateralized open account arrangements or open credit facilities. Whether mortgage notes, as collateral security, needed to be held in pledge by the creditor to preserve his priority status was a question that was not answered until after the Civil War. The partners in the Burbridge firm clearly thought that the credit facility afforded McKneely was adequately secured.

The fact is that both of the instruments just described accomplished the purpose for which they were intended. The Burbridge mortgage encumbered property with a liquidated value of at least fifty thousand dollars. Neither firm expected to commence foreclosure proceedings when they accepted their respective mortgages from their debtors. They did not, in other words, lend on collateral. In the unlikely event of a default, however, they were more than adequately secured for credits that represented substantial sums of money in the antebellum period. Per capita income in the United States in 1860 was a little more than one hundred dollars a year. Ten thousand dollars was the combined annual income of ten middle-class households.

One of the largest loans financed through the credit facilities of a New Orleans commission merchant that utilized a mortgage on slaves alone was one executed personally by John Y. Mills and Alexander Mills and by their firm of John Y. Mills & Brothers. The firm of Wills & Rawlins of New Orleans had accepted six drafts drawn by John Y. Mills & Brothers, five for three thousand dollars and one for one thousand dollars. "To secure the full and punctual payment of the said drafts and to secure and hold the said Wills & Rawlins harmless and indemnified against any and all loss, damage, or injury which they . . . [might] incur or be put into by, through or on account of their acceptance of said drafts, and being compelled to pay the same as acceptors thereof—without being furnished with the necessary funds by said John Y. Mills & Brothers," John Y. Mills, Joel H. Mills, and Alexander Mills mortgaged to Wills & Rawlins four slaves belonging to John Y. Mills, five slaves belonging to Alexander Mills, and five slaves belonging to Joel Mills. They also bound themselves to send their next crop of sugar to Wills & Rawlins and to pay attorney's fees of 10 percent on any outstanding balance in the event of a default.[46]

The magnitude of the credit facilities furnished the Mills brothers by

Wills & Rawlins obtains some perspective from the liquidation, the following year (1855), of the property of the succession of Leonora Perry. Her fifteen-hundred-acre sugar plantation was sold with 150 shares of Citizens Bank stock, subject to a loan from the Citizens Bank, for five thousand dollars and a six-thousand-dollar loan from Lowe & McCall of New Orleans. The purchaser, her surviving spouse, bought the plantation for three thousand dollars cash, the assumption of the debts described above, and one thousand dollars financed on two years' credit. The liquidation of 110 slaves brought $70,373.[47]

The Mills brothers resorted to local credit sources in the years following their arrangements with Wills & Rawlins. On April 24, 1855, they executed two promissory notes to Abel Norwood for $18,725 secured by a mortgage on seventy-six slaves, thirty mules, and 1,050 acres.[48]

Slaves sometimes provided additional collateral for a vendor, especially when an entire plantation was sold on credit. On June 4, 1855, Susan Brewer sold S. M. Thomas her Cottage Hall Place, consisting of nine hundred acres, farming utensils and equipment, and fifteen slaves, for fifteen thousand dollars at 8 percent interest payable over five years. She reserved the right of "requiring payment of a portion of said principal, but not to exceed the sum of twenty-five hundred dollars any one year."[49] The land and improvements were released from the mortgage, however, and she accepted in substitution a mortgage on a slave family, composed of six members, who belonged to her vendee. It seems probable that the paper she received in this transaction was much more likely to be negotiable at something close to par than the prior mortgage on land and slaves. In truth, the fifteen slaves represented about 80 percent of the purchase price. By obtaining a mortgage on additional slaves for the credit portion of the sale, she was protecting herself in the event one or more of the slaves subject to her mortgage died during the term of the loan.

On August 1, 1855, there was the rather extraordinary transaction in which Benajah D. Doughty and his two partners, Thomas Dixon and Robert Brown, secured the purchase price of a steam engine from Lyon & Bell of Cincinnati with a mortgage on slaves. The three acknowledged their indebtedness to Lyon & Bell for $1,260 for the steam engine, boiler, and sawmill gearing. They gave a note to Lyon & Bell's representative payable at the counting room of James Robb in New Orleans on January 1, 1856, with 8 percent interest thereafter. Dixon mortgaged Noah, aged 22; Doughty mortgaged Maria, aged 22, and her four children; Bob, aged 8; Phil, aged 7; Charley, aged 4; and Andy, aged 2. The notary paraphed the note payable at Robb's office with the act of mortgage.[50]

Frequently, mortgages to New Orleans factors accomplished a consolidation of a planter's debts. Daniel C. McMillan entered into an arrangement with Wright & Davenport of New Orleans, represented by Hamilton L. Wright, wherein the firm agreed to accept the following drafts, all of which evidenced antecedent debts contracted by McMillan: a draft to W. H. Letchford & Co. for $1,279 at twelve months; two drafts in favor of A. Levi, Bloom & Co. of Clinton for $850 and $147, respectively, at ten months; and a draft in favor of Frank & Pool of Clinton for $500 payable in twelve months. The arrangement provided for "further acceptances and advances, not to exceed $6,000."[51] To secure his new credit facility, McMillan gave a mortgage to Wright & Davenport on twenty slaves. He agreed to pay a 2 1/2-percent commission on any drafts accepted by the commission merchant. Interest was charged at the rate of 8 percent on the unpaid balance.

A few observations about the last decade before the Civil War are in order. First, the number of formally collateralized credit transactions was growing, and the size of the credit facilities seemed to be increasing. Whether there was an upsurge in new borrowings by parish planters, however, is far from certain. A consolidation of credit facilities within the region at New Orleans would have perforce led to a formalization of lending arrangements that in prior decades would have subsisted on personal relationships without collaterals. The growth in the use of collaterals may be more indicative of the appearance of a secondary market for mortgage-backed securities.

It is unlikely that loan growth in the 1850s diverged significantly from improving income streams during those years. In the case of Louisiana at least, Green concluded that the symptoms of financial instability were not in evidence before the 1857 panic. Of course, Green's analysis was from the perspective of the commercial banks and thus does not contemplate the role of factors as investment bankers. The assets of the commercial banks were highly liquid, whereas those of factorage firms were relatively less so. Still, the panic seems to have occasioned relatively little hardship in the locality or at New Orleans. This would seem to support the conclusion that loan growth in the 1850s did not diverge significantly from improving income streams.[52]

Improving income streams were, however, a direct consequence of the increasing demand for staples during the 1850s. Wright observes that this demand stagnated in the decades after 1860, so presumedly debt levels would have had to contract to comport with a declining income stream. It is unlikely that the shock would have been severe, however; most borrowers were not leveraging assets.[53]

What distinguishes the 1850s from the 1830s is the quality of the collateral backing the loans. The property bank mortgages of the 1830s, for example, collateralized considerable acreage but relatively few slaves. If the credit transactions of the 1830s were thinly collateralized, those in the 1850s were well secured in an economy that was growing in wealth, sophistication, and size. There were practically no direct bank loans by New Orleans banks in the area in the 1850s, and the banking capital in the city certainly was not much larger than it had been in the 1830s.

Second, local lenders, whether of cash or credit on accommodation en-dorsements, continued to be important sources for credit. Such local lenders accounted for about 30 percent of the dollar amount of all formally collater-alized transactions in the years covered by this examination. One inescapable conclusion, however, is that the credit system was becoming more consoli-dated, while its capacity to support even larger loans, and more of them, was growing.

Third, it must be remembered that formally collateralized transactions represented only a minor percentage of all credit transactions in the area. The marketing of a cotton crop, for example, required a substantial amount of thirty-, sixty-, and ninety-day credit, all of which was collateralized by opera-tion of law without written or recorded instruments, except for bills of ex-change, drafts, or a merchant's book entry of debits and credits.

In passing, it should also be noted that an extensive market for negotiable instruments existed both in the locality and at New Orleans. It is common-place, for example, to find notices such as the following in the Clinton news-papers:

> All persons are hereby cautioned not to trade for a certain promissory note drawn by me in favor of Zachariah Worley on order for fourteen hundred and twenty-four dollars and 40 cents on the 20th March, 1856, and due January 1, 1857, drawing eight percent interest per annum after due till paid as the consideration for which said note was given has failed. I am deter-mined not to pay it unless compelled by law.
> April 12, 1856, A. Woodward.[54]

Woodward was not denying that he was liable for the face value of the prom-issory note to a holder in due course. He was, however, threatening pro-tracted litigation if a third party negotiated the paper. His threat had little behind it except nuisance value.

Conclusion

With the advantage of hindsight, it is logical to conclude that southern slaveholders attempted to collateralize their credit relationships with slaves. Slaves were portable, they could be transferred to other parts of the South and sold, and on average they constituted about 80 percent of the wealth in places such as East Feliciana Parish. They also produced income, in a rela-tively regular and predictable stream, that would support long-term loans.

What were the most general characteristics of collateralized credit trans-actions in East Feliciana Parish? Slaves represented 80 percent of the security, even in transactions in which mortgages were executed on land and slaves. Collateralized credit transactions probably represented only a small percentage of all credit arrangements in the antebellum period, but they regularized a structure for making large loans for long periods of time. The arrangements evidenced in these transactions suggest a much higher level of sophistication about credit and long-term loans than the kind indulgences of local accommodation endorsers or New Orleans commission merchants accepting new paper for old each year at planting season.

It appears that the markets for land and slaves differed greatly from each other. The slave's value was in cash, whereas land commonly sold on credit, with illiquid paper constituting the medium of exchange. The import of this reality weighs heavily when evaluating the overall importance of slaves in collateralizing credit relations.

The patterns observed in the locality relative to credit relationships emerge with even more clarity in the New Orleans money market. A large secondary market for plantation debt is evident in the last two prewar decades. The instruments brokered in this secondary market were analogous to modern industrial bonds; they guaranteed an income stream by collateralizing the assets that produced that stream. Investors did not purchase equity interests and share in the risks of plantation agriculture.

In such a debt market, borrowers' creditworthiness would have borne little relationship to their plantations in terms of acreage cleared or improved, buildings, or even crops, whether staples or corn for home consumption. Rather, the capitalized value of the income stream from slaves would have been the paramount consideration. Those who bought plantation debt were not looking for capital gains on their portfolios of paper securities. They were, however, looking for income and security.

The unique character of the local and regional debt markets reflects the unique conditions of the slave market—its regionwide geography and cash nexus. If plantations had been capable of sustained productivity gains, then it seems likely that some type of investment arrangement would have emerged to allow third parties to share the risks and thus reap the rewards. That bond financing remained the primary vehicle for financing long-term investment in slave plantations says something about the character of those operations. It also says much about the central role of slavery in shaping the configurations of southern debt markets.

It must be remembered that the people contracting these arrangements involving slaves were rich, but not as rich as the local accommodation endorsers who lent cash or credit. The richest families in East Feliciana rarely collateralized their credit relationships. The few who did were making large capital investments in their estates, not financing that year's planting. They were very rich by any contemporary standard. The price of a male slave in his twenties in the 1850s was the cost of a fine house and lot in the town of Clinton, or the cost of a complete college education at Princeton.[55]

4

The Nemesis of Prewar Debt

I subsequently noticed by the copy of his [John Slidell's] will . . . that he owned
only $17,000 worth of Negroes, hence it was no consequence to him pecuniarily
whether Planters of the South were or were not deprived of their slaves,
upon whose labor they relied to pay millions of their debts
and the ruin of thousands have consequently followed.[1]

Henry Marston

THERE IS NO BETTER vantage point for gaining insights into a defunct society than the aftermath of the cataclysm that engulfed it. An endless variety of relationships, often spanning generations, emerges in a panorama as spectacular as the events that occasioned the ruin. A frenzied speculation precedes the final collapse; everyone with anything of value attempts to reify property rights with layers of security or convert abstract claims into commodities or precious metals. Mortgage notes representing a range of collateralized financial relationships become objects of speculation. Mortgages are good to fall back on and are much to be preferred to currency or note issues of state and local governments. There is, however, no prescription that will safely inoculate everyone from ruin, so a mad dash for remaining scraps ensues after the winds of misfortune cut a final swath in a ravaged landscape.

The Civil War occasioned a staggering loss of life in the South as well as substantial physical damage to production facilities in the region's agricultural economy. Emancipation of the slaves, however, substituted a whole new calculus in financial relations and left holders of property rights in human labor with unenforceable claims. The Thirteenth Amendment to the federal Constitution simply outlawed slavery with no provision for compensating those who had owned the slaves or those who had lent on the certitude of such collaterals.

Roger Ransom and Richard Sutch have argued that the outlawing of slavery "did not destroy the 'capital' embodied in the black population" but transferred the ownership of that "human capital" from slaveholder to former slave.[2] Their analysis, however, proceeds in another direction from the one taken in this study. Slave property was so integral to a variety of financial relationships that uncompensated emancipation effectively bankrupted many prewar producers in the locality and left many others heavily in debt. In consequence of antebellum practices for financing purchases of land and the postbellum lawsuits, most improved acreage in the parish was heavily encumbered with conventional and legal mortgages. Land had not been the basis of wealth before the war, and it did not fill the vacuum left by emancipation. The loss of wealth was not imaginary: it impacted planters far more significantly than by merely altering the conditions under which they obtained labor. Two consequences were a massive loss of liquidity in the financial system supporting plantation agriculture and the inability of growers of every description to spread risks over a period of years beyond a single planting season.

Shortly after William Silliman's death in 1868, Samuel Silliman wrote his lawyers in Clinton that the war had "cost [William] 200,000 in gold but that he had [had] enough left to last him through and help others that were needy."[3] The inventory of his estate revealed more than $400,000 in property, making him one of the richest men in the postbellum South. The bulk of the fortune, however, was not invested in plantation agriculture; it consisted of commercial real estate in New Orleans, bank stocks, and bonds in northern railroad companies. Silliman's losses from emancipation and wartime vicissitudes were substantial, but he was still able to leave sizable bequests for a number of charities. He was the exception in East Feliciana Parish, and the inventory of no estate in the parish would show so much property again until after World War II.

In the months after the end of the war, wave upon wave of suits were filed in the district court, the overwhelming number of which were debt collection proceedings. By the end of 1866, the docket had swelled by more than one thousand cases, most of which ended in default judgments in favor of plaintiff creditors. The debts were mostly prewar ones; the capacity of the financial system to generate any loans during wartime had been severely curtailed. Most of the plaintiffs were living in the parish.

An extensive examination of individual suit records leads to the inescapable conclusion that families of the parish who had been among the richest families in the country in the antebellum period were in the throes of debt distress. Indicators of that distress will be examined more closely, but suffice it to say that property separations between husbands and wives provide one of the most sensitive indicators of debt distress within individual households.

How had the fortunes of even the wealthiest families been so severely diminished by the war, other than by the emancipation of the slaves? In 1871 Henry Marston recounted to J. U. Payne, his New Orleans factor, just how the war had wrecked his finances. The recitation was occasioned by Marston's complaining to Payne about the firm's transfer as "collateral security" of an unsecured promissory note, executed by him during the war, to a Mr. Wilson, "a friend of the firm," or as Marston wrote Payne, "your friend." It is clear from Marston's correspondence with Payne that the annualized interest costs were about 20 percent. The note was pledged to Wilson as security; each year Marston paid whatever it cost the Payne firm to carry this indebtedness on their books, which was the short-term cost of money. Twenty percent was reasonable considering prevailing conditions. Had the note been discounted at the Union Bank and not pledged, Marston contended, the debt could have been discharged on far less onerous terms. Instead, he still owed most of the principal, "nearly $3800 and which show[ed] a clear loss of $4400 by the transfer of . . . [the] note to your friend Mr. W."

Other losses occasioned by the war included eleven thousand dollars in outlawed claims on individuals outside the Marston family who were able to pay but refused to do so. Twelve thousand dollars had disappeared in the worthless note issues of Confederate and state governments, and rebel soldiers had burned eleven thousand dollars' worth of cotton on the Red River plantation. If only a portion of these debts could be collected, Marston continued, he could "pay the balance due upon the unfortunate note and release your firm of that much of the claim of your 'over exacting' friend."[4] The fortunes of families such as Marston's had not only been decimated by the outlawing of one species of property, slaves, which constituted the bulk of most planter estates, but also by that of another, Confederate currency and bonds and debt instruments in general.

Marston may well have wished that the infamous note transferred by his factor to Wilson as collateral security for a loan made by Wilson to the firm had been discounted at the Union Bank on far more generous terms. In truth, however, the city's banks had stopped discounting factors' paper from the onset of secession in 1861, precipitating a credit contraction throughout the lower Mississippi Valley. What financing there was during the war years was obtained through commercial agencies for seasonal plantings, or from friends and family. Although collection suits by New Orleans banks in the months after the war were not unknown, they were relatively rare and the sums sued for rather paltry.

The Bank Act of 1842 had ensured the stability and liquidity of the state's banks, at the price of retarding the formation of banking capital during the antebellum period, but those banks did weather the war years and emerge with their specie holdings intact. The banks held in their portfolios trade acceptances, short-term factors' paper, some stocks and bonds, and in the case of the remaining property banks, a limited amount of capitalization collateralized with mortgages on land and slaves.[5] The banks, then, had only limited exposure to the agricultural economy, and concomitantly, their capitalization was less than 5 percent of the total gross wealth in the state. Their note issues were small and always redeemable, and their capital was inadequate to be of much assistance in providing long-term financing for rebuilding the devastated agricultural economy.[6]

Suit records can be most illuminating in providing information about the condition of a particular institution in the months immediately after the war. The Union Bank, for example, sued one Isaac Jackson in 1866 on a three-thousand-dollar mortgage note.[7] Jackson had given the note to Wright, Allen & Co. on December 17, 1861. This transaction was one of a number of similar ones negotiated by the firm during the first months of the war. Wright, Allen was liquidating its accounts with its customers in the parish by obtaining mortgage notes from them to settle bills receivable on their open accounts; these mortgage notes were subsequently discounted at the bank.

Only wartime financial exigencies would have forced Wright, Allen to obtain mortgage notes in settlement of relatively small balances owed by their customers, who were prevented from disposing of their 1861 cotton crop and liquidating balances. Jackson, and others like him, were providing "collateral security" to Wright, Allen for antecedent debts—small unsecured loans contracted at the onset of the new planting season. The steps taken by Wright, Allen probably provided some short-term relief for hard-pressed country customers who were still attempting to purchase supplies in New Orleans in late 1861 and early 1862. In this instance, Wright, Allen had discounted Jackson's note at the Union Bank, and by endorsing it, rendered it that much more secure for the benefit of future holders, including the immediate transferee—the Union Bank. However, Wright, Allen had failed by the time the war was over.[8]

Jackson filed an exception to proceedings contending that the Union Bank could not properly maintain a cause of action against him because it had tacitly forfeited its charter by having suspended specie redemptions of its note issues. Although the exception was overruled by the district court, Jackson was allowed to propound interrogatories to the bank's chief officers in New Orleans. The president, Alfred Penn, responded to the question about whether the bank had suspended making specie redemption, admitting that it had indeed suspended at the end of December 1864 and had never resumed. Its debtors were unable or unwilling to pay their loans. When the bank suspended, it had $499,802.30 in liabilities. The directors and officers hoped that redemption in United States currency, if not specie, could resume when the securities deposited with the United States government in 1854 were returned to the bank's possession. Those securities had now arrived in New Orleans, and the bank would soon begin redemptions in currency, or greenbacks.[9]

It can be seen, then, that the bank's circulation was quite small; the total note issues of New Orleans banks by the end of the war had contracted substantially and probably were no larger than specie reserves. The capital of a single large commission merchant house in 1860 ranged somewhere between $100,000 and $500,000 and up.

Because they were limited to discounting short-term commercial paper and were severely circumscribed in lending long term on property mortgages before the war, the banks of the city preserved their solvency and their capital. The mortgage paper endorsed by commission merchants that was held by institutions such as the Union Bank probably was viewed either as short-term merchants' paper or paper simply held in pledge as security for loans to the commission merchants. Consequently, the city's banks could shrink their total assets without impairing capital at the commencement of the secession crisis. Their very solvency after the war lends credence to contemporary accounts of a massive credit contraction in the lower Mississippi Valley in the months before and after Louisiana's secession from the Union.[10] The city's banks seem to have survived the war in a state of limbo.[11] They could do little to cushion the impact of wartime vicissitudes on the agricultural economy. After the war they continued to operate, but they were too small to have a substantial role in reviving the ruined financial system, which more than anything else required long-term loans of capital.

Indeed, the banks wasted no time in disposing of what mortgage notes they held in their portfolios. On July 11, 1865, the Bank of Louisiana, in liquidation, sold four mortgage notes to Joseph W. Dougherty of East Baton Rouge Parish for what was owing on the underlying indebtedness plus the accrued interest. All four notes were drawn for amounts far greater than what was actually owing, an average margin of three dollars of security for every dollar loaned. All four loans had been guaranteed by New Orleans factor James W. Burbridge, and the instrument states that he accepted the transfer of the notes for Dougherty. Burbridge probably had prevailed on Dougherty to purchase the loans as a speculative investment when he himself was called upon by the bank to pay them off after the principal obligors defaulted.

One of the mortgaged plantations was in East Feliciana. Dougherty filed suit against John F. McKneely and his wife, Maria Margaret Scott, at the end of the 1865 shipping season. Originally, their indebtedness had been secured by a mortgage on their sugar plantation and slaves, an estate worth upwards of $100,000 in 1860. Dougherty obtained a default judgment against the McKneelys, but the district court afforded them some relief by staying its execution for the whole principal amount of ten thousand dollars until December 1, 1866. The court, however, granted Dougherty "a special privilege upon the crop to secure the payment of the installment." The court further stayed portions of the judgment for up to six years, provided the McKneelys paid one-sixth of the principal indebtedness plus the total accrued interest each year. Dougherty probably acquiesced in the judgment allowing the McKneelys six years to pay off the debt; nevertheless, he had the whole property seized and sold three years later when the McKneelys failed to meet the terms of the stay, and he purchased the plantation at sheriff's sale for what was then owing—seven thousand dollars.[12]

The McKneelys' plight was typical of that of many large planters; relative to their prewar wealth, their debts had been insignificant. However, emancipation, currency depreciations, and failure to service loans during the war years all worked together to erode their wealth and make their debt burden intolerable. That the McKneelys reduced the principal amount of the judgment by about one thousand dollars a year in the three years before the seizure also elucidates another problem of the postbellum agricultural economy. Production was more risky, even though commodity prices were high in the years after the war. It appears that adequate income could not be generated using free labor, whether because of high labor costs or squeezed profit margins, to service the prewar loans.

The McKneelys' failure to make the transition from the antebellum to the much-altered postbellum agricultural economy was repeated many times in East Feliciana Parish in the five years after the war. The more or less complete collapse of the antebellum plantation production organization in those five years was the beginning of a period of disintegration that was to stretch into the twentieth century. Production units shrank in size, and the credit system for financing the annual plantings consumed a much larger share of the gross income; moreover, there was virtually no long-term lending for improving production.

The kinds of suits filed in the months immediately after the war leave no doubt about who the real losers were in economic terms. For the white population of the parish, emancipation was a social and economic disaster of unimaginable proportions. To that event, however, had to be added both the complete repudiation of a currency in which many held substantial liquid wealth and the crushing burden of prewar debts.

Various defenses were available to embattled debtors in consequence of decisions of the Louisiana Supreme Court and the new constitution of 1868.[13] All were asserted at various times by defendants in East Feliciana proceedings. The administrator of the estate of Evander White, for example, sued two succession debtors on obligations contracted at probate sales of White's property. One defendant asserted that the slave he had purchased at the sale in March 1861 was "addicted to theft." Emancipation had rendered it impossible for the defendant "to tender a return of the slave." The defendant prevailed.

White's administrator also sued White's widow on debts she had contracted by purchasing succession property at probate sales. She answered that she had had a complete settlement with the plaintiff on August 17, 1863, paying all debts owed by her to her husband's succession. She further averred that at the time of the settlement the notes being sued on "were in the possession of plaintiff's . . . [lawyers] McVea and Hunter, and that said attorneys were absent from the Parish in the Military Service of the Confederate States, and that said notes could not be obtained at the date of the settlement."

The administrator then executed an affidavit stating that he had signed the August 17, 1863, agreement, but that the "money was Confederate Treasury interest bearing notes." Moreover, he then consulted several creditors of the White estate, "and they refused to take the money [Confederate Treasury Notes] in payment of their claims." According to the administrator, "the circulating medium of the . . . [Clinton] community at that time was a little mixed. Some persons refused to take Confederate money. The Circulation consisted of Confederate Money, Bank money, and a few green backs." Part of the debt owed by White was for a slave she had purchased at the probate sale. The administrator said that had he had possession of her paper at the time of the settlement in 1863, he would have surrendered it to her. The district court dismissed the portion of the claim that pertained to the slave sale but gave judgment for the balance.

White ultimately sought relief from the Louisiana Supreme Court. There, she objected to the admission of testimony at the trial court proceeding in regard to circumstances surrounding the 1863 settlement that contradicted the administrator's own written acknowledgment. She contended that "no witness could be heard to prove that [the administrator] . . . had violated the law and given aid and comfort to the rebels in arms by giving currency to their so-called Confederate Treasury notes." The supreme court held that her objection had been properly overruled, saying that "a receipt for money . . . [was] not conclusive between the parties, but [was] . . . open to explanation by parole especially as to consideration."[14]

In virtually every instance where a planter family was bankrupted by the war, as evidenced in suit records, the name of an especially distressed commission merchant house was usually to be found. In February 1867 the firm of A. Miltenberger & Co. sued Mary Purnell, the administrator of the estate of George Purnell, on the mortgage indebtedness earlier identified in connection with the development of Louisiana's unique collateral mortgage. The debt was fifteen thousand dollars plus interest and 5 percent attorneys' fees. Purnell had executed a new mortgage to Miltenberger in 1859 that secured three mortgage notes of five thousand dollars each, payable one, two, and three years after date. In February 1861 Purnell advised Miltenberger that he had executed two more notes of five thousand dollars each that were payable in 1863. The new notes were given as a continuation of the notes that were payable in 1860 and 1861. Purnell authorized Miltenberger to hold the old notes in pledge until the two new notes, "or any renewal thereof," should have been paid. A. Miltenberger & Co. obtained its judgment and eventually purchased the property at probate sale in 1870. They sold it the following year to K. P. Muse for $17,500. Muse paid seventy-five hundred dollars cash and the balance in promissory notes payable in one, two, three, and four years.

A. Miltenberger & Co. transferred the paper for the credit portion of the sale by endorsement to the New Orleans Insurance Company. Muse defaulted on the obligations in 1879 after having paid only fourteen hundred dollars on the debt by January 1878. The New Orleans Insurance Company bought the property at sheriff's sale and sold it on November 30, 1879, to Archibald McLaurie for thirty-five hundred dollars—two thousand dollars cash and the balance payable in three equal annual installments. The insurance company's mortgage was reinscribed in 1890, an indication that the debt had not yet been fully liquidated. An estate that had been worth in excess of $100,000 in 1860 had been reduced to 3 percent of its former value by emancipation, war, postwar debt distress, and asset deflation.[15]

Neither was the plight of the Purnell family all that unusual. Richard Pritchard, for example, a partner in the New Orleans commission merchant firm of Pritchard and Flower, sued Henry Perkins and Alex Smith on various evidences of indebtedness that aggregated to $9,787.20. Perkins and Smith had purchased a valuable tract of land in Point Coupee Parish in 1859 from Richard Flower for $10,053.25. The purchasers had drawn three promissory notes of $2,234 each, all payable in 1861, on the firm of Slaughter, Smith, & McRae of New Orleans, of which Smith was a partner, and the notes were accepted by the firm. The partnership's acceptance of the notes made all three partners individually and personally liable for the entire indebtedness. In addition, Perkins and Smith drew a note for $1,959 payable in 1862 as part of the consideration for the sale price, and they assumed a debt of $1,125.96 owed by Flower to the firm of A. & J. Dennistoun & Co., the original vendor of the property.[16]

Especially interesting about this case are the intricate connections between Perkins, the planter, and two commission merchant firms with close economic and personal ties to the area. Flower was a resident of the parish, a planter as well as a city merchant; his wife was a member of one of the oldest and richest planter families in the area. Perkins's partner in the transaction was a city merchant as well as an East Feliciana resident. Perkins's family was closely allied through marriage and politics with the Norwood family, one of the richest families in antebellum Louisiana.

The property in Point Coupee was sold for a fraction of what was owed on the debt, and Pritchard obtained a judgment against Perkins and Smith for the deficiency as well as judgments against the assuming partners of the now defunct firm of Slaughter, Smith, & McRae. Within a short time the wives of both Perkins and Smith had separated in property from their husbands.[17]

The antebellum firm of Payne, Harrison, & Co. had other clients in the parish besides Henry Marston, some of whom were much wealthier and owed the firm considerable sums. In 1856 Joanna McManus's husband and a business partner purchased a valuable sugar plantation from the firm for $115,000, a credit sale evidenced by four promissory notes of $28,750 each and four promissory notes of $9,200 each for the accrued interest. In 1861 only one of the notes for $28,750 remained unpaid; nevertheless, the firm filed suit against Mrs. McManus, then a widow, in September 1866, obtained a judgment against her, and had the plantation in Plaquemines Parish sold for what was owing on the debt. The judgment included attorney's fees of $1,497.15.[18]

Edward Nalle & Co. was another New Orleans firm with close ties to the Clinton area. The firm appears to have relocated its operations to Clinton after the federal occupation of New Orleans. One of the firm's partners, Richard Cammack, attempted to serve the needs of long-standing clients during the war years. On May 2, 1866, the firm sued Mrs. R. B. Dunn, administrator of her husband's estate, on a prewar debt of $2,217. The Dunns conducted their transactions with the firm through a middleman in Clinton, W. W. Chapman & Co. One communication from W. W. Chapman & Co. to Edward Nalle & Co. was filed in the suit record. Dated July 18, 1861, it informed the Nalle firm of R. B. Dunn's death. The Nalle firm was to forward a barrel of flour immediately to Dunn's widow, care of W. W. Chapman & Co. She had a fine crop of cotton and would need bagging and rope for one hundred bales.

The suit record also contained a statement of the firm's open account with Dunn during the 1861 planting season. To a balance of $1,071.25 owing from the previous year had been added charges for supplies furnished in the first seven months of 1861, causing the account to aggregate to $2,221.32, an amount that included interest and a commission of 2.5 percent for cash advances. Dunn, like the many clients of Wright, Allen, had executed a promissory note to the firm on January 7, 1861, for $1,230; the note had been discounted at New Orleans for $1,085 and the proceeds applied as a credit to the balance owed. It is likely that the execution of the promissory note was highly unusual and was intended as a temporary solution to liquidity problems that plagued New Orleans commission merchants in the wake of secession. The 12 percent discount seems fairly reasonable, given prevailing commercial circumstances, but what is significant is that Dunn shipped no cotton to New Orleans in the fall of 1861. Very likely the Nalle firm advised her not to ship because the market there was a poor one; moreover, the Union blockade was already more or less effective.

West Feliciana, La
January 2nd 1871.

$250.00

On _____ years after date I
promise to pay to my own order
the sum of _____ _____ Two hundred _____ for value received
with eight per cent per annum
interest thereon from date until
paid.

R. P. Mills

2 Feby 1876 Received Two hundred fifty dollars a/c of Interest
Jany 6/77 Received Three hundred fifty dollars on a/c of Interest
                                        correct
                                    R. P. Mills

R. P. Mills

The front and back of a promissory note (a mortgage note) executed by K. P. Muse on January 2, 1871, for twenty-five hundred dollars. The original creditor was A. Miltenberger & Co., whose unqualified endorsement appears on the back of the note. When the Miltenberger firm failed (apparently sometime in 1874 or 1875), the New Orleans Insurance Co. came into possession of the note. The New Orleans Insurance Co. foreclosed on the property in 1879 after Muse defaulted on the obligations. The original note reads:

West Feliciana, La
January 2nd 1871

$2500⁰⁰

Four years after date I promise to pay to my own order the sum of Two thousand five hundred dollars for value received with eight per cent per annum interest thereon from date until paid.   K. P. Muse

Nalle sued Dunn's widow on the plantation account, on which $987 was owing, and the firm claimed a privilege on the 1861 crop for supplies furnished during that year. They also sued on the promissory note of $1,230 and obtained judgment against the Dunn estate for both claims. If Mrs. Dunn indeed produced one hundred bales of cotton in 1861 and kept them secure for the duration of the war, she was a wealthy woman. Apparently, this was not the case. Cammack testified that "no particular items made up the account of $1071.25 [on the open account]. . . . On the 7th of January, 1861, [his] . . . account for supplies and drafts amounted to $4254.68. Up to that date, the credit on his account, which accrued from sales of cotton, amounted to $3,183.43." The balance owing was $1,071.25.[19]

Before the war, the Dunns had been a well-to-do planting family with valuable assets and little debt except for the annual supply bill that accrued during the planting season, a short-term debt that was liquidated when the cotton was sold. That they owed a balance at the end of 1860 was not surprising; most of the cotton grown that year would not have been sold until the winter and spring of 1861. Preparations for planting the 1861 crop, on the other hand, would have commenced in January of the new year, and their supply needs would have been greatest in the months when the prior year's crop was being sold. Like many others that year, they apparently chose to hold rather than to sell.

In February 1866 Payne, Harrison & Co. sued John L. Singletary on a promissory note of $1,487.80, at 8 percent interest, dated November 22, 1858. In this instance, the firm probably had held the note in pledge as collateral security for the open account. Like the Dunn note, this note was not collateralized with a mortgage on either land or slaves but was held as security for the open account for supplies invoiced during the planting season. The claim had primacy by operation of law; the note, however, could be discounted or pledged to secure Payne, Harrison's debts to New Orleans banks of other merchants.[20] Such had been Marston's arrangement with the firm. Payne obtained a promissory note from Marston in December 1862 as collateral security for an unpaid balance on Marston's open account. It grieved Marston that Payne then pledged the note to Wilson as collateral for the firm's debt with the latter.[21] In the case of Singletary, the district court afforded him some relief by staying the execution for half of the judgment for twelve months. The other half was stayed for eighteen months.

The firm of Roser, Prothro, & Co. discounted at the Citizens Bank a substantial number of "collateral security notes" that had been transferred to them as security for plantation accounts. The bank instituted suits on a number of such notes, all for debts smaller than five hundred dollars. Ten years later, the bank still had not collected what was owing on the judgments and found it necessary to have its judicial mortgages reinscribed.[22]

As has been reiterated many times, the New Orleans factors who serviced the area had close personal ties to the community (i.e., family, friendship, religion, and politics). Also, the largest plantation operations were achieving a degree of vertical integration: planting, processing, and marketing cotton were being amalgamated into a single business operation. Such operations sometimes were composed of groups of individuals who effected a merger of activities in a series of interlocking partnerships. At least three wealthy families in the parish had consolidated their operations into such combinations by the late 1850s. Most notable of these were the widow and children of Elias Norwood. Abel J. Norwood not only managed four plantations in different parts of Louisiana but was a major commission merchant in New Orleans, as well.[23] The family fortune, which aggregated to something in excess of $1 million in 1860, was owned by the three children and the widow of Elias Norwood as indivision owners. A final division of the property was not effected until 1880, after Mrs. Norwood's death.[24]

At the end of the war, the Norwoods were still wealthy, but their fortune had been diminished by at least 80 percent; moreover, Abel Norwood's factorage activities had exposed all of them to the possibility of creditors forcing a partition by licitation of their several plantations. Norwood had extensive liabilities in the New Orleans money market, to holders of paper endorsed by the firm of Hawkins and Norwood and accepted in the course of trading activities, and to depositors who had accounts with the firm. His partner, Gilbert S. Hawkins, was dead, and Hawkins's insolvent estate was being liquidated for the benefit of creditors.[25]

In the suit records, it is not clear how Norwood kept his numerous creditors at bay and salvaged a portion of his inheritance. Litigation commenced in May 1866 with a suit by the Union Bank of Tennessee against J. B. Smith and Norwood on a promissory note of $1,163.95, drawn by Smith on February 7, 1862, and endorsed by Hawkins and Norwood.[26] The bank eventually obtained default judgments against both men, but in the meantime, Norwood's mother and brother-in-law had obtained substantial judgments against him. Catherine Norwood filed three suits against her son and took judgments for debts that aggregated to fifty thousand dollars.[27] Dr. Lewis G. Perkins took a judgment for $8,559.39 against his brother-in-law.[28] The records in all four suits indicate that both Mrs. Norwood and Perkins had substantial funds on deposit with the firm at the time of its insolvency. Mrs. Norwood's suits were on promissory notes sold to her through the firm's agency, drawn by third parties and guaranteed by Hawkins and Norwood. Also, she ran a substantial surplus with the firm in her open account, which showed income from a variety of sources, including sale of cotton, but primarily from interest and discounts on trade acceptances in which her son had invested her substantial and idle funds. The same was true of Perkins.

In all of the proceedings, James G. Kilbourne represented both Mrs. Norwood and Perkins. He was Perkins's brother-in-law, and he successfully defended Norwood in a number of collection proceedings later on.[29] It appears, however, that the judgments taken by Mrs. Norwood and Perkins fully encumbered whatever remained of Norwood's interest in his father's estate. Because of their timeliness, the judicial mortgages that flowed from these suits outranked all those subsequently obtained by creditors; hence, there was no reward for a creditor who seized such an interest and had it sold. Mrs. Norwood and her son-in-law could always buy the indivision interest at a sheriff's sale for what was owed to them. All the paper sued on in the collection suits against Norwood was collateralized with nothing but the signatures of the makers and the firm's endorsement. No part of Norwood's estate was mortgaged to secure such debts; hence, the judicial mortgages of mother and brother-in-law presented a formidable obstacle to any creditor attempting to seize what remained of his property. Mrs. Norwood, Perkins, and all the judgment creditors were unsecured creditors; the timely filing of collection proceedings by mother and brother-in-law insulated from attack what remained of a great family fortune.

The Mechanics and Traders Bank of New Orleans also sued Smith and Norwood on a promissory note drawn by Smith and endorsed by Hawkins and Norwood. The defendants, however, prevailed, claiming that the note had prescribed. Such a defense would not have been sustained in the federal court system; nevertheless, the plaintiff bank never attempted to reopen the proceeding after that decision was rendered. Smith was ruined, and Norwood was judgment-proof.[30] The same bank took a judgment against Norwood on another note for twenty-five hundred dollars by default in 1867.[31] In 1870 the bank caused a writ of fieri facias to be issued to Richard Flower, who was also a commission merchant in New Orleans, for any property belonging to Norwood remaining in his hands. Mrs. Norwood, however, had caused a writ to be issued a few days before the bank's and had apparently seized whatever property was in Flower's hands, because the bank's writ was returned with the sheriff's notation that no property was to be found. Probably, Flower had held the proceeds from the sales of cotton and sugar produced on the Norwoods' plantations, and Norwood was entitled to a portion of them. Where wives and family members were judgment creditors, a portion of a debtor's property could be placed beyond the reach of ordinary general creditors.

In January 1867 the Citizens Bank filed suit on three promissory notes that aggregated to six thousand dollars.[32] Two of the notes had been drawn by Hawkins and Norwood to the order of the Citizens Bank; a third note had been drawn by S. M. Thomas, accepted by Hawkins and Norwood, and discounted at the same bank. Kilbourne filed an answer on Norwood's behalf, claiming that the three evidences of indebtedness had been paid when the bank had accepted three more notes, drawn by various individuals, that had not been accepted by the firm of Hawkins and Norwood. It is likely that Hawkins and Norwood placed the latter notes in the hands of the bank's cashier either as "collateral security" (i.e., in pledge) or for the purpose of permitting the plaintiff bank to recover what it could on the notes and apply the proceeds toward the liquidation of the original three promissory notes.

When paper was transferred between factors or between factors and bankers as "collateral security," the prevailing view in the marketplace seems to have been that the transferee of such paper held it in pledge, not in ownership. The holder could not transfer it, in the event of default on the underlying obligation, to a third party, even though the paper had been transferred for the purpose of securing or collateralizing another indebtedness. However, pledge agreements usually authorized a public or private sale of such notes without recourse to the courts. Holders who sold such paper could still sue their debtors and obtain judgments where money was owing. This custom or usage, neither judicially recognized nor legislatively approved, was contrary to Louisiana's law of pledge.[33] That the holder of such a note could sell it for a valuable consideration and apply the proceeds to another debt without novating the original obligation was something of an anomaly.

Such paper was in fact held in pledge as collateral for an underlying indebtedness. If the holder disposed of the paper when the debtor defaulted on the underlying obligation simply by selling it without a judicial proceeding, a fundamental principle of Louisiana's system of civil law was violated. It is tempting to conclude that the economic exigencies of the times were the root cause of such commercial practices, but the more likely explanation is a phenomenon significantly more complex. The New Orleans money market traded paper from all parts of the United States and Europe. Disposal of collateral securities, without recourse to courts, probably was an accepted practice in other commercial centers, and it simply prevailed in the New Orleans region independent of state municipal laws.

The Citizens Bank had already placed the three collateral security notes in the hands of attorneys for collection. The bank had then sued on Hawkins and Norwood's three promissory notes. Kilbourne averred that the collateral security notes, already sued on by the bank, were "the property of the Citizens Bank." Moreover, the Bank had "by its act [of suing on the collateral security notes] appropriated said notes—and [could] . . . not . . . return them. . . . [The] plaintiff now h[eld] as owner properties . . . the said notes, received from the defendant for a greater sum than the notes of the defendant." The plaintiff moved to dismiss the proceeding in 1871 with costs assessed to itself.

Nothing, it appears, was ever recovered on the collateral security notes transferred by Hawkins and Norwood.[34]

In 1866 and 1867, the New Orleans firm of A. Levi & Co. and its Clinton
subsidiary, Bloom, Kahn & Co., filed suits on promissory notes and open accounts that aggregated to something in excess of $100,000. Both firms were
in various stages of liquidation, and a few of the suits were filed in the name
of an unofficial liquidator for the Bloom, Kahn entity. Later, the partners
individually undertook to wind up the affairs of the two firms and had themselves substituted as parties plaintiff in the suits instigated by the liquidator.[35]

None of the New Orleans firms active in the area before the war had
survived into the postbellum era without severe problems. The capital of
most was totally wiped out. Most partnerships, like that of Hawkins and
Norwood, owed far more in unsecured debts than they could ever collect
from their planter clients. Fortunes grounded in financial paper and slaves
had simply vanished. A few firms—Payne, Huntington & Co., for example—
had reorganized and attempted to conduct business as they had before the
war, but the world they operated in was far riskier, and the condition most
characteristic of subsequent decades was the constant pressure for liquidity.
In this regard they partook of the same ill fortune as their planter clients
and, indirectly, thousands of sharecroppers and tenant farmers.

It would be a mistake, however, to conclude that commission merchants
suffered only because planters could not or would not pay their debts. Commission merchants were an integral part of the antebellum economic order,
and they suffered along with everyone else. The firms that survived the war
often remained on good terms with defaulting debtors, and such debtors
sometimes permitted consent judgments to be entered against them. For example, when Payne, Harrison sued John L. Singletary in 1866, Singletary
allowed the firm to enter judgment against him provided the execution was
stayed for eighteen months.[36] He signed a confession of judgment and agreed
to 8 percent interest on the unpaid debt. The firm never found it necessary
to have a writ of fieri facias issued on any of Singletary's property, so, presumably, the debt, with interest, was paid eventually. Singletary could have
objected that the note had prescribed; that he did not suggests that some
individuals wanted to pay what they owed regardless of the legal enforceability of such obligations. W. W. Dunn permitted Byrne, Vance & Co. to
have judgment on an open account on which $1,466.99 was owing.[37] In re-
sponse to the plaintiff's petition Dunn simply accepted service, waived all
delays, and confessed judgment.

Virtually every firm was in liquidation by 1868. Few found a salubrious
business climate in years to come and were suing on notes and accounts
contracted after the war within a very short time. The firm of Wright, Allen

and its local representative, R. O. Draughon, never recovered. The wealthy East Feliciana planter, David Pipes, sued the partners of Wright, Allen in the Sixth District Court of Orleans Parish on his account and obtained a judgment of $5,757 for money owed him in 1861. Such a large balance probably reflected what remained of the net proceeds from cotton sales in the spring of 1860. Pipes recorded his judgment in East Feliciana only because the firm owned immovable property in the parish.[38]

Across the whole spectrum of rules and customs that had made up the antebellum economic and social orders, tensions and cleavages rapidly appeared. Siblings sued each other, wives sued husbands for property separations, parents sued children, and children pressed whatever legal claims they had against parents. A daughter alleged that her mother was insolvent and unable to pay what was owed to her from her father's estate.[39] Ruth Johnson sued her son-in-law, Henry Marston, on a debt of fifteen hundred dollars, and her heirs, including Marston's wife, had the judgment reinscribed ten years later.[40] Marston sued the executor of A. D. Palmer's estate for a share of the executor's commission.[41] Marston's good friends, Payne, Huntington, sued his son, John, and took a judgment against him for $3,741.90.[42] The Palmer estate sued Marston on a promissory note that Marston successfully defended in the United States Supreme Court.[43] His defense, of course, was that the consideration for the note had been the sale of a slave, a consideration that was now reprobated.

In the two years after the war, claims amounting to $1 million were reduced to judgments in the district court of East Feliciana Parish. A large number of other claims were defeated by pleas of prescription and illegal causes in the underlying transactions. Many more claimants endeavored to work with their debtors in hopes of restoring vanished fortunes. The number of properties seized for debt after judgments were taken was relatively small. Well into the 1870s, the Boyce brothers were grudgingly continuing to agree to receive only partial payment of the interest and no principal each year on their antebellum debt with Marston. Marston's plantation was a valuable property, and the Boyce brothers were much pressed themselves by creditors; still, they were loath to "close the judgment."[44]

It is probable that the total indebtedness in the parish exceeded the value of all the property that remained after the Civil War, and the ratio of debt to assets only worsened as planters sought credit to resume their operations. Credit was very dear in 1866 and 1867. Marston was paying two and one-half times the legal rate on the note that had been transferred by Payne, Huntington to Wilson. That he paid what the market demanded is indicative of the times. It also says something about legal institutions overwhelmed in a marketplace fraught with risks.

Defenses to Debt Collection Proceedings: Impairment of the Obligation of Contract and Federal Courts

It is surprising that scholars of the economics of slavery and the post-bellum order generally have not examined closely the problem of debt distress in the two decades after the war. From 1865 to 1870, the trend in collection suits was toward liquidating prewar debts, and the consequences for already embattled planter families were devastating. In subsequent decades, collection activities mirror a radically different economy with an emphasis on high-risk, short-term, small loans collateralized with crop liens of tenant farmers. Debt distress had simply "trickled down" to those recently freed from slavery.

Initially, the postwar collection suits were instituted by New Orleans commission merchants, their local counterparts, and those holding security interests in real estate (i.e., a vendor's privilege, or a mortgage securing the credit portion of a sale of land). Suits on mortgages, wherein the consideration was the credit portion of a slave sale, were not unknown. The state supreme court considered the consequences of the outlawing of slavery for such contracts in the 1867 decision of *Thomas Wainwright, Administrator v. Mrs. Alice Bridges, et al*. The Sixth District Court of St. Helena Parish had ruled that the credit portion of a slave sale executed before emancipation was still owing, even though slavery per se was now outlawed. The vendor of the slave, seeking to enforce the contract, contended that his warranty did not extend "to fortuitous events that happen[ed] after the contract had been entered into." The supreme court reversed the district court's decision in a three-to-two vote, holding that slavery "was never, strictly speaking, established in . . . [the United States] by positive law."

Once the majority had reached this conclusion, it was a simple matter of resorting to that amorphous concept, natural law: "freedom was . . . a pre-existing right; slavery, a violation of that right." In confronting the more difficult issue of the United States Constitution's prohibition against states enacting laws impairing the obligation of contract, however, a majority showed that they could deviate wildly from natural law in the space of a few paragraphs. The prohibition against impairing the obligation of contract, they reasoned, had "no application to the sovereign power." The "power and efficacy extended to . . . laws [regulating slavery] . . . [were] granted, and exist[ed] only by the will of the sovereign." When the sovereign will of the United States declared that African slavery should no longer exist within its borders, "an unavoidable result was, that the laws which had theretofore sustained the institution of slavery and given their sanction to and enforced contracts, the objects of which were the sale of slaves, ceased to exist." The extent of that sovereign power apparently was boundless. It could "release the contracting parties" and "set the bondman free. . . . With the ownership perished the obligation to pay the price which was the consideration stipulated for that ownership." The courts were powerless to enforce obligations such as the one sued on by the Wainwright succession representative.

The *Wainwright* decision was a lousy one. It provided little relief for planters distressed by debt, but it rendered a great deal of their commercial paper worthless, of no value even to speculators, who might have added liquidity to the wracked New Orleans money market. By far the better opinion was that of dissenting justice J. Ilsley, who said, "Whether the traffic in slaves was in conflict with natural law, or violated any canon of ethics . . . [was] an abstract question," the answer to which it was unnecessary to determine for resolution of the issue at hand. The general warranties in contracts of sale did not contemplate "nor extend to losses of . . . the thing sold by force majeure which the act of the sovereign . . . [was] deemed to be." According to Ilsley, there was no power in the sovereign "to annul the *title* for any anterior vice in it." He cited a decision of the Missouri Supreme Court made the year before stating that such contracts had never warranted against emancipation of slaves by the sovereign power. Abolition was "the mere enunciation of one great fact, that the status of slavery was extinct. . . . It had no retroactive bearing whatever on contracts which had been entered into, in relation to that species of property." Ilsley was satisfied that the plaintiff had every right to recover from the defendants, a right "founded in law, not withstanding the ingenious and plausible theories submitted to us to sustain the pretensions of the defendants. They soar too high for the judicial mind to contemplate."

He concluded with one important observation, weighted with the jurisprudential authority of the court's previous fifty years: the legislative will (meaning the accumulated wisdom of ancient precedents) "cannot be made to yield to every change of circumstances or events, and it is the sacred duty of Judicial tribunals to carry out and apply recognized principles of law, upon all occasions and to all cases." Citing Article 21 of the Civil Code, he reminded his brother justices that equity only spoke in Louisiana's legal system when the law was silent. In the case before the court, the "rules of law" were "too plain to be misapprehended or misapplied." Ilsley's eloquent defense of the rule of law was sadly out of place with the times in which he lived.

Carried to its logical conclusion, the majority's decision made everyone who had ever sold slaves, and their heirs, liable in warranty to their vendees where such slaves were alive at the moment of emancipation. It also raised the question of whether holders in due course of commercial paper secured by mortgages on slaves could sue their immediate endorsers, or the makers of such notes, and be barred from recovery because the collateral securing such paper was slaves.[45]

Initially, the state supreme court indicated, in the case of *New Orleans Canal and Banking Co. v. Samuel Templeton*, that a holder in due course would be protected where the consideration given for such paper was slaves. Not surprisingly, Ilsley authored the decision, concluding that the policy of the law was "favorable to the holder of negotiable paper," and it required "very cogent evidence to convict him of bad faith." However, it is hard to imagine how third party holders of negotiable instruments with notarial paraphs to mortgages on their faces could logically be protected when original holders were barred from collecting from their debtors. Nowhere was the *Wainwright* decision of the previous year mentioned in the decision of the case.[46]

The issue of protection for holders in due course of paper grounded in slave transactions was back before the supreme court in 1869, in the case of *Edward Groves v. K. M. Clark and R. H. Carnal*. The author of the majority decision in *Wainwright*, Justice J. G. Taliaferro, again wrote for the majority, this time relying on Article 128 of the recently enacted state constitution of 1868. Asking rhetorically whether "the commercial law [was] paramount," he answered, "Certainly not." There was, he concluded, no reason for the insertion of Article 128 in the new constitution if the framers had not "intend[ed] to assert more broadly the doctrine of the Wainwright case, and to leave no question as to their intention to render null and abortive in the hands of any holder whatever all obligations" that had the trafficking in slaves as their cause. The decision in *Canal and Banking v. Templeton* was explicitly overruled.[47]

The defenses asserted in this line of cases by defendants pressed with collection proceedings started to appear in the district court of East Feliciana Parish in the first wave of filings in the year after the war. Other defenses included the nonenforceability of contracts denominated in Confederate money and the statutory prescription of five years for suits on promissory notes. The legal issues raised by these defenses, especially the federal prohibition against the impairment of the obligation of contract by state action, eventually were raised before the United States Supreme Court, but more than five years elapsed before holders of such paper obtained any relief.

Perhaps it is indicative of the commercial importance of East Feliciana Parish that one of the earlier federal cases setting aside the interpretation of Louisiana courts on the running of prescription during the war years originated in a debt dispute between a New York wholesaler and a Clinton commercial firm. A. T. Stewart and Co. of New York commenced suit on April 16, 1866, against Bloom, Kahn & Co. in the Fourth District Court of New Orleans on a promissory note made in New York in August 1860 for $3,226.24. The note was payable seven months after date and plainly was given as payment on an open account. Bloom, Kahn asserted that prescription had run on the indebtedness, a defense recognized by the state district court and affirmed by the state supreme court.

The plaintiffs in this case had relied on a congressional enactment that authorized an interruption of the running of prescription when cases could not be prosecuted because of the Civil War. They next proceeded to the United States Supreme Court on a writ of error arguing that the act of Congress relative to the running of prescription applied to cases pending in state courts as well as federal ones. The federal Supreme Court agreed and reversed the judgment of the Louisiana Supreme Court, remanding the case to that court, "with directions to overrule the plea of prescription." Justice Swayne noted that "it would be a strange result if those in rebellion, by protracting the conflict, could thus rid themselves of their debts, and Congress, which had the power to wage war and suppress the insurrection, had no power to remedy such an evil, which is one of its consequences." The congressional enactment was "within the canons of construction laid down by Chief Justice Marshall. *McCulloch vs. Maryland*, 4 Wheat. 316."[48]

In April 1872 the United States Supreme Court rendered two decisions nullifying provisions in the postwar constitutions of Georgia and Arkansas that had made debts grounded in slave transactions unenforceable. Both cases had proceeded on writs of error, and in the Georgia case some rather imaginative arguments were made for sustaining the decision of the state supreme court. First, it was argued that when Georgia adopted its constitution in 1868 it was not a state of the Union but a conquered territory, and "the inhibition . . . to pass any law impairing the obligation of contract had no application to her." Second, the Georgia Constitution did not affect the contract per se but rather forbade any court of the state from taking jurisdiction of contractual disputes in which slaves had been the consideration. Third, Georgia had been coerced by Congress into adopting its constitution, so the state constitution itself was an act of Congress, and Congress could impair the obligation of contract. Swayne again authored the opinion, which stated that Georgia and the other Confederate states were at no time "out of the pale of the Union"; hence, the arguments sustaining the state provision were without merit. Swayne wrote: "The late Rebellion was without any element of right or sanction of law."[49]

In the Arkansas case, Swayne's opinion practically tracked Ilsley's dissent in *Wainwright*. Swayne wrote that the seller was not "bound to warrant the buyer against acts of mere force, violence and casualties, nor against the act of the sovereign, 1 Domat, part 1, Book I, tit. 2, sec. 10, paragraph 4." Moreover, he said, there was no merit to the argument that because the institution of slavery had been contrary to "natural justice and right" and was only sustained by positive law, once it was abolished, "all such contracts and the means of their enforcement . . . [were] thereby destroyed." Though slavery was "contrary to the law of nature it was recognized by the law of nations." To render such contracts unenforceable would "shake the social fabric to its foundations and let in a flood tide of intolerable evils." Swayne concluded:

Whatever we may think of the institution of slavery viewed in the light of religion, morals, humanity, and social political economy—as the obligation here in question was valid when executed . . . we have no choice but to give it effect. We cannot regard it as differing in its legal efficacy from any other unexecuted contract to pay money made upon a sufficient consideration at the same time and place. Neither in the precedents and principles of the common law, nor in its associated system of equities jurisprudence, nor in the older system known as the civil law, is there anything to warrant results contended for by the defendants in error. Neither the rights nor the interests of those of the colored race lately in bondage are affected by the conclusions we have reached.[50]

The thrust of both decisions made the *Wainwright* decision and Article 128 of the Louisiana Constitution of 1868 untenable.

During the October 1873 term, the Supreme Court rendered its decision in the case of *Boyce, Plaintiff in Error v. Tabb,* a case that had come before the Court on a writ of error to the circuit court of the United States for the district of Louisiana. Tabb had sued Boyce on a promissory note, the price of a slave, and the suit was unsuccessfully resisted by Boyce on the grounds of a failure of consideration. Boyce objected to the judge's charge to the jury that it was not a legal defense to a suit on a promissory note "to allege and prove that such note was given as the price or a part of the price of slaves sold to the maker." Plaintiff in error argued that since Louisiana's highest court had refused to enforce such contracts for reasons of public policy, the federal courts were obligated by the 34th section of the Judiciary Act of 1789 to follow that rule of decision. Justice Davis, writing for the court, held that such an argument was completely erroneous, citing *Swift v. Tyson,* a seminal decision in the development of federal common law. The judgment of the circuit court was affirmed.[51]

In all probability, these decisions came too late to salvage the fortunes of those holding paper grounded in slave transactions. The bulk of such paper was uncollectible; either prescription or the death of the maker would have ensured a significant erosion of value. Also, by 1870 such paper was very stale for collection purposes.

It is ironic that the plaintiff in error, the estate of Henry Boyce, was one of Marston's largest creditors. Marston's debt was not, however, grounded in a slave transaction but rather was the unpaid portion of the purchase price of a large tract of land on the Red River.[52] It is easy to see how debtors and creditors were very much one and the same in the antebellum financial world and how debtors' relief measures often penalized the very people they were intended to help.

Marston himself was before the United States Supreme Court in 1872 in a case that had more than passing significance for debts grounded in slave transactions. The executor of the estate of Archibald D. Palmer sued Marston in the district court of East Feliciana Parish on a promissory note executed by Marston and given to J. O. Fuqua. Fuqua had transferred the note by endorsement and without recourse to Palmer during the war. This note was the source of much grief and worry to Marston, and his correspondence on the subject of its enforceability is extensive. While the matter was pending before the Supreme Court in the winter of 1872, he wrote his son at Ashland Plantation on the Red River, the same plantation purchased from Henry Boyce before the war, that counsel for the Palmer estate had taken a writ of error to the decision of the Louisiana Supreme Court in his favor. Marston complained that Judge Edwin Merrick had grounded his writ of error in Article 128 of Louisiana's 1868 constitution. Merrick's argument was that the provision violated the federal Constitution and presented the United States Supreme Court with a state court decision based, not on that court's own jurisprudence, but on a state constitutional amendment. In all prior cases, the Supreme Court had refused to take jurisdiction because no proof had been presented that a statutory enactment specifically impaired the obligation of contract.

Marston contended that the Louisiana Supreme Court decision was based on the prior decisions of that court, previous to the adoption of the 1868 constitution. His case conformed "to the previously established jurisprudence of the state as settled *before* that Constitution went into operation." If the judgment went against him, however, he reckoned that it would increase his debts by fifteen hundred dollars and add that much more to his burdens. He complained that he had "offered to pay every dollar of this debt to Mr. Fuqua in Confederate money but he refused to receive it, although he was one who voted for the Ordinance of Secession and plunged the *South* into the forlorn condition into which she has fallen." His "great error" had been to "not *compel* him to take it."[53]

Marston repeated his tale of woe to Jacob Payne:

> I have not time at present to enter into a recital of all the reasons of my refusal to pay the balance of the debt due to Fuqua, but will merely remark that I offered to pay the *whole* amount in *Confederate* money, which I had not refused to receive for *debts* due to me in gold and silver and which as an *advocate* of the Secession movement he was *doubly* bound not to have refused to receive it.[54]

Marston even approached Payne about executing a mortgage to secure his indebtedness (i.e., a collateral security note the firm had transferred to Wilson). He requested Payne to forward a power of attorney to Judge L. M. Pipkin, Payne's attorney in Clinton, authorizing him to accept a mortgage in favor of Payne, Huntington & Co. on Marston's Clinton property. He

assured Payne that it was his belief that he would prevail in the Supreme
Court, "but owing to the 'glorious uncertainties of the law' it m[ight] . . .
perchance be decided against . . . [him] and [he had] therefore concluded to
give [Payne] this lien, prior to the *possible* reversal of this case by the United
States Court."[55] Even more than a century ago, debtors knew a great deal
about making themselves judgment-proof or giving preferences to friendly
creditors.

Marston complained bitterly to his attorney in New Orleans, James H.
Muse, himself a former Clinton resident, that his fee was too high, that the
printing of his briefs could be done more cheaply in Washington than in
New Orleans, and that Marston's cousin there could accomplish many savings
in the course of the appeal. He prevailed on his cousin, S. J. Randall, a
member of Congress from Philadelphia, to undertake various agencies for
him at the nation's capital. Judging from Marston's correspondence to Randall, it may be said that Randall was a patient, understanding relative.[56] In
one letter to Randall, Marston accused Judge Merrick, a former chief justice
of the Louisiana Supreme Court and member of the Feliciana bar, of "pal-
pable misrepresentations" in his supplemental brief, as bad as "the falsification
of Record in his first brief."[57]

The writ taken by the Palmer estate, however, was dismissed for want of
jurisdiction. According to Justice Swayne, "The provision of the state Constitution upon the subject of slave contracts was in nowise drawn in question.
The decision was governed by the settled principles of the jurisprudence of
the state. In such cases th[e] court ha[d] no power of review." Neither party
had claimed that a positive provision of Louisiana law violated the federal
Constitution. The Supreme Court, then, refused to take cognizance of the
case. Swayne cited the recent case of *Bank of West Tennessee v. Citizens Bank of
Louisiana* for the proposition that the Supreme Court could not take jurisdiction under the judiciary act when the writ of error proceeded from a jurisprudential finding by a state court.[58]

Marston, it seems, was extremely lucky; not so, his creditor, Boyce,
whose case the following year was arguably the same in every respect. On
grounds of public policy, Louisiana courts had refused to enforce contracts
grounded in slave transactions, and the absence of a positive state law vio-
lative of the federal Constitution left the federal Supreme Court without
jurisdiction. Attorneys for Boyce argued as much. However, Justice Davis
held that such questions were of a general nature and "not based on a local
statute or usage."[59] The decisions, then, of state courts were not conclusive
authority.

The last major pronouncement by the Louisiana Supreme Court relative
to either Articles 127 or 128 of the state constitution of 1868 came in the case
of *Henderson v. Merchants' Mutual Insurance Co.* The issue that brought the

case on a writ of error before the United States Supreme Court was ancillary to the main demand and involved a judicial mortgagee whose security interest in immovable property flowed from an obligation that had been contracted in Confederate currency. The Louisiana Supreme Court had held that to grant relief to the judicial mortgagee would, by virtue of Article 127 of the 1868 constitution, have had the effect of enforcing a prohibited agreement. It is significant that the complainant, J. T. Delmas, had obtained his judicial mortgage prior to the adoption of the 1868 constitution. Justice Miller, writing for the federal Supreme Court, stated what would be reiterated in the Boyce decision in 1873. The nation's highest court was not bound to follow state court rules of decision in every instance; otherwise, Miller reasoned, a constitutional provision "could always be evaded by the State Courts, giving such construction to the contract, or such decisions concerning its validity, as to render the power of . . . [the Supreme Court] of no avail in upholding it against unconstitutional State legislation." The Supreme Court ordered that the judgment of Louisiana's highest court dismissing Delmas's demand be reversed and that judgment be had in his favor. The Louisiana Supreme Court complied in a terse one-paragraph decision in 1873.[60]

Even though creditors were able to prevail in federal courts against unconstitutional state laws and decisions, which had created a variety of defenses to prewar debts, it does not necessarily follow that all such creditors eventually overcame defenses such as the contract grounded in slavery, the debt contracted in Confederate money, or prescription having run. The bulk of these claims had already received final dispositions by the time the United States Supreme Court considered the constitutionality of such exceptions to the enforceability of contracts. It is not at all clear, either, whether state courts followed the decisions of the United States Supreme Court even after pronouncements such as *Boyce*. A creditor who sought relief by means of a writ of error had to have a substantial claim with a high probability of being collected after judgment. By 1872 most antebellum claims were indeed prescribed, and the collectibility of even large ones was highly questionable.

Deep Distress: Suits for Property Separation

While the volume and total value of collection proceedings in a locality are important indications of overall economic conditions, such information rarely provides insights into how a particular household or class of households fared in the years immediately after the war and whether debt distress was generalized or concentrated in one or more economic classes. In the case of Louisiana, however, debtors had at their disposal a remedy that permitted them to place a portion of the household wealth beyond the reach of general creditors. The property regime that was tacitly contracted by most spouses at marriage in antebellum Louisiana was the community of acquets and gains. The husband was head and master of the community between the spouses, and the assets acquired during marriage belonged to his patrimony. Community property could be seized by an antenuptial creditor of the husband to satisfy a separate debt. The wife, however, enjoyed substantial protection for whatever property she brought with her to the marriage in dowry and as paraphernal property. Property inherited by the wife or donated to her during marriage was also her separate property, and she would in certain instances retain the sole administration of such property.[61] Although the income of the wife's separate property inured to the community of gains between her and her husband, she might also in certain instances receive the income from such property.[62]

Louisiana's law of matrimonial regimes provided substantial protection for the wife's paraphernal and dotal property when the husband became insolvent and was sued by his general creditors; moreover, the wife had a legal mortgage on all the husband's immovable property for the restitution of her dowry and her paraphernal property at the dissolution of the community of gains.[63] When the husband mortgaged a community immovable, only the wife's subordination of her legal mortgage would allow the mortgagee to obtain a ranking superior to hers. Louisiana's municipal law prohibited the wife from binding herself for her husband's debts. However, the charters of the property banks of the 1830s and 1840s deviated from this general principle and permitted wives to bind themselves personally with their husbands and contract debts secured by mortgages on community and separate immovables.[64] Wives were relatively free of debt when the war ended; only in cases in which an exception existed by positive legislation were wives likely to be personally encumbered with debts. It must be remembered, however, that even separate property was not immune to the deleterious effects of emancipation and wartime inflation.

No sooner had the district court commenced operating in late 1865 than there was a wave of suits filed seeking separation of property. A wife could petition for a separation of property "whenever her dowry [was] . . . in danger, owing to the mismanagement of her husband, or otherwise, or when the disorder of his affairs induc[ed] her to believe that his estate m[ight] not be sufficient to meet her rights and claims."[65] Virtually all of the wives' petitions declared that the latter condition prevailed (a husband's affairs had endangered paraphernal property), the institution of dowry being highly exceptional, as was the case with antenuptial contracts in general. The judgment of separation was null if it was not accompanied by a settlement between the spouses for restitution of dotal and paraphernal property, to the full extent of the husband's patrimony.[66] So far as community and separate immovables of the husband were concerned, the wife's legal mortgage was superior to that of any other claimant unless she had availed herself of one of the rare exceptions at some time during the marriage and subordinated her mortgage to that of another creditor. A judgment of separation ended the community of gains between the spouses, although the husband's creditors could object to a separation of property judgment "and even [an] executed [judgment]" where it was to defraud them.[67] The wife, having obtained a separation of property, was bound to contribute to the household expenses and to the education of the children, and to bear those expenses alone where there remained nothing to the husband.[68] The wife still had to obtain her husband's consent when disposing of her immovable property.[69]

It is difficult to estimate what percentage of East Feliciana households availed themselves of property separations. According to the 1860 census, fully one-third to one-half of all the free households in which both spouses were still living and able to take advantage of such a partial solution to their difficulties apparently did so. Such a high percentage is indicative of a general bankruptcy of monumental proportions. What survives of the correspondence of families whose situations were not so desperate as to warrant separations of property suggests a never-ending press to liquidate antebellum debts and obtain enough credit to provide for the next year's planting. When it is remembered that a separation of property suit was useless unless the wife could establish her claim to separate property, it becomes clear that even families who had been among the wealthiest before the war were either in reduced circumstances or simply ruined. What is also clear is the horrendous psychological jolt delivered to the southern psyche by such a complete bankrupting of families who for generations had known themselves to be wealthy. Such ruin, carried to every economic level of a society, is without parallels in American economic history.

Emily Stanley sued her husband, James B. Smith, on February 9, 1866, for a separation of property. Smith was a lawyer as well as a planter, and the family's wealth probably totaled something in excess of $400,000 in 1860. In the wake of the war their fortune was gone, and both sons had died before Richmond fighting for the Confederacy. Stanley claimed three contiguous tracts of land, about fourteen hundred acres in all, and the proceeds of the 1836 crop. The couple had married in 1836, and she averred that she had made twenty-five hundred bushels of corn, two thousand bushels of potatoes, and ninety-five bales of cotton that year. At the date of her marriage, she had also had a large stock of horses, cattle, oxen, and hogs. Her husband had also received the proceeds of a promissory note of seventeen hundred dollars that belonged to her. She had sold a black man, Peter, for five hundred dollars, and her husband had received and used the money. Such proceeds had been received by her husband "and appropriated to his own use and benefit." Her husband "was very much in debt and greatly embarrassed," and she believed him to be insolvent. She had cause to believe "that her paraphernal property and right [would] . . . be endangered on account of the great pecuniary embarrassment of her husband." In the same petition she renounced "all interest and claim in the community of acquets and gains heretofore existing between herself and her husband."

Stanley asked for a separation of property, for a dissolution of the community of gains between herself and her husband, and for recognition of her ownership of the three tracts of land and the stock of cattle and hogs still on the property. She asked for judgment against her husband "for the sum of Twelve Thousand Dollars with interest thereon from the filing of [the] . . . petition until paid." She claimed a mortgage on the real estate of her husband that secured the restitution of her paraphernal property and was effective from the date when he had received such sums of money and appropriated them to his own use. Finally, she asked the court to grant her "the free use and control of her property with her writ of possession and that she have her execution against her said husband."[70]

Stanley's several obligors filed affidavits supporting her claims that her husband had received payments from them on various evidences of indebtedness. Certified copies of conveyance instruments were filed in the proceeding that definitely substantiated her claim to the three tracts of land as separate property. Other affidavits established her claim to $9,900 of the $12,000 she claimed, whether for notes paid to her husband or for the proceeds of the 1836 crop. Four days elapsed between the filing of the petition and rendition of judgment in her favor on every claim prayed for in the petition. No creditor ever attacked the proceeding at a subsequent time.

More than a century after Stanley filed her suit, Louisiana's matrimonial regime law still contained the same provisions that afforded her some relief after the Civil War; nevertheless, a chorus of reformers echoed a much earlier criticism that such protections afforded the wife were "anti-commercial." A powerful supplement to this argument came from feminists, who were offended by the designation of the husband as "head and master" of the community of acquets and gains and various provisions that gave the husband more or less exclusive control over marital property in community with the wife. Nevertheless, it should be remembered that such laws once had a vital function and did much to alleviate family hardships in the desperate times that followed the Civil War.

Mary Woodward Steadman, the daughter of an old and wealthy planter family in the parish, returned with her husband and children to East Feliciana from Mobile, Alabama, either during the war or shortly thereafter, pursued by creditors. Although she obtained a judgment separating her in property from her husband, the Mobile firm of Walsh, Smith & Co. sued both Steadman and her husband individually on two promissory notes evidencing a combined debt of $4,784.80. Both Steadman and her husband had executed the notes in 1861, but under Louisiana law as it then stood, the wife was strictly prohibited from binding herself for her husband's debts, even if such debts were contracted for the benefit of the community. This was true whether she was separated in property by antenuptial contract or by judgment or was still in community with her husband. The only exceptions were the legislatively posited ones in the charters of the property banks.

The plaintiff, perhaps correctly, insisted that Alabama law governed the transaction and that the district court was bound to enter judgment against Steadman as well as her husband. A default judgment was taken against the husband within one month of the filing of the proceeding, but more than a year later the suit against Steadman was dismissed. In her answer, which was filed shortly before the dismissal of the claim against her, she asserted that "the debt [was] . . . solely the debt of her husband. . . . the notes [had been] . . . made by him in business transactions [that] relate[d] to him exclusively, and [she had] . . . received no consideration whatever for said notes."

Her husband initially claimed that he had not been properly notified, and when that defense failed, he claimed that the notes sued on were prescribed. Here, however, he lost to another peculiar provision of Louisiana law. A prescribed debt is an adequate cause, or sufficient consideration, for a new obligation. Allowing the default judgment to be entered against him, it appears, was sufficient for claiming he had acquiesced to a natural obligation to pay the debt even if it was prescribed. He had, in effect, contracted a new obligation by failing to answer to the suit with a timely plea of prescription. The judgment against him was revived in 1878, the same year he died.[71]

The Bank of Kentucky was more successful when it sued Mary C. Kirkland on a note she had made in 1861. The bank alleged that at the time Kirkland made the note she was separate in property from her husband, but he had authorized her to sign the note, and "the same [had been] . . . for the benefit of her separate property." The transaction, then, was not one of those reprobated by Civil Code Article 2,411. The judge granted a default judgment against her after appropriate delays. It is interesting how far her note had traveled during the war. She had transferred the note to A. S. Shotwell & Son in New Orleans, and this firm discounted it at the Citizens Bank. Sometime during the war, the Citizens Bank and the Bank of Kentucky swapped quantities of paper, and the note passed into the possession of an institution nearly one thousand miles from East Feliciana Parish. It is clear that private negotiable paper was an important part of the nation's money supply.[72]

Plaintiff wives were sometimes very direct in enumerating the cause of a husband's financial distress. Alex Smith's wife, for example, stated in her petition that "by the results of the late War her said husband ha[d] become embarrassed in his pecuniary and financial affairs. Her father had left her a large estate, and her paraphernal rights were in danger of being lost to seizing creditors."[73] Sara Dixon attributed her husband's pecuniary embarrassment to the "losses and suspension of business caused by the war." Having obtained judgment, she caused writs of fieri facias to be issued and seized thirteen bales of cotton from the 1866 crop, 320 acres of land, and "all the growing crops consisting of about thirty acres of corn, sixty acres of cotton, and three acres of potatoes, together with all the cotton picked."[74]

Some petitioners provided highly detailed information about the family's planting activities before the war. Eliza J. Winter, for example, contended that she had substantial funds in her possession when she married her husband, A. F. Currie, in 1852. In that year, she averred, she had two thousand dollars in cash, the proceeds of the 1851 cotton crop. The various witnesses supporting her money claim all testified that in the year before her marriage, "she had 18 to 20 hands big enough to work." So many slaves, they reasoned, surely established the validity of her claim to a large income in bygone days.[75]

Wives usually prevailed in such suits, and general creditors rarely attempted to attack separation judgments that placed most of what remained of family property beyond their reach. In at least one instance, however, a creditor intervened, attacked the proceeding, and prevailed. The firm of Letchford & Co. and R. E. Carr sued John Shelton in separate proceedings in December 1866.[76] Mrs. Shelton subsequently filed for a separation of property, claiming that Shelton had used thirty-nine hundred dollars from her separate estate for his own benefit. His affairs, she claimed, "were dreadfully embarrassed and . . . she [was] endangered of losing altogether her paraphernal rights."

She claimed that her mortgage securing the restitution of her separate property outranked all claims of all creditors, including those with judicial mortgages. James A. Cobb intervened in the proceeding, asserting that the "pretensions of the plaintiff . . . [were] injurious to him . . . that he ha[d] an interest in contesting the same . . . [and] that the defendant [was] . . . perfectly solvent and able to pay all his debts." Cobb sought a jury trial on his intervention, but the judge refused because the jury "was to be discharged for the term on the day which the case [had been] . . . assigned." According to the judge, granting the intervenor's motion for a jury would have retarded the proceeding indefinitely, or "at least until the next term of court."

The intervenor then amended his petition, alleging that the plaintiff "at the date of her pretended marriage with the defendant was the wife of James M. Stokes." She was not divorced but was only separated from bed and board with Stokes, and her marriage to Shelton was a nullity. In response to these inflammatory allegations, the plaintiff requested the court to dismiss the suit against Shelton, saying that "she had never authorized any such judicial proceeding."[77]

The case, however, was highly unusual, and it is unlikely that the plaintiff acted in bad faith when she sued her putative husband for a separation of property. Mrs. Stokes's name appeared in the 1860 census, but she was already separated from her first husband and was the head of a household with minor children. It is easy to see how her efforts to obtain a final divorce during the war might have miscarried; moreover, as a general creditor of Shelton, her claim had no preferential ranking vis-à-vis other creditors. Her lawsuit brought her nothing but public humiliation.

Separation of property suits were endemic in this postwar community. Women who, before the war had been in the highest economic stratum, filed them; so did women from middling to wealthy backgrounds and women who had known far less fortunate circumstances in the antebellum period. Emily Stanley had known great wealth; so had a host of others: Ann Relf Chambers, Maria Margaret Scott, Sarah Dubose, Mary Draughon, Mary Taylor, and Adelia L. Atkinson.

Bythella Haynes was the daughter of a wealthy Clinton planter and lawyer and had already inherited substantial property from her mother's succession when the war came. She had married a well-to-do merchant, Lewis Nauman, and lived in a fine house in Clinton. The Naumans' difficulties began in 1861 when the Confederate government seized all of the Nauman firm's accounts payable to New York wholesalers.[78] Those claims amounted to more than eight thousand dollars. Nauman paid the funds over to a representative of the Confederate government under a writ of garnishment as he liquidated his stocks.

Creditors did not simply vanish because the defunct Confederate government had already levied on the accounts. Haynes filed her suit as soon as the district court commenced operations in the summer of 1865 because her "husband's affairs ha[d] become so much involved as to endanger her paraphernal rights."[79] She prayed for judgment dissolving the community of gains and empowering her to administer her separate estate. She asked that her legal mortgage on her husband's property be recognized to secure her paraphernal property. Her brother testified regarding the extent of Nauman's business obligations and his inability to honor them, specifically enumerating some of those obligations. The particulars were a recapitulation of the judgment taken by the Confederate government confiscating the property of enemy aliens in Nauman's hands.

Catherine Gore sued her husband and reclaimed the $150 and a buggy she had brought to the marriage.[80] In her suit, Ann Elfrith, the wife of a master mechanic, claimed two thousand dollars, the value of the family residence in Jackson and most of the household furnishings.[81] The wives of merchants, doctors, lawyers, plantation overseers, mechanics, druggists, farmers, planters, and college professors filed suits in hopes of saving even a small sustenance.

For surviving spouses with minor children, the law afforded some protection in the form of a legal mortgage that encumbered all of a tutor's immovable property during the period of tutorship.[82] This mortgage, like the wife's legal mortgage for the restitution of her dowry and paraphernal property, secured the minor's property for as long as the property was administered by the tutor. In 1868 the parish clerk of court made a concerted effort to cull from all pending tutorship proceedings the inventories of minors' property filed by their tutors and to record the extracts of these inventories in the mortgage records.

Husbands whose wives never filed separation of property suits nevertheless executed affidavits recognizing their indebtedness to their wives' separate estates. James G. Kilbourne and his brother-in-law, Dr. Lewis G. Perkins, filed such affidavits in the mortgage records in 1868.[83] H. B. Chase, the mayor of Clinton, executed an affidavit acknowledging his indebtedness to his wife, Emily Blossman, for more than eight thousand dollars, money he had received from her father, Sampson Blossman.[84] Such were the times, and few escaped the financial distress that afflicted people of every station.

5

The Truncation of the Factorage System

IT IS IMPOSSIBLE to generalize about the factorage system in the postbellum South outside the lower Mississippi Valley on the basis of this study. However, it appears that the collapse of the credit system during the war and its failure to revive afterward played havoc with factors generally. As Harold D. Woodman and others have argued, transportation and communication improvements contributed to the attenuation of factors as the primary market makers for commercial agriculture.[1] Nevertheless, the horrendous contraction of capital and credit resources in the decades after the war hastened their demise.

Michael Wayne has attributed the persistence of the old elite in the Natchez district to "the general deterioration in the real estate market." That former slave owners "remained economically ascendant in the district points not to their own prosperity but to the relative impoverishment around them."[2] Factors, too, cut poor profiles in the wrecked landscape of city and hinterland that before the war had yielded easy fortunes. Most either failed or became cotton brokers, wholesalers, or specialists at the newly opened cotton exchange. Their clients had lost most, if not all, of their financial capital: their services as investment bankers were anachronistic.

By the end of the antebellum period, the relative value of services performed by factors had undergone dramatic changes. They had become the principal conduit for capital investment in huge agribusinesses. They still marketed crops, but the investment services they provided were their most profitable area of operation.

In the antebellum period, the system that connected approximately three hundred planters in the parish with their factors, whether in New Orleans, Port Hudson, Clinton, or Jackson, comprehended a fairly ordinary set of arrangements. At least one hundred of the wealthiest planters, those with wealth greater than forty thousand dollars, carried on a direct correspondence with a New Orleans firm. During the last two decades of the antebellum period, such firms plainly were evolving into private investment banks, following a pattern similar to English commercial firms in the last decades of the eighteenth century. In fact, investment banking was fast becoming the most profitable area of operation for many large firms.

Factorage firms in New Orleans continued to provide marketing services

to their planter clients; that is, they purchased for them in bulk various con-
sumer items—food, clothes, furniture, bagging for cotton bales, even reading
materials. They collected a 2.5 percent commission on all purchase orders and
on bales of cotton, barrels of corn, and hogsheads of sugar consigned to
them for sale when these products were sold. Commissions collected on sales
had been the primary source of income for factors in the early decades of the
nineteenth century. Commissions on purchase orders were less important because planters rarely seemed to consume more than one-third of their gross
income in ordinary years, and the wealthiest expended something less than
that on living expenses for their families and slaves.

In the last three decades of the antebellum period, most planters spent a
significant part of gross income on debt service (i.e., principal and interest
payments on long-term and short-term debt). Most wealthy planters serviced
their debts through their factors' agencies. When a planter gave a draft to a
creditor in payment of a debt, he made it payable either on demand or at
thirty days, sixty days, ninety days, or six or more months after the date of
the instrument. If payment was postponed six months or more, the instrument usually bore interest at the legal rate, typically 8 percent. The holder of
such a draft could sell it to a third party at a discount and obtain bank notes
or other liquid paper. More often, he remitted the draft to his factor to hold
for collection. In the meantime, the factor held such paper in pledge as collateral security for debts owed to him by the remitter. When the debtor drew
on his factor to pay a debt, the holder of the draft presented it to the drawee
within a short time, but before maturity, for acceptance. Acceptance simply
meant that the drawee endorsed the draft, making himself primarily liable
with the drawer for the eventual payment of the debt. A factor charged a
commission of 2.5 percent of the amount of each draft drawn on and accepted
by him in this fashion. When he advanced money to a client to pay a draft,
he charged 2.5 percent.

Only toward the end of the antebellum period did planters begin to keep
large cash balances with their New Orleans factors.[3] In prior decades, the
scramble to expand planting operations had necessitated running large current account deficits with factors, but with the improving business climate of
the last fifteen years of the period, East Feliciana planters had substantial
surplus income that had to be reinvested.

Much of that surplus income found its way into debt instruments that
had gravitated to New Orleans from all parts of the lower Mississippi Valley.
Some surplus income was invested in railroad stocks and bonds as well as
New Orleans bank stocks. Planters who had been able to contract long-term
debts in the 1830s by means of the property banks showed great reluctance to
hasten the liquidation of such obligations, preferring instead to invest their

surplus income in other interest-bearing debt instruments.[4] Part of the reason for this psychology may have been the highly profitable commercial banking operations of the property banks. In the 1850s, a planter who had subscribed to stock in earlier decades typically found that his dividends alone were sufficient to meet all interest and principal payments on loans secured by stock pledges.

Factors collected interest and principal payments, as well as stock dividends, for their clients. When the planter with surplus income lent money in the locality, he drew on his factor. Once again, the factor charged a commission for accepting or paying such a draft. Similarly, a planter who had contracted a loan, whether with a bank or an individual, through the agency of his factor, made interest and principal payments through his factor. The factor likewise charged a commission for these services. The total of all debt in the parish, short-term and long-term, probably approached $2.5 million in the last decade of the antebellum period.[5] This was double the gross value of all agricultural products shipped from the parish in a good year in the last decade before the war. Assuming an average rate of interest of 8 percent and principal payments equal to 10 percent of the gross debt, factors' commissions on debt service amounted to at least 50 percent as much as commissions collected from selling bales of cotton, barrels of corn, and hogsheads of sugar.

Commissions for servicing debts probably represented more than half of a factor's total commission income. Even in long-term debt arrangements, planters paid the prevailing cost of money, which varied from year to year. If a firm had to advance money to a client to meet a debt installment, interest costs often exceeded 12 percent, inclusive of discounts.

Although factors often bought and sold commodities on their own accounts, no commissions were collected on such transactions. Commission income from selling consignments from country merchants had to be shared with the consignees, and commission income from purchase orders certainly was much smaller than income earned from debt service arrangements.[6]

Promissory notes, drafts, and bills of exchange all commanded commissions when negotiated through factorage agencies. The legislative impediments to bank expansion, moreover, ensured that factors continued to enjoy a large and permanent role in the development of the New Orleans money market.[7] It must be remembered, also, that the hinterland that traded through New Orleans was shrinking, even in the last decade of the antebellum period. Private banking services provided by factors were destined to expand in importance if for no other reason than that the growing pool of savings in places such as East Feliciana inevitably gravitated toward New Orleans in search of profitable investments.

Changed Circumstances

In the 1850s no less than twenty New Orleans firms had observable profiles in the parish.[8] As previously noted, the largest planting operations were taking on the appearance of vertically integrated enterprises. After the war, most of these firms were in liquidation; few survived into the postwar period. Former partners organized new firms and attempted to reestablish old ties with their clients in the country. Henry Marston, for example, maintained his connection with Jacob Payne throughout the war years and continued to transact his business through the new firm's agency well into the 1870s. Marston wrote his son, Bulow, in the fall of 1870 that their family had "not a better or truer friend" than Payne.[9]

Not all of Payne's clients felt as kindly disposed toward him, especially in light of his wartime activities. Payne had not only converted firm claims against clients into promissory notes, which he had then pledged to firm creditors, but had also liquidated many of the payables with Confederate money in 1862 and 1863. Within months of the restoration of peace, one disgruntled creditor, Daniel Brown, wrote him to complain of the losses he had sustained in consequence of taking Confederate money in satisfaction of his claims. Brown believed that Payne had been in a much better position to realize value for Confederate money during the war than he had been. All those to whom Brown had loaned gold had repaid him "in Confederate Bonds and Treasury notes amounting in all at the time the Confederacy fell, to the amount of $150,000 leaving me [Brown] with this amount of Confederate Bonds & c and $12 *in specia*, and this after being robbed of negroes and a large portion of my stock of all kinds." Without relief from Payne and his partners, Brown expected to lose his "last foot of land . . . to pay off the Succession claims," leaving him "without a home and *not a cent in my pocket*."[10]

Brown was the executor or administrator of a succession. He had not completed his liquidation before the start of hostilities and had relied on the good agency of his factor to manage funds received in payment of succession claims. Payne had succeeded in relieving his firm of all liability for this agency by paying out such claims in Confederate money. Brown, however, was still liable to the heirs for all funds collected during his administration, just as if the debts had been paid with legal tender.

The deterioration of Marston's own relationship with the Payne firm is a good barometer of worsening financial conditions for both planters and factors in the first postwar decade, in part because the cotton crops were short, and because prices dropped precipitously from their initial postwar highs. In February 1871 Marston received a statement of account for sale of the 1870 crop showing net proceeds of $5,847.32 for ninety-five bales of cotton. He wrote Bulow: "In this a/c they [Payne, Dameron & Co.] bring me to their *debt* $240.40 by charging $2,000 paid to their friend Mr. Wilson on account of my note transferred to him. This has been done without any consultation with me as to my abilities to make so large a payment—But they state that from the information they have from you, there will be from 50 to 75 bales more to come."[11]

Marston was especially anxious that the payment requested in 1871 by the Boyce family, toward liquidating the prewar debt incurred in the purchase of Ashland Plantation, be met. On March 4, 1871, he wrote Payne to complain about the firm's levying on his account without first seeking his approval. He considered Wilson's demand that year of a payment of $5,800 to be exorbitant, and the charge on his account had made him a "*mutual* sufferer, in order to satisfy the rapacity of an individual whom it would seem . . . can have but very little feeling in these hard times for the sufferings of his fellow men."

To add to his troubles, the Boyce brothers were demanding a payment of three thousand dollars and additional funds sufficient to purchase six mules, which would take another thousand dollars. Michael Boyce had proposed that Marston make payment on a note drawn by Boyce that had been dishonored. If Marston could arrange the matter with the holder of the note, Boyce had agreed to excuse him from making any payment during the ensuing year, and he therefore felt "anxious that it should be made—as it is so uncertain in regard to the number of bales that are still to be sent forward, and the amount of funds they will nett [*sic*]." Marston thought it would "have been more appropriate to have advised with me, as to my ability to pay . . . any more than the *interest*" due on the infamous note transferred to Wilson.[12]

Marston had had gross income in 1870 of $6,079.83 after the agricultural laborers received their share of the cotton. His cash labor costs that year, as well as provisions and insurance connected with his planting operations on the Red River, amounted to seventeen hundred dollars. That year his total interest costs in connection with the unpaid balance on the mortgage note held by the Boyce family and the note transferred by Payne, Dameron & Co. to Wilson as "collateral security" were $1,679.80. After the exempt income was subtracted from gross, he had taxable income of only $376.31.[13] The interest costs alone on two debts were almost as much as the gross expenses of running a cotton plantation, which might produce 150 bales in a good year—interest costs without one penny allocated to principal repayments.

Marston's total debts amounted to approximately fourteen thousand dollars, about 10 percent of his prewar worth.[14] In 1870 those debts equaled at least two-thirds of what remained of his fortune. Improvements at Ashland before the war had amounted to about thirty dollars per acre. As land values fell throughout the 1870s, Marston doubted that he could recoup anything close to what he had spent building levees that fronted on the Red River, even if the plantation could be sold.[15]

By May 1871 it was clear that Marston would have difficulty paying even half the amount demanded by the Boyces. By this time Michael Boyce owned the entire indebtedness, having settled for it with his coheirs in the Succession of Henry Boyce. Boyce agreed to receive fifteen hundred dollars in satisfaction of the 1871 payment, although he himself was much pressed in consequence of his commission merchant having failed. Boyce had had funds with Joseph Hoy & Co. when it suspended payments, and now his drafts on the firm were being dishonored in consequence. Marston wrote him: "In regard to your friends . . . Hoy & Co. I have learned that the Banks in the city came to their relief and have advanced them $200,000, which has enabled them to go on with their business, and therefore trust that yourself and others will be able to obtain from them all the assistance you may require independent of the little aid that it may be in my power to render."[16] Unfortunately, Marston's intelligence was mistaken.

The Marston family was pressed in other ways. Bulow Marston had set up a plantation store at Ashland and was selling supplies on credit to his own hands, and to the neighbors as well, but he encountered much difficulty collecting on the accounts. Consequently, he owed substantial sums to wholesalers in New Orleans. Marston admonished him: "Excepting those [goods] supplied to the Negroes [at Ashland] the remainder should have been sold for *cash* or *cotton*. . . . To be compelled to use the proceeds of the crop to settle these debts will prove disastrous indeed."[17]

Marston's relations with both Bulow and Payne were much strained at this time. He attributed all of his difficulties with the latter to the note "transferred . . . as collateral to their friend Wilson."[18] He complained to Bulow that that transfer had made him "a mutual sufferer with themselves to satisfy the avariciousness of their friend Mr. Wilson."[19] The two thousand dollars paid on that note by the firm without his authority out of the proceeds of the 1870 crop especially irked him. He vowed to "endeavor to guard against a repetition of such a proceeding again, on the part of Payne, Dameron and Company."[20]

Marston was especially anxious to pay the fifteen hundred dollars requested by Boyce on the antebellum indebtedness for the purchase of Ashland. He wrote Payne in the summer of 1871 that the amount asked for by Boyce was "just one half of the sum" demanded the previous year. He proposed that Payne should authorize him to draw a draft for "not less than $1000, or . . . for the amount required" on the firm, which the firm would accept in favor of Boyce, and added that "not withstanding business is dull, I understand that money is plentiful and therefore trust that it will not be inconvenient to let me have the amount."[21]

Payne replied that the "season . . . [was] too hard and [would] . . . continue to be so until relief [was] . . . had from the next crop." The firm could accept no orders except to pay "the absolute wants and necessaries to carry [both the firm and the Marston family] into the next shipping season." Payne concluded: "And we hope that you will be able to satisfy Mr. Boyce, that this is one of the years to be indulgent. It will be just as much as we can do to make both ends meet and run into the new crop season, and if the wants of planters were not much less this, than the last year owing to more economy and lower prices of provisions we should not be able to do that much."[22]

A liquidity squeeze characterized conditions at New Orleans. Financial stringency pressed the Payne firm and weighed on its clients in the country. Boyce went himself to New Orleans to plead with Payne the necessity of permitting Marston to draw for the thousand dollars, but such importuning was to no avail. To Bulow, Marston wrote that the Payne firm had declined "accepting a draft in *his* [Boyce's] favor," but unfortunately had conveyed to Boyce the impression that they would still accept small drafts drawn by Marston for plantation and household supplies. Marston believed that this had been the source of Boyce's wrong idea that he owed the firm little or no money, and in consequence Boyce was now demanding a payment of five thousand dollars the following January. Boyce was not only importuning Marston for money, but the Payne firm as well, complaining that he could get nothing from his failed factor, Hoy and Co. By this time the creditors of the Ashland store had begun entreating Marston to pay on their open accounts. He could do nothing but promise some payment when the next crop came to market.

Relations with Bulow became anything but cordial. Marston took umbrage with a remark made by Bulow that he hoped that he might "never be the Butt of such another year as the last." Such an impudent statement, Marston said, required explanation. The times took a terrible toll on family and friends.

Marston and his son next contemplated the sale of Ashland as their only course of relief from debt woes, even if such a sale meant sacrificing fifteen years of work and more than thirty thousand dollars spent on improvements: "The time has arrived when something must be done—What do you think of putting up the Plantation in a lottery? It is a suggestion of your dear mother—Could 2000 tickets at $20 to $25 be disposed of in N.O. . . . at $35 per acre it would bring $44,500. . . . Allowing 10% for expenses it would yield $40,000—nett [*sic*]." By 1872 Marston's wife was planting cotton, having turned half of her flower garden over to growing the cash crop. Marston had undertaken an insurance agency in the area to raise extra income.[23]

The difficulties the Marstons encountered with their country store were not unlike those of New Orleans commission merchants or others who opened country stores. Everyone wanted cash, and credit was very dear. To Bulow, Marston wrote: "What is to be done about making collections? If other people commence suits against us, we shall be compelled to follow their example for self-protection."[24] Elsewhere he advised Bulow: "You will be compelled to look after your lawyers or they will not look after your debtors."[25] As the Marstons soon discovered, it was far easier to sell on credit than to collect on past-due accounts.

One complaint that permeated Marston's correspondence with both Bulow and the Payne firm was the imprudent haste with which bales shipped to New Orleans were sold. Before the war, cotton bales shipped to New Orleans in the fall and winter were held for sale in the late spring and early summer. Prices usually rose toward the end of a shipping season, and it was well worth waiting for a penny rise in the price. Postbellum economic conditions did not afford such a luxury. According to Marston, planters were forced to sell as soon as the cotton arrived in New Orleans. In February 1872 he wrote the following to Payne, Dameron & Co.:

> I fear that the cotton has been prematurely sold—I am of the opinion that middling cotton will command by the 1st April to 1st May at least 25 cents which upon 80 to 90 bales would probably make a difference of $800 to $1000 in the nett [*sic*] proceeds of the crop—This amount would have been worth saving, but we who are unfortunately in debt must submit to the dictation of our creditors—I was not aware that my son was shipping forward the whole of the crop at this time, or I should have begged of you to hold on if in your power.[26]

Marston knew the firm needed to reduce cotton to cash as soon as it arrived in the city to meet its own pressing commitments. Another problem he encountered with the firm, without precedent in his long relationship with Payne, concerned obtaining timely statements of account, especially statements regarding bales disposed of at New Orleans.[27]

Payne, Dameron & Co., like its country clients, barely survived from season to season. The trends documented elsewhere in the postwar southern economy—of difficulty in obtaining credit even to do the next year's planting and the pressure to liquidate the crop as soon as it came to market—are evident here. These desperate conditions did not abate in the 1870s but became worse. Families such as Marston's were able to hold on and continue planting simply because of luck (i.e., the forbearance of creditors). Marston wrote Boyce on February 13, 1872, that whether there would be a payment that year on the debt rested with his son and Payne, Dameron & Co. Whatever they proposed to do, he would accept. "You know the immense amount of labor and expenses incurred in the opening of the Ashland plantation and the thousands of dollars that have been paid on account of it; and if the toils of the last fifteen years are to be sacrificed God will support me in the hour of trial."[28]

Marston was nearly eighty years old when he wrote this letter. Eighteen months before, his son, James, had died as a result of a wound received while fighting for the Confederacy. His bitterness over the South's plight manifested itself everywhere in his correspondence. An antisecessionist Whig, he wrote Bulow shortly after James's death that "your *dear dear* brother, and *thousands* of *others* . . . were sacrificed to gratify the whims, the fancies, the caprices, and the unholy ambition of *Jefferson Davis*."[29]

As early as January 1869, Marston had pleaded with Boyce for forbearance, urging his own opposition to secession as a reason for being as generous as humanly possible in pressing the claim:

> The terms which you have prescribed seem somewhat exacting. . . . A *portion* of the crop must necessarily be reserved for the support of myself and family—When we look back to the heavy misfortune that has befallen us all, by the disastrous result of the late most unfortunate war, we should be disposed to be as lenient as possible to each other. I was strongly opposed to the suicidal policy of Secession, the fruits of which have involved the whole South in one common ruin from a state of the most unexampled prosperity—Our own people destroyed 100 bales of cotton for me, the proceeds of which would have canceled the debt I owe you—Look at the overflows, and consequent loss of crops which have since been encountered, and the immense expense of levees.[30]

Marston was still optimistic enough in 1869 to hope that he might obtain new financing by means of a mortgage on Ashland and compromise the debt to Boyce for cash. He expected to deduct four years' interest from the balance for the war years and pay about half of what remained in cash. He thought three thousand dollars would suffice, but he had no hope of obtaining mortgage financing from a Louisiana source. In the fall of 1869, he traveled to the North, primarily for the purpose of obtaining such financing, but found no one willing to lend on such a security.[31]

The fact that Marston expected to receive a 50-percent discount on the unpaid loan balance from Boyce, if he paid cash, reflected the antebellum perception of land prices. Acreage, it will be remembered, almost always sold on terms of three, four, and five years.[32] When land was purchased for cash, the average per-acre price was 50 percent below that of land sold with financing for a period of years.

Despite the pressure on profit margins, Ashland generated between eight and twelve thousand dollars of income annually. The claims on that income have already been enumerated. Suffice it to say that interest costs consumed as much as 25 percent of Marston's share of the income in any given year after the war. Marston also complained to Payne about factorage charges in the postbellum environment, and the few insignificant mortgages contracted after the war evidence the legitimacy of such complaints. He suggested that the merchants of New Orleans had the power "by combination to *control* the charges of drayage, storage and especially rates of insurance in offices in which so many of them are Directors."[33] Drayage and storage charges had doubled from prewar levels and now amounted to seventy-five cents per bale. If the increase was due to "the depreciation of the currency, according to the same mode of reasoning you [the merchants] would be entitled to the same advance upon your [the merchants'] commission for selling."[34] Factors were attempting to squeeze as much as possible out of commission income. Marston had simply failed to calculate the rise of that income in consequence of the effects of inflation on cotton prices.

Whatever prosperity planters and factors enjoyed in a reviving economy after the war proved illusory. By 1868 and 1869, factors were suing on open accounts contracted since the war and on promissory notes. The impression is a subjective one, but there seems to have been a measure of liquidity at New Orleans in 1866 and 1867 in consequence of high cotton prices. The cessation of hostilities brought many bales produced during the war to market, and they commanded high prices. Some planters and local merchants either smuggled cotton to New Orleans during the war or were able to warehouse a precious hoard in the countryside until they could bring it to market in the winter of 1865. The Marstons appear to have sold twenty thousand dollars' worth of cotton in the spring of 1865, but they used the money to buy merchandise for the Ashland store rather than to pay off debts.

In any event, the old firms that had serviced the area's planters, newly reorganized and striving to hold on to prewar clients and keep their own creditors at bay, were able to provide fairly generous credit to those who had always constituted their basic clientele. In 1866 and 1867, William Fellows had permitted Isabel Fluker to draw on him for more than five thousand dollars to pay for plantation supplies. Before the war, she had been one of the richest planters in the parish, with a fortune of perhaps $500,000. At the end of the selling season, in May 1867, Fellows obtained from Fluker something he would never have asked for before the war—"a collateral security note."[35] The note was secured by pledge "of the proceeds of the crop of said plantation by privilege." She waived citation, the usual delay, and confessed judgment. Fellows sued on the note two years later and obtained a judgment by default. By this time, however, Fluker had lost her most valuable plantation and was hopelessly burdened with antebellum and postbellum debts.

Several generalizations can be made about postwar factors' dealings with planters in the parish. Most had been members of now-defunct prewar firms with close personal ties to the area. Those prewar firms had guaranteed a substantial amount of the debt used by planters to expand their operations in the 1850s. In consequence, they faced ruin when much of that debt proved to be uncollectible after the war. Compared to their antebellum counterparts, reconstituted firms were thinly capitalized. Moreover, they lacked the means to sustain long-term loans to the plantation economy they had served so faithfully before the war. Their financing arrangements increasingly reflected little else than providing the necessary supplies for each year's planting season. The factorage system, then, did not simply yield to postwar improvements in transportation and communication; rather, it eroded with the rest of the agricultural economy. The process that was clearly under way in the 1870s, both in plantation agriculture and factorage, might best be described as a long-term crumbling. The reduction in size of planting units will be discussed in the next chapter, but suffice it to say that attenuation in planting units manifested itself in the factorage system by a transfer of the supplying and financing activities to the locality. The capacity for planters to prosper along antebellum lines was gone. With this disintegration came the eventual disappearance of the traditional factorage system.

Factors with judgments often worked with their debtors, attempting to resuscitate what life there was in a plantation operation. A few were lucky enough to dispose of their judgments to someone in the locality. Byrne, Vance & Co., for example, obtained a two-thousand-dollar judgment against John Collins in 1866, but its execution was stayed for two years, providing Collins paid one-half of the balance in each of the two years. In March 1870 they sold the judgment to Joseph M. Young, Collins's son-in-law. Young foreclosed on his mortgage in 1876, thereby shutting out an inferior mortgage creditor who had sold supplies to Collins on credit in prior years.[36]

A common practice of New Orleans factors both before and after the war was to arrange for the purchase of cotton from small growers through mercantile agencies in Clinton, Jackson, and Port Hudson. Before the war, Byrne, Vance & Co. had arranged its purchases through George A. Neafus & Co.; Wright, Allen & Co. through R. O. Draughon & Co.; Oakey, Hawkins through Mills and Cleveland; Payne, Harrison through Abraham Levi & Co.; W. A. Andrew & Co. through Frank and Poole; Carroll, Pritchard & Co. through Harris & D'Armond; and McRea, Coffman & Co. through M. Bloom & Co. These were just the Clinton firms that bought for New Orleans factors.[37] They and their counterparts in Jackson and Port Hudson purchased the production of about two-thirds of all the growers in the parish. The value of cotton handled just by the Clinton firms was in excess of $300,000 annually.

New Orleans firms attempted to revive these arrangements after the war. All of the antebellum Clinton firms, like their New Orleans counterparts, were in liquidation in the late 1860s. Richard Pritchard attempted to arrange cotton purchases through the newly formed firm of Doyle and Cocoran with disappointing results. In the first year after the war, he supplied them with more than eight thousand dollars in cash and goods. Cash advances alone were made in two-thousand-dollar increments. He had advanced Doyle and Cocoran "cash and merchandise which they sold and converted the proceeds to their own use." According to interrogatories propounded to Pritchard's clerks in New Orleans, the firm had "furnished cash and supplies to the defendants to advance on cotton to be shipped to the plaintiff [firm]." An examination of the accounts revealed that Doyle and Cocoran had shipped bales of cotton to Pritchard as early as July 1865. Each bale had brought an average price of $160, four times the average price in the 1850s, and three times the average price of a bale from the parish in 1870. Within one year's time, the firm was in debt to Pritchard in excess of five thousand dollars. Pritchard's pleadings contained a veiled accusation of fraud. Pritchard eventually got his judgment in 1870.[38]

In his study *King Cotton and His Retainers*, Woodman took exception with Alfred Holt Stone on a number of points concerning factors' financing arrangements with planters:

> Valuable as it is, Stone's article unfortunately contains a number of serious errors which have regularly found their way into subsequent studies. The evidence does not support his insistence that commissions often exceeded 2 1/2 percent, that interest was often charged for the entire year regardless of the length of time borrowed money was held, and that factors required planters to send a given amount of cotton to them, charging a penalty commission for failure to meet this stipulation.[39]

Although there is no evidence of such practices in antebellum arrangements, they did occur in postbellum credit relations. No effort was made to conceal them, either; they were to be found in postbellum mortgage instruments.

On May 5, 1879, for example, Ann Relf Chambers, represented by her son, James R. Chambers, granted a supply privilege on her 1879 crop to the New Orleans firm of Frankenbush and Borland. The supply privilege secured a promissory note of $250, payable on demand, at 8 percent interest until paid. Frankenbush and Borland were to have exclusive consignment of all her cotton, "including any cotton [paid to her] as rent or on shares or otherwise." If she defaulted, there was to be an automatic sequestration of her entire crop, and the firm was "empowered to sell the [crop] . . . at the current market prices and hold the net proceeds after deduction of all costs, charges, expenses, commissions, and attorney's fees." The net proceeds would then "stand in lien of the property sequestered."

In other words, the firm would sell the sequestered property, without appraisal, at the market, and hold the net proceeds after paying all their commissions and expenses, pending a resolution of the matter in controversy. Chambers further waived her "right to bond and the delay granted therefor and consented that the sequestration bond [should] . . . stand in place of the release bond required by law." Sequestration would issue "at the option of the holder of the promissory note, without notice or citation of any kind." She confessed judgment and waived all notices and citations required by law as well as the right to appeal. Her recitals in this instrument were her answer and confession of judgment in any future proceeding resulting from her arrangement with the firm. Attorneys' fees were to be assessed at 10 percent of principal and interest. As additional security, the firm could insure the buildings on Oakhill Plantation, charge the premiums to her, and keep any script rebated from the same. The firm's commission was set at the usual 2.5 percent, but she was required to ship a minimum of thirty bales. She was to pay to Frankenbush and Borland "commissions and brokerage on the amount . . . stipulated whether the crop reach[ed] the quantity and amount or not—[the firm] being authorized to charge additional commissions and brokerage [if] . . . the crop exceed[ed] . . . 30 bales." If any part of the crop was shipped to another house, or if she failed to ship when ordered to do so, the "whole" of the open account would be immediately payable, and the crops could be sequestered if the firm so ordered.[40]

It is not possible to determine from the instrument itself whether the firm's interest charges exceeded the legal rate, but Chambers had conceded so much discretion over the handling of the crop to the firm that they may well have charged their 2.5 percent on drafts drawn against net proceeds. She was charged interest on the full amount of her promissory note of $250 for the period of time in which any part of the open account remained unpaid.

In 1879 New Orleans factors contracted only four formally collaterized commercial arrangements with local planters in the parish. The amount of debt thus collateralized was less than 5 percent of the average dollar total in the 1850s. Loans on mortgages, whether by factors or banks, had become practically extinct.

Joseph M. Young, who was one of the most successful of the postwar planters, gave a mortgage to Nalle, Cammack on fourteen hundred acres to secure a promissory note of five hundred dollars due in six months. He also granted the firm a supply privilege and exclusive consignment rights to all his crops and agreed to pay 10 percent attorneys' fees on principal and interest in the event of collection proceedings. In a separate instrument, he borrowed eighteen hundred dollars on the same terms and mortgaged the same property. Nalle, Cammack also advanced cash to him under the arrangement, as well as supplies furnished directly by the firm, enabling him to secure cotton from black tenant farmers in the area. As such, much of the credit furnished to Young by the firm was actually attributable to a quasi-agency relationship, rather than a traditional commercial arrangement between factor and planter.[41]

Amedie Delambre secured twenty-five hundred dollars from Jacob M. Frankenbush, represented by two promissory notes payable in October and November 1879 and secured by a mortgage on two plantations with an aggregate size of thirty-four hundred acres.[42] He also agreed to consign his crop to no one but Frankenbush and agreed that any collection proceedings would be by executory process, with the property to be sold at sheriff's sale for cash. Delambre, like Young, was one of the few East Feliciana planters to prosper in the postwar period.

This was the extent of "commercial arrangements" in 1879 between New Orleans factors and East Feliciana planters that were formally collateralized. A few very rich planters continued to conduct their business through New Orleans firms, and did so without having to collateralize their credit arrangements with mortgages. Most, however, like their black counterparts, dealt directly with a store in one of the towns. The mortgages enumerated above all involved credit arrangements for another year's planting. There simply existed no long-term financing for capital improvements of any kind. The amount of credit available even to the best risks was scant indeed. The credit system, mirroring the rest of the economy, was becoming more and more attenuated.

The plight of the Chambers family from 1869 to 1880 reflects what was happening to large-scale planting units during those years. The Chamberses typified Louisiana's antebellum Creole-American aristocracy. Ann Relf Chambers was the daughter of Richard Relf, one of New Orleans's leading financiers, and the granddaughter of a former colonial Spanish mayor of the city.[43] Joseph Chambers, a native of Maryland and a West Point graduate, came to Louisiana in the early years of statehood. After their marriage, the couple moved to Oakhill Plantation in East Feliciana Parish, a property that was part of Ann's dowry from her father. The Chamberses subsequently acquired Hopewell, a sugar plantation near Port Hudson, and erected there a huge sugarhouse. Their financing for plantation operations was arranged through family connections, and in 1858 they borrowed twenty-five thousand dollars from the Bank of Louisiana, mortgaging Hopewell and 56 slaves.[44] The loan was guaranteed by Ann's brother, Stephen Z. Relf, and the mortgage was never canceled. It is not clear whether the Relfs continued to service the loan during the war and afterward, but it appears that the bank never foreclosed on its mortgage. The Chambers family managed to hold on to the property until 1880, but Hopewell was virtually destroyed during the siege of Port Hudson.

The value of the Chambers properties in East Feliciana in 1860 exceeded $150,000. Like many wealthy families in the parish, their prospects appeared somewhat sanguine in the first two or three years after the war, but in December 1869 Joseph Chambers filed an affidavit in the mortgage records acknowledging his indebtedness to his wife's separate estate.[45] He acknowledged that she had received $10,457.08 from the succession of her grandmother, Maria Quinones, in August 1830, and he had used those funds for purposes unrelated to the preservation and enrichment of her separate property. Her claim, however, was subject to a credit of $8,830 repaid to her in subsequent years by her husband.

After Chambers died in 1874, his widow and his son, James, continued planting activities on both plantations for another five years. During those years, what remained of the family fortune simply melted away. Before his death, Joseph Chambers had given a mortgage for $9,960.75, on Hopewell, to James; the mortgage was reinscribed in 1879.[46] It seems that James had advanced money to the family during and after the war, and his father may have been attempting to secure for him a priority position vis-à-vis general creditors. Perhaps, however, he was merely trying to secure a debt with all of his remaining property.

Weeks before his death, Joseph Chambers granted a mortgage on Hopewell to the New Orleans firm of Jurey & Gillis to secure a debt of twenty-two hundred dollars incurred by James.[47] By this time, James was conducting all of the family's planting operations, an arrangement similar to the one between Marston and his son, Bulow. The debt had been contracted for plantation supplies for the 1874 planting season. In the mortgage instrument, Joseph Chambers acknowledged that the property was encumbered already with mortgages to his son and to John R. Gaines of New Orleans to secure a twelve-hundred-dollar note. The debt to Gaines was already three years old. In the same instrument, James subordinated his two mortgages to Jurey & Gillis's mortgage, and Ann Relf Chambers waived the security interest she had for restitution of her dowry and paraphernal property.

The crisis year for the Chambers family and other planting families in the parish appears to have been 1874. Theft of cotton from the fields reached epidemic proportions, as this letter from James to Gaines represents:

I was compelled to pay, the demands for the years advances before settling other claims—The time I was called away from home was a critical one for the crop—As the freedmen had collected a considerable cotton, & notwithstanding I had left an agent to attend to my business, they succeeded in getting off a good part of their crop—no one residing on the place—The consequence was that the crop did not pay the year's supplies—although it was a good one—I deferred writing to you, expecting to get something from the clerk's office, and have come up here for the purpose—Capt. Lanier tells me he has cost bills to the amount of $2000 from which he cannot get enough to live on—My regret at not being able to meet the very modest demand from you, amounts to mortification after I had felt so sure of doing so—My present situation is that I do not see when I am to get supplies for the *family*, the coming year—Should the cost Bills be collected in part, I will forward you whatever I have over a bare support.[48]

The debt to Gaines antedated the current planting year, so he had no privilege on the crop. Jurey & Gillis had insisted on being paid first, a preference to which they were entitled by law. James had not been able to make collections from the freedmen he had furnished. He was in no position to pay any part of Gaines's older claim.

The Chamberses still had friends in the city who could afford them relief. On September 2, 1875, Ann Relf Chambers purchased Hopewell at her husband's succession sale.[49] She sold it three months later to the Right Reverend Joseph P. B. Wilmer, Episcopal Bishop of Louisiana, for six thousand dollars. She reserved the right, however, to redeem the property within six years. The arrangement was simply an interest-free loan to the Chambers family by the bishop to be repaid within six years. The purchase price included $3,500 in United States treasury notes and $825 in supplies and mules already received from Wilmer.[50]

In January 1876 James gave Wilmer a lien on four mules, purchased from a third party for $630. The instrument recited that the lien was to "act as a vendor's privilege."[51] At this time, there was no such thing as a chattel mortgage in Louisiana law; the only way to effectuate a security interest in movables was by means of a vendor's privilege. A vendor's privilege on movables, however, only secured a vendor; it did not apply to a third-party lender unless the lender also sold the secured property to the debtor. Such arrangements, involving livestock, were confected in the postbellum period.[52] Regarding the mules, Wilmer's security interest appeared less than certain.

James executed two "commercial arrangements" with two New Orleans factorage firms in 1876. For $330 in supplies, he gave Nalle, Cammack a privilege on his 1876 crop and exclusive consignment rights to that crop. To John Chaffe & Sons he gave a privilege on all the crops grown at Hopewell, as well as the livestock thereon. The Chaffe firm eventually acquired Hopewell at sheriff's sale, subsequent to Wilmer's reconveyance of the property to the Chambers family. The Chaffe firm sold Hopewell in 1885 for forty-five hundred dollars.[53]

John Chaffe & Sons had sued James in 1879 and obtained a judgment of $243.33 with interest from February 1877. Wilmer had conveyed Hopewell to James, rather than his mother, on February 9, 1877, and Chaffe obtained an order for the seizure and sale of Hopewell to satisfy its judicial mortgage.[54] The judicial mortgage had already been inscribed in the mortgage records when Ann Relf Chambers executed her agreement with Frankenbush and Borland respecting the crops produced on the Oakhill property.[55] In May and June, James recorded three of his rental contracts with tenant farmers, which he subsequently assigned.[56]

Another of James's creditors, C. L. Walmsley & Co., recorded its judicial mortgage in November 1879 for twenty-five hundred dollars.[57] This debt was already four years old, but the Walmsley claim was secured by a conventional mortgage, which perhaps explains why the firm had resisted suing James immediately. Moreover, the debt was subject to a credit of $875; James had therefore managed to service the loan partially during the interim. Chaffe recorded another judicial mortgage the same day Walmsley made its recordation in the mortgage records, this time for a debt contracted on an open account, a promissory note, or both, for one thousand dollars.[58] Finally, James's wife recorded her judgment decreeing a separation of property between herself and her husband and recognizing her claim against him for $1,350 for restitution of her paraphernal property.[59]

The incident that was probably the immediate cause of the judgments taken out against James by the Chaffe and Walmsley firms was his transfer of a one-half interest in the Hopewell property to George B. Croft. The Walmsley suit named Croft as a codefendant with James, and their judgment ordered Croft to surrender his one-half interest for sale. Apparently, the transfer had been a simulation. Compounding the affliction borne by the Chambers family in 1879 was the death of Ann Relf Chambers. Hopewell was sold at public sale on December 20, 1879.[60]

On June 8, 1880, James filed a declaration of homestead exemption, claiming 160 acres of another tract of property as exempt by law.[61] He also claimed exemptions on livestock and provisions to the full extent allowed by law. All of these claims, however, were disallowed, and he was assessed fifty dollars in damages for enjoining the sale of the property that he claimed was exempt by law. So ended a story that in most respects typified the condition of formerly wealthy planter families and their city factors in the postwar period. The price received by the Chaffe firm in 1885 for the property hardly justified their having held it for five years, but a rosy optimism seems to have pervaded the first decade and a half after the war. Most believed that cotton prices would reach fantastic highs in the years ahead and restore fortunes that had vanished with the war and emancipation. The price of cotton, however, was not what ailed the economy.

Marston's relationship with Payne grew more strained as the 1870s progressed. His proposal to mortgage his property in East Feliciana to secure the firm in the event judgment went against him in *Worthy v. Marston* was too favorably received: indeed, Payne nagged him for just such a security even after a favorable judgment was reported. Marston complained that he was loath for the community in which he lived to learn how large a debt he owed.

When Payne persisted in writing him about the mortgage, fearing that Boyce might attempt to satisfy his debt out of Marston's Clinton property, Marston responded that he considered such a possibility highly improbable. Boyce was amply secured with the Ashland property. A mortgage in favor of the firm on Marston's residence would only damage his credit in the community. The advantage accruing to the Payne firm was far outweighed by the injury it would cause him. Those with whom Marston had "been upon such intimate business transactions, for so large a number of years" probably would withdraw that "lenity" he had come to expect and on which he relied.[62]

Marston and Bulow were both concerned that the Payne firm would make another unauthorized levy on the proceeds of the 1872 crop to service the collateral note pledged to Wilson in 1865. Bulow proposed shipping part of the crop from Red River for the account of Michael Boyce as a safeguard against such a levy. Marston thought it a good idea but cautioned that "great care [had] . . . to be observed in order that [the firm] . . . should not become offended." Payne had acquiesced to Marston's request to forgo a mortgage on the East Feliciana property and had "simply required the renewal of [the note] . . . from the date of the last payment." Marston proposed giving Boyce a six-month draft of two thousand or twenty-five hundred dollars, provided the Payne firm would accept it; acceptance would guarantee payment by the firm at maturity. Marston advised Bulow that he had only drawn on Payne, Dameron for four hundred dollars during the 1872 planting season for necessary household expenses. He owed some small balances on open accounts at local stores, but he had curtailed his living expenses to about one-quarter of their prewar levels.[63]

The difficulties experienced by Marston with Payne, Dameron were typical of the times. Most cases were a great deal more extreme. Debts on open accounts accumulated unpaid balances from season to season and became impossible to service in years of poor harvests. Many planters attempted to switch firms, leaving their old factors with unsecured debts. It is clear why factors began demanding collateral for open accounts that before the war rarely had been collateralized. It also explains why formal agreements consistently provided for exclusive consignment arrangements between planter and factor.

The factorage system did not simply vanish; it did, however, respond to what was happening in the whole agricultural economy. Excepting the first two or three years after the war, factors in the postwar period shed their investment banking role and financed little else but short-term commercial credit for each year's planting. Such operations were far more risky and not

The Marston house in Clinton, circa 1900. The structure was built in the 1830s to house the Clinton branch of the Union Bank and became the Marston family's residence in the 1850s. (Marston House Collection, Clinton, Louisiana. Photograph courtesy of the Louisiana State University Library)

nearly so remunerative, which probably explains why factors sought to squeeze every penny from commission income. To justify long-distance relationships, moreover, necessitated certain economies of scale that were conspicuously absent from the postwar agricultural economy. The new imperative stressed smaller production units and numerous credit relationships. A New Orleans commercial firm could not afford several thousand open accounts with tenant farmers who shipped five or six bales of cotton each to market annually. The problem centered on evaluating the creditworthiness of numerous small borrowers and absorbing the high default rate characteristic of such open accounts. What remained of the old line business was not enough to sustain the plethora of antebellum firms.

As late as 1885, East Feliciana planters still contracted formally collateralized credit relationships with New Orleans firms. Twenty-one such arrangements appear in the mortgage book for that year, most for relatively large sums of money by postwar standards. Anna R. DeLee, separate in property from her husband, mortgaged seventy-five acres to Frankenbush and Borland to secure a debt of three hundred dollars for supplies for the 1885 planting season. She had obtained a judgment ordering a property separation one week before contracting with Frankenbush and Borland. She had to ship not less than thirty-five bales and pay $1.25 per bale on any deficiency. The mortgage also secured antecedent and future advances by the firm. The supplies purchased through the firm were specifically enumerated: "5 barrels pork, 5 barrels meal, 3 barrels flour, 75 bushels of corn, 25 bushels oats, 5 barrels mess pork, and 5 barrels of meal to be furnished during March, April, May and June—freight to Clinton pre-paid."[64]

G. W. Munday mortgaged 370 acres to J. L. Harris & Co. to secure a planting debt of $569.[65] Amedie Delambre contracted an arrangement with Lehman, Abraham, & Co. in which he acknowledged an indebtedness to the firm of three thousand dollars, represented by a promissory note payable in eight months. The note was secured by a mortgage on twenty-five hundred acres and all the livestock on the plantation. He also gave the firm a crop pledge, exclusive consignment rights, and the authority to sell at the market at any time. Lehman's authority included discounting the note in the money market "at a rate not to exceed 12%" and crediting the proceeds to Delambre's account. Delambre had, in other words, contracted an arrangement whereby he paid interest on the whole three thousand dollars for the full eight months, not when charges were incurred on the open account.[66] His actual costs ranged as high as 20 percent, depending on the rate of discount. He no doubt paid the firm a commission for endorsing his note.

The firm of H. & C. Newman contracted no less than sixteen of the twenty-one mortgages taken by New Orleans firms in 1885. The total value of their collaterized loans that year was twenty-two thousand dollars, a very large sum by postbellum standards. The Newman firm was the successor of the antebellum firm of A. Levi & Co. of Clinton and New Orleans.[67] Consequently, the Newman brothers had a ready-made clientele, but unlike their predecessor, Abraham Levi, they collateralized with mortgages and crop pledges and recorded such instruments in the public records. On February 19, 1885, H. A. Lea contracted a commercial arrangement with the Newman firm for "advances in money and goods and necessary supplies to the amount of

$1000" for the 1885 planting year. "For every $10.00 which H. & C. New-man . . . advanc[ed] . . . [Lea] promis[ed] to ship one bale of cotton . . . the said commission . . . [being] $1.25 on every bale" not shipped. Lea gave the Newmans exclusive consignment rights to all of his crops with complete discretion to sell as they deemed advisable. The debt was evidenced by a promissory note, due and payable on October 1, 1885, that was accepted by the firm and immediately discounted to a third party. Lea, then, was obliged to ship at least one hundred bales to pay back the entire thousand dollars in 1885; if he failed to ship the requisite number of bales, he paid a penalty charge of $1.25 a bale.[68] Like Delambre, he paid interest on the entire thousand dollars for the full term of the loan, and discounts probably doubled the cost of the loan.

The Newmans contracted a three-thousand-dollar arrangement with Ada S. Beauchamp. Her quota of one hundred bales was less onerous than the arrangement with Lea, but the Newmans could stop making advances on the open account at any time should a "disaster" threaten the year's cotton production.[69] If the Newmans found it necessary to discount Beauchamp's note, the rate of discount was fixed at 2.5 percent. This charge, however, was in addition to the 8 percent interest the note bore. Moreover, she was borrowing the money for nine months; the effective rate of discount was closer to 3 percent on an annualized basis, and this charge was in addition to the 8 percent interest rate on the whole three thousand dollars. Each time she drew a draft on her account, the Newmans charged her 2.5 percent for accepting it and 2.5 percent for advancing the money to pay it. Interest was payable on the whole three thousand dollars for nine months, not from the time when charges were actually incurred on the open account. Failure to ship the requisite number of bales resulted in an additional charge of $1.25 a bale for any deficiency.

Such commercial arrangements typically provided for an open account secured by a promissory note bearing interest from date until maturity; the factor could discount the note if the need arose. Before the war, credit facilities had not been collateralized in this manner. Factors rarely asked for authority to sell the collateral security: they generally pledged such notes, seldom disposing of them to third parties.

Debtors now paid interest throughout the term of the agreement, not when charges were actually incurred on the open account. Discount charges added to such costs, so a premier credit risk in the agricultural economy in 1885 paid 15 to 20 percent interest on an annualized basis, and more when commissions for accepting and advancing were charged. This rate was at least double the average borrowing cost in other parts of the economy.

It is important to remember that all of these arrangements were for financing short-term loans for planting purposes. Such loans would almost never have been formally collateralized in the antebellum period; moreover, the debts that were collateralized before the war were for capital investments in the plantation economy. Loans on mortgages in the antebellum period generally were on terms of up to ten years. The aggregate value of such outstanding loans in 1860 was in excess of $1 million. The mortgage loans contracted in the first prosperous decade after the war probably aggregated to no more than fifty thousand dollars.

The reasons local growers continued to cultivate relationships with New Orleans firms were obvious. Credit costs were far more reasonable than those contracted through a local store, the costs of buying in bulk at New Orleans were wholesale, and the prices of cotton were higher in the city, even after allowing for freight charges and insurance. However, the factorage system, like the plantation economy in general, was contracting. Production units were shrinking in size, and with the decline of large-scale agriculture came diminished income for city factors. There was no financing for capital investment in the decades after the war. Servicing investment loans to the plantation economy had been the fastest growing source of income for factors in the last decade before the war. The loss of such business accounted for at least a 50-percent reduction in income after the war.

Marston's relationship with the Payne firm steadily declined. By the summer of 1873, the firm had advised him not to draw against them even for household expenses. Marston replied angrily to the firm's admonition, quoting "an old Georgia friend." He had " 'economized to the living point' and it was with this essential fact in view, that prevented me from accompanying my daughter to your city [New Orleans] during her late visit." His wants would be few until the new crop could be harvested and sold, except for his state and local taxes, which were "beyond endurance." He had drawn a draft in favor of a St. Louis merchant who would expect payment when the draft was presented to the Payne firm for acceptance.[70]

In a subsequent letter, Marston reminded Payne of their long association. For three years there had been an understanding between himself and the firm that he should be accorded the "privilege of drawing for all incidental expenses including taxes, expenses of myself and family." He hoped the firm would "rework . . . [its] present determination," adding that few of Payne's patrons could claim a relationship that spanned twenty-eight years.[71] The economies that had held the old system together were gone.

The Payne firm suspended operations in June 1874, Jacob Payne having failed entirely in his business. Marston conveyed his condolences to Payne but advised him that he and his family were making other arrangements pending a resumption by his firm.[72] Bulow negotiated an arrangement with J. W. Burbridge & Co. that provided for a thousand-dollar open account so the Marston family could obtain badly needed supplies. One of the firm's partners, George Robinson, subsequently purchased the judgment from Michael Boyce for something less than fifty cents on the dollar and compromised the collateral note in the hands of the Payne firm's liquidator.[73]

This, then, is how one family's fortunes were salvaged more than ten years after the war, but not before the Payne firm in liquidation issued a writ of attachment in East Feliciana and seized the Marstons' residence. Seventy bales of cotton, in the hands of J. W. Burbridge & Co., were also seized. The pledgee of the collateral security note retransferred it to Payne in exchange for a sugar plantation. Three years elapsed before this claim was finally settled.

The Burbridge firm, of course, had had extensive commercial relations in the parish before and after the war. What may well have proved crucial in this firm's decision to rescue the Marston family after the suspension of the Payne firm was the almost reckless abandon with which Bulow planted cotton on the Red River during the 1874 planting season. He leased adjoining properties and planted more than eight hundred acres in cotton, a very risky strategy considering the river's propensity to overflow, labor problems, and the costs of credit. A disastrous epidemic killed many horses and mules in East Feliciana but did not spread to the Red River. Gross proceeds exceeded forty thousand dollars.

With money, the Marstons strengthened their negotiating position and compromised the collateral note on far more favorable terms than Payne had been prepared to offer before his firm's suspension. Marston still believed that he owed an obligation of loyalty to Payne, a feeling Bulow did not share. Congenial relations between planters and their prewar agents belonged to the past, along with slaves and regular income streams. Every planting was a gamble, and no claim older than the prior year had any moral right to share in the winnings.

6

Decline and Default

I return, without my approval, to the Senate, in which it
originated, an act entitled "An Act to exempt from seizure and sale,
under execution, property, real or personal, to the value of $1,250., stating
the manner, and how said valuation shall be ascertained, and prescribing
penalties for the violation of any provisions of this act." . . .
It seems to be unnecessary and unwise to permit this bill to become law. . . .
Such a law, in my opinion, would be of doubtful benefit, if not an
actual injury, to the poor man, whose interests it is doubtless intended
to subserve. It is far more important to him that he should be able to obtain
credit from time to time than that he should be able to escape the payment of
obligations which he may incur. Any law which in effect forbids a prudent
tradesman or landlord to give credit deprives the poor of this greater
benefit. It seems to me that the law should rather aim at securing
the greatest certainty in the enforcement of all obligations.
In the long run more good to the larger number
will be in this way secured.[1]

William P. Kellogg, Governor
January 5, 1874

ONE VIEW OF postbellum credit arrangements seems to be that the system
that had evolved before the war for supplying planters more or less
vanished with the cessation of hostilities, and in its place there sprang up a
plethora of country stores vying for the trade of recently emancipated slaves.[2]
Because such people could not obtain credit in their own right and owned no
property, country merchants carried them through the planting season in
exchange for liens on their crop shares. There was, however, nothing new or
strange about these arrangements.[3] New Orleans factors and their Clinton
representatives had regularly taken promissory notes from small growers as
collateral security for supplies shipped to them during the winter and summer months. Such notes were never collateralized with mortgages; they were
simply notes collateralized by operation of law.

These "collateral security" notes only obtained a measure of visibility in
the postwar suit records; evidence of such transactions is not to be found in
the mortgage records. On the face of such a note would be the all-too-com-
mon notation "for supplies, 1861." This type of note evidenced not only the

debt but a privilege as well, provided the crops had been consigned to the commission merchant or factor or were still in the grower's possession.

Antebellum Security Devices and Postbellum Innovations

In the 1825 revision of the Civil Code, consignee privilege was codified, thus giving a commission merchant a privilege on agricultural production consigned to him up to the amount of advances made by him to the consignor. This privilege outranked other security encumbrances on a consignor's property, including conventional, judicial, and legal mortgages, provided the consigned property was in the hands of the consignee merchant who had made actual advances in supplies and cash. Such property was deemed to be in the hands of the consignee if he had received an invoice or bill of lading previous to any attachment by another secured creditor. Article 3214 of the Civil Code was amended in 1841, at the height of the depression that had begun in 1839, to remove any ambiguity regarding the application of this privilege, not only to amounts owing for supplies furnished but for any general balances owing on open accounts as well.

Article 3184 was amended in 1843 to provide for a privilege on "the product of the last crop and the crop at present in the ground . . . for *necessary* supplies furnished to any farm or plantation." This privilege was at least concurrent with a lessor's privilege for rents of immovables and the hire of slaves "in working the same." It was, however, inferior to an overseer's claim for wages against the same property.[4]

Under the antebellum scheme, free laborers were simply general creditors with no privilege equal or superior to that of consignee merchants, overseers, or lessors of immovables, insofar as crops were concerned, whether standing or already consigned to a merchant.[5] The legislature remedied this deficiency in 1867 with Act 195, which restricted the privilege provided commission merchants in Article 3184. For debts due "for necessary supplies . . . and debts due for money actually advanced, and used for the purchase of necessary supplies" privilege only extended to "the crops of the year and the proceeds thereof." The old privilege had included "the product of the last crop and the crop at present in the ground." However, the privilege was extended at this same time to cover cash advances actually made. Moreover, the privileges granted to overseers, furnishers of supplies, and parties advancing money "necessary to carry on any farm or plantation" were henceforth to be ranked concurrently. Such privileges were, however, superior to those of any prior mortgage creditor and survived a seizure and sale of the land while the crop was on it. Much of what was legislated up to this point simply reflected developments in antebellum jurisprudence, but the 1867 act also created a privilege in favor of agricultural laborers that was then ranked as the first privilege on the crop.[6]

A sharecropper who leased on shares was not an agricultural worker within the meaning of amended Article 3184; he was a tenant. If his contract provided for the payment of shares in lieu of wages, however, he was an agricultural worker and covered by Civil Code Article 3184 as revised in 1867.

Individual contracts often were ambiguous about whether the arrangement was a lease on shares or a contract of employment with shares in lieu of wages. The situation was especially confusing when the parties contracted that the tenant would cultivate the landlord's property three days out of the week in return for land the tenant could cultivate for himself during the remainder of the week. The tenant's status was ambiguous, and it became even more so if he obtained supplies or credit from his lessor or employer, a merchant in the town, or a cotton buyer for a New Orleans firm in expectation of whatever share of cotton he might obtain in his own right. A true agricultural laborer had no ownership interest in the crop, and it is doubtful that he could confect a security interest in favor of a supplier other than his employer. However, tenants of every description could contract for supplies with furnishing merchants, and such advances were protected by Article 3184.

Article 123 of the 1868 constitution attempted a draconian reform in the operation and effect of Louisiana's law of privileges. Henceforth, "no mortgage or privilege [would] . . . affect third parties, unless recorded in the parish where the property . . . affected [was] situated."[7] Moreover, existing tacit mortgages and privileges would cease to have any effect against third persons after January 1, 1870, unless an instrument was recorded that evidenced such a mortgage or privilege. The 1869 legislature then adopted a recordation provision that put into effect the policy enunciated in Article 123.[8] This legislation is the reason more than two hundred recordings were filed in the mortgage books in 1870, but the recordations accounted for no more than 15 percent of all the planting units in the parish that year.

Recordation was not a solution, however. Most privileged creditors failed to record any evidence of their privileges on standing crops, the reason being that most holders of privileges were not vis-à-vis other third parties. Lessors, tenants, and furnishers all had contractual relationships with each other that obviated much of the necessity of making recordings. There were few, if any, parties outside a given set of relations who could claim third-party status. A furnishing merchant to whom money was owed from a prior year might attempt to seize the crop to pay his debt, but his claim was still inferior to that of the lessor and furnisher who claimed valid privileges on the present year's crop. Agricultural laborers took precedence over all other creditors.

The first wave of recordings of crop privileges lacked any formal definition insofar as Louisiana law then stood; the recordings were simply acknowledgments of the existence of various privileges. In 1870 it is probable that recorded privileges in favor of furnishers in fact collateralized antecedent debts. At that time, there was simply no device available to a creditor that would permit a securing of a prospective debt on a standing crop. A mortgage on land and crops was possible, but most production units in the parish were not grounded in land ownership.[9]

Insofar as such makeshift privileges afforded any protection to a creditor, a recording of such an instrument probably put other parties on notice and discouraged them from contracting more obligations with barely solvent debtors. The recordings may well have been limited to only the most risky credits extended by local merchants and others to growers, or exclusively to antecedent debts.

Quite a few supply privileges, however, were recorded in the years from 1870 to 1875, the majority to local merchants. It appears that by 1870 the essential postbellum growing arrangement between planters and their former slaves had fully evolved. Initially, in the two or three years after the war, planters attempted to conduct their operations much as they had done before the war. Cash wages probably were never an important feature of planting arrangements in postwar East Feliciana Parish. Planters contracted with agricultural laborers on halves, providing everything necessary for planting, including supplies. The costs of the supplies, of course, were borne by each laborer's share of the crop. If the crop was a short one, the planter could fail even to meet expenses; such an occurrence foretold ruin to many. It was at this point that many planters either recognized the need to spread risks and downsize their exposure or found themselves unable to supply their laborers.[10]

Indeed, it is possible to trace planters' growing awareness of the need to spread risks to credit consumers in the correspondence of Henry Marston to his son, Bulow, on Ashland Plantation. As early as the 1868 planting season, the Marstons were growing cotton on halves at Ashland but supplying their hands and selling to them through their store on the plantation. Most of the merchandise sold through the store was exchanged for cotton. The store, however, carried its own risk. Marston advised Bulow of his concerns about using revenues from planting to subsidize the store. He was chagrined to learn that earnings from the 1868 crop had been used to settle claims with wholesale vendors. Bulow still owed Payne, Huntington & Co. for advances made for the benefit of the store, and he was in debt to suppliers, who were growing impatient. Marston queried him about the amount of stock on hand and outstanding debts. The store, he wrote, "should be made to contribute as *much as possible* towards the payment of the debt due [the Boyces] for the plantation—for of what value is the store without the plantation?"[11] Although the store eventually made money, it was a risky venture. Marston urged his son to extend no credit but to accept only cash or cotton.

The actual planting arrangements were a combination of cash and share wages. None of their workers were tenants. Marston continually queried his son about such arrangements, giving advice on the latest developments concerning them:

> I held a conversation with Dr. Ball formerly of Shreveport, who is cultivating one of the finest tracks [*sic*] of land . . . in West Feliciana. He tells me he has hired hands to work for him 4 days in the week and *two* for themselves, he finding them rations of meat and team and plows to work the crop—This appears to be more favorable terms than you have hired a portion of yours if I am not mistaken.[12]

In February 1871, in response to Bulow's advising him that four mules had been lost during the 1870 planting season, Marston responded that "the Negroes should be compelled to furnish half the mules and other stock and farming utensils."[13]

It is clear that the Marstons were supplying their workers under the terms of a labor agreement, and they were selling to them through the Ashland store on credit. Accounts were settled in January of each year; the laborers received cash, cotton, or store credit for any balance owed to them after their charges for the prior year had been deducted. Marston advised Bulow that difficulties with the Payne firm were not the cause for delays in settlement of such accounts:

> You speak of "the complications arising and *never having heard*, of the cotton, the *first part* of the crop shipped in your name, the negroes have no settlement, and swear they will never let the cotton out of their sight until they see the cash." Now it just so happens that I received only duplicates of the sales of the first 26 bales sold on the 4 Dec., the *originals* having been handed to you, and therefore *the fault* is with yourself alone, that "no settlement has been made with the Negroes"—My calculation has been that the *originals* of copies of not only *all* a/sales of cotton, but of bills of supplies would be handed or sent to you, whereby it would have been in your power to have paid the Negroes the cash that was due to them over and above the amount owing by them to the store or for the supplies of meat and c furnished according to *your* agreement with them and by reference to the Payne, Dameron Co A/current, amounts to nearly $2000! independent of what they be owing to the store.[14]

Based on this quote, it appears that the predominant relationship between the Marstons and their workers was one of employer-employee, not tenancy. The workers were supplied specific items such as pork rations under a labor agreement, and they could buy additional supplies on credit from the store.

As the Marston family's financial condition worsened in the 1870s, Henry Marston began to contemplate other arrangements, whereby more of the risks could be spread to the sharecroppers. He suggested to Bulow an out-right lease of the land to the workers as tenants "for 100 lbs. or more of clean cotton per acre." The tenants could then supply "themselves in *everything*—teams, ploughs, provisions." Such were the terms "upon which the planters in Bolivar County, Mississippi, conduct[ed] their plantations."[15] Marston certainly considered his son's arrangements with the sharecroppers far too generous. When Bulow advised him that the plantation required "hands, mules, horses, or money," he answered that of the last three he had none to offer; nevertheless, he thought hands could be persuaded to leave East Feliciana and settle at Ashland for the terms then being offered by Bulow.[16]

In 1869 and 1870 Bulow attempted to establish himself in a factorage business in New Orleans. This venture was doomed for a variety of reasons, including the premature death of his brother, James, in whose hands he had entrusted the management of the plantation. Nevertheless, from the correspondence with his father concerning cotton consignments from East Feliciana, it is clear that black tenants and agricultural laborers had cotton in their possession at the end of the growing season and were free to dispose of it. His father advised him that he "had better send up the *cash* that will be necessary for this purpose [to advance on consignments]—Negroes cannot be dealt with in any other manner than the *money* paid into their hands."[17] On October 6, 1870, Marston wrote: "Every day Negroes are bringing in their cotton and could I say to them that I could pay them $25 to $30 per bale, they might be induced to ship—Many of them however are in debt to stores in town and consequently some feel bound to give their creditors the preference."[18]

Black tenants and workers were not yet formally bound by debt arrangements to local storekeepers. Privileges, unlike pledges and mortgages, did not preclude alienation of the crops to the prejudice of creditors. In the last half of the 1870s, crop pledges almost always provided for exclusive consignment arrangements, whereby indebted farmers pledged all of their crops to the furnishing merchant and were thus prevented from disposing of any portion to a third party.

It is not surprising that the distinctions between agricultural laborers and tenants tended to get blurred. Laborers often worked for a share of the crop; tenant farmers paid their rentals in cotton, sometimes on shares and other times in pounds per acre. The dichotomy, to the extent that it can be distinguished at all in such labor relationships, probably is not very valuable in estimating the extent of control exercised by planters over their former slaves. Where landowners simply furnished land and nothing else, the relationship, on the surface at least, partook of lease. However, even in the case where the laborer was paid in cotton, the relationship contained many of the elements of a lease arrangement.

The 1870 recordings of supply privileges to furnishing merchants were a small percentage of those recorded in 1879. In such an instrument, a debtor acknowledged the receipt of supplies from a furnishing merchant, effectively creating a privilege in favor of the merchant. The debtor was attempting to collateralize the debt with the crop then being brought to market. The privileges that were recorded were dated in the winter, during the planting season, but not recorded until the fall, during the harvest.

The supply privileges recorded in 1870 represented an attempt to collateralize debts that were already at least a year old. No provision in Louisiana's then-existing system permitted the collateralization of debts from prior growing seasons with encumbrances on growing crops. Furnishing merchants solved this problem by closing out a prior year's balance with a promissory note. The furnishing merchant then advanced money to a client on the new year's account to liquidate the note. The advance was protected by the privilege on the growing crop.

During the antebellum period, liquidating old open accounts with promissory notes was a fairly common practice; another was collateralizing such accounts with pledges of interest-bearing notes. In the case of the former, the factor or storekeeper could discount such paper, with or without recourse, convert short-term debt into long-term debt, liquidate his accounts with minimal risks, and at the same time aid in the vast credit expansion that was a key factor in the growth of plantation agriculture in the late antebellum period.

Failing planters, white farmers, and black freedmen, however, had little with which to collateralize their credit relations after the war. They needed to be able to encumber their crops in advance of the harvest for debts incurred during the planting season. Privileges protected everyone, but they did not obligate a tenant, for example, to deliver his cotton to the furnishing merchant who had advanced supplies to him. Privileges also were not very effective when cotton was stolen from the fields and transferred to innocent third parties. The problem was not one of conflicts between creditors of the same rank with concurrent privileges. As a practical matter, the incidence of tenants obtaining supplies from both landlords and furnishing merchants probably was quite small. Similarly, the incidence of agricultural laborers obtaining supplies from sources other than their employers must have been practically nil.[19]

Act 66 of 1874 authorized the pledging of a crop for prospective advances of cash and supplies, and it resolved the conflict between creditors with identical privileges. Henceforward it was permissible to pledge or pawn a "growing crop of cotton, sugar, or other agricultural products for advances in money, goods, and necessary supplies" required in the production of such crops. There had to be a writing specifically pledging the crop, and it had to be recorded in the office of the recorder of mortgages of the parish where the crops were to be produced. The pledgee obtained a right, "the same as if the said crop had been in the possession of the pledgee." In other words, he obtained the rank of a consignee to whom the crop had been properly consigned. This right of pledge was, however, subordinate "to that of the claim of the laborers for wages and for the rent of the land on which the crop was produced."[20]

Michael Wayne describes a change that occurred in the Natchez district in the mid-1870s in the practices of furnishing merchants vis-à-vis landlords and the provisioning of tenants. In East Feliciana, that change dates from 1874; most credit arrangements thereafter appear to be between tenants and furnishing merchants. Before 1874, if the Meyer brothers' ledgers are any guide, credit was extended to white landowners who in turn supplied their sharecroppers and tenants. Probably, most planting relationships before 1874 were grounded in sharecropping but were in fact rentals on shares. The contract was one of tenancy, but it included a provisioning agreement with the landlord. Sometime before 1874, many landowners lost the ability to provision their workers.[21]

Whether tenants were renting on shares or for a fixed rental in cotton per acre is not important. Both before and after 1874, furnishers had a privilege, for supplies furnished, on the crops of tenants of every description. After 1874 tenants could pledge a standing crop to a furnishing merchant as well, but subject to the landlord's superior privilege and the superior privilege of an agricultural laborer.

The right of pledge conferred by the 1874 statute and Civil Code Article 3217 must be construed together. Under Article 3217, the landlord and the furnisher still had concurrent privileges, and the agricultural laborer had a superior privilege to either of them. After 1874 arrangements among furnishers, tenants, and landlords were still regulated by this provision, but the tenant could now pledge his crop as well to secure advances made by a furnisher.[22]

The 1874 statute had no application to true agricultural laborers, except that it confirmed their superior privilege in all contracts between tenants and furnishers. It applied to tenants (whose arrangements predominated in the mortgage records after 1874) and sharecroppers who were in fact tenant because they rented on shares. The statute contemplated relationships between tenants and furnishers; landlords were secondary in that scheme. A such it is an important indicator of the declining importance of landlords i furnishing arrangements.

Enacting the 1874 statute had something to do with prevailing econom conditions, specifically, growing unemployment among the masses of agricu tural laborers. Furnishers could now contract for a pledge of the standir crops, a stronger security than a privilege. The furnisher held the pledged property subject to any unsatisfied claim, and his claim survived a fraudulent transfer. Cotton was being stolen from the fields and sold to third parties, and the privilege usually did not survive such transfers; a pledge did. It was a question of degree, of the quality of the security obtained by the furnisher. The 1874 statute permitted a pledge of property that before could only be protected with a privilege. It certainly was not intended to defeat the rights of agricultural laborers. The pledgor, however, was now bound to deliver his cotton to the pledgee.[23]

Louisiana's approach is apparently exceptional and inconsistent with what historians have said happened about the same time in other southern states after redeemer governments came to power. The agricultural worker's privilege continued to be recognized as superior to all other classes of creditors, landlords and furnishers included. Moreover, the 1874 legislation was enacted by a legislature composed of radical Republicans, and it survived the redeemers.[24]

The reason behind the 1874 legislation is obscure. It clearly contemplated tenancy, not a relationship based on shares in lieu of wages. Conditions had worsened considerably with the onset of the 1873 depression, and there are numerous accounts of seed cotton being stolen from the fields, probably by unemployed and starving agricultural laborers. The 1874 legislation made it more difficult for cotton buyers to purchase seed cotton that had been stolen. A buyer bought the cotton subject to the pledge and was responsible to the pledgee.[25]

It is probable that this legislation was enacted primarily at the behest of the furnishing merchants, who had risked their solvency by supplying tenants during the growing season. They were hardly consoled when customers sold "their" cotton to cotton buyers or competitors who were less than scrupulous about recognizing and protecting their claims. The lien, or privilege, would have afforded them little protection. Now a tenant who pledged his crop to a furnishing merchant could deliver his entire production to that merchant, subject to any superior privileges in favor of landlord or agricultural laborer. The pledge gave the furnishing merchant effective control of the entire production. Landlords, of course, were in a good position to police the disposition of the cotton once it was harvested and packed and could insist on their rental payments before tenants made delivery to their furnishers.

The 1874 legislation deterred purchases of cotton in fraud of the preexisting rights of furnishers. It was not the work of a redeemer legislature controlled by old planter elites. What was going on was considerably more complicated than a simple dichotomy of triumphant planters and obsequious merchants, and it is difficult to believe that Louisiana was exceptional.

Act 66 also clarified one important technicality regarding the nature of the privilege obtained by consignees when crops had been properly consigned to them and they were owed by the consignor for advances of cash and supplies. Such products were now held by the consignees in *pledge* "from the time the bill of lading . . . [was] put in the mail, or put into the possession of the carrier."

The third section of Act 66 codified what had evolved jurisprudentially in the antebellum period in connection with the relationship between two consignees. For example, a Clinton merchant in failing circumstances had consigned cotton to a factor in New Orleans to whom he owed on a general balance of account. The cotton had been obtained from a local grower on consignment and had not been paid for by the Clinton merchant. The Clinton merchant failed, and the grower attempted to recover his cotton from the New Orleans factor, but the factor claimed a consignee's privilege on the cotton because the Clinton merchant owed him money at the time of his insolvency. The general balance of account owed by the Clinton merchant to the New Orleans factor was completely unrelated to the relationship between the Clinton grower and either consignee, yet antebellum cases had held that the consignee's privilege outranked the grower's consignor's privilege.[26] This jurisprudential rule was codified in the statute, conferring the status of pledgee on the subsequent consignee, but with the provision that the laborers' and lessors' privileges for wages and rents survived all subsequent transfers and retained their superior ranking.

Act 66 simply permitted the pledging of a crop, and for a merchant or factor to be fully protected, the amount of the debt being contracted had to be stated in the instrument that was recorded. The new law clearly was grounded in the antebellum system of privileges, which arose by operation of law, but in substance it partook of Louisiana's law of mortgages. It deviated from Louisiana property law in one important respect, however: it allowed for the encumbering of a standing crop separate from the land itself. In property law, standing crops were considered part of the land; hence the mortgaging or pledging of them apart from the land was a theoretical impossibility. However, Louisiana's legal system has always proved to be flexible when confronted with practical necessities.

The Case of Joseph Embree

How the critical shrinkage in the basic unit of credit came about in the years immediately after the war can be traced in the planting arrangements of one East Feliciana planter. Before the war, Joseph Embree had had small-scale operations in the Clinton area and in the vicinity of Woodville, Mississippi. He resumed planting in the winter of 1866 with supplies furnished by the New Orleans firm of Flower and Maes. As previously mentioned, Richard

Flower had close personal ties to the area; he had lived in the parish before the war, even as he carried on his factorage business in the city, and his wife was a member of one of the oldest and wealthiest planter families in either East or West Feliciana Parish.[27] Embree owed a small balance of no more than one hundred dollars to Flower after his cotton from the 1866 planting year was sold in the winter of 1867. He expected Flower to carry him through the next planting season, which Flower did to the extent of his slender resources.

Embree purchased most of his supplies for himself and his sharecroppers from Clinton firms, settling with drafts drawn on Flower and Maes. Flower furnished him some corn, pork, and bagging for cotton bales but often advised him to obtain his supplies from local sources because many items were either scarce or unavailable in the city. In May 1867 Embree drew on Flower for $250, payable at sight, in favor of Packwood and Harris, a Clinton firm. Flower was much agitated by the appearance of the sight draft at his counting room. He advised Embree of its payment but admonished him that in such "hard and alarming times, [it was] . . . advancing . . . on a very uncertain state of things." He told him not to draw any more drafts at sight "until there [was] . . . some prospect of [the firm's] . . . being able to get accommodations from the banks or capitalists." He added ominously that the funds of clients then in his hands could not be used for "any purpose whatever and it [had] . . . taken every dollar [they] could raise to furnish supplies to enable [the firm's clients] . . . to make a crop."[28]

It is clear from Embree's account current for 1866 and 1867 that cotton produced by himself and his employees was shipped under his name alone. Embree drew again on Flower in favor of Packwood and Harris, this time for $420, in the summer of 1867. Shortly thereafter Embree advised Flower that he had poor expectations for his crop and could promise little with which to settle his substantial debt—more than eighteen hundred dollars—to the firm. Ever willing to work with clients, Flower advised Embree that whatever cotton could be produced and shipped would receive his utmost attention in selling, and that he would make the proceeds reach as far as possible in settling outstanding accounts. He also wrote: "We will try and help you again next year—We have been more liberal with you really, than with any other *customer* in the parish, and we have not advanced as much to anyone person as we have to yourself, thinking it would all be right."[29] Embree, however, defaulted, and Flower filed suit against him on December 13, 1867.[30]

The most likely reason for Flower's haste to file suit was Embree's attempt to ship what there was of a short crop to another factor. As mentioned previously, by this time he owed Flower eighteen hundred dollars, and he had little prospect of settling his account and paying any portion of the next year's expenses. In the meantime, Embree's wife filed suit for a separation of property, obtained a judgment against him, had the plantation seized to satisfy her claim, and bought it at sheriff's sale.[31] There was little that Flower could do to collect Embree's debt. All future crops would be grown in his wife's name, and none of the privileges extended to crops in the ground owned by a third party.

Flower, however, was ever hopeful. He wrote Embree on November 25, 1868, advising him that he had written "to Mr. Kilbourne [Flower's lawyer] not to disturb you at all for I thought if you had a chance you would pay me and I had no disposition to distress you—If you have *corn* and *team* I would be willing to assist you next year, provided you obligate to pay me at *least part* of the old debt."[32] It is clear from this communication that Flower recognized that he was an unsecured creditor, but he was willing to let bygones be bygones provided Embree collateralized part of the old debt, probably with a crop privilege. The language "obligate to pay me" in this context is crucial. Embree was already a judgment debtor of Flower, so the only way he could obligate himself to pay a portion of the crop was to collateralize the debt with a privilege on future crops. Such an arrangement was, legally speaking, impossible to confect at this juncture in Louisiana's legal history; nevertheless, it was being done.[33] It seems fairly certain that most of the crop privileges recorded in 1870 were intended to collateralize just such antecedent debts.

Embree then made an arrangement with Abraham Levi. It was probably to Levi that he had shipped the cotton that had been destined for Flower in 1868. By 1869 Embree was conducting his planting activities with I. D. Wall.[34] All of their tenants had arrangements with the Meyer brothers, who operated a Clinton firm, in the form of short-term credits extended one or two months prior to the shipment of the cotton.[35] Embree and Wall dispatched most of their cotton directly to Levi; their tenants, however, delivered their cotton to the Meyer firm, which then shipped it to Levi in New Orleans. It seems fairly obvious that Embree had been able to shift a small portion of his risks in supplying his sharecroppers to the Meyer brothers, although their risks were fairly small at this point in time.

Embree died in 1874 or 1875, his estate probably insolvent. Flower's judgment was never paid.

The Meyer Brothers' Store, Clinton, Louisiana

Only a small portion of the credit arrangements entered into in 1870 were ever recorded in the mortgage records, and these obviously collateralized debts from the prior year. There were at least thirteen stores in Clinton alone in 1870, and one of the more important of these was the firm of Emanuel and Henry Meyer.[36] The Meyers commenced operations in Clinton in 1866, both as furnishing merchants and as cotton buyers for Abraham Levi.

Levi had lived in Clinton for many years before moving to New Orleans to establish himself as a cotton factor shortly before the Civil War. He was a partner in the antebellum Clinton and New Orleans firm of Bloom, Kahn, & Co. and provided most of the capital for the enterprise, the activities of which included furnishing local planters and buying cotton for resale in New Orleans. Bloom, Kahn dissolved voluntarily in 1862, shortly before the Union Army occupied New Orleans.[37] The former partners undertook to liquidate the firm's assets voluntarily after the war, but it is obvious that most of the partners had been ruined by the war. Levi's own factorage firm commenced suits against numerous planter clients after the war, with only limited success in making collections.

The Meyer brothers' arrangement with Levi, like so many other postbellum ones, had its essential grounding in the antebellum commercial environment. Their relationship with Levi was identical to Levi's with Bloom, Kahn, except that Levi was not a partner, either limited or general, in the Meyer firm. There were, then, two sets of transactions that characterized the Meyer brothers' operation. One was the conduct of a retail merchandise business to local consumers, who included the inhabitants of Clinton, a few planters, and a large number of black sharecroppers; the other was buying cotton from local growers for A. Levi & Co. in New Orleans. The relationship between the city capitalist and the local retailer was similar in every respect to the Marstons' consolidated enterprise, which included a large plantation and a country store.

The Marstons, however, had capitalized their retail operation on Red River with twenty thousand dollars, money obtained from the sale of hidden cotton bales brought to market in 1865.[38] The Meyer brothers were without such a hoard of money to begin their operation, and they depended on the credit facilities of Levi to finance their inventory of merchandise. In the decade after the war, the Meyers purchased from dozens of wholesale vendors, many in New Orleans, as well as some in New York, St. Louis, and Cincinnati.

Emanuel Meyer was constantly making excuses to his vendors for being so tardy in settling accounts with them, and in numerous instances he transferred an interest-bearing collateral security note to satisfy the demands of a particularly difficult creditor. This, again, was typical of credit arrangements between local furnishers and their wholesale vendors in the antebellum period. The brothers paid hundreds of dollars of interest each year to their primary wholesale vendors in the decade of the 1870s.[39] Times were so hard for the brothers in 1867 that Levi refused to honor their drafts, and various wholesale vendors had some of their drafts protested for nonacceptance. In the fall of 1867, Emanuel begged Levi to accept, without discount, his draft, which had been drawn against a consignment of eight cotton bales shipped to Levi.

Emanuel's talent for holding his wholesale vendors at bay was truly remarkable. He made partial payments, he made excuses, but he also always responded promptly to the complaints of his creditors with reassuring words. When Levi did not accept his drafts, the likely reason was not any commercial impropriety by the Meyer brothers; rather, the Levi firm itself was pressed for liquidity.[40] The difficulties encountered were practically identical to the ones experienced by the Marstons in their dealings with Payne, Huntington. The Meyers bought cotton from local growers and consigned it to A. Levi & Co., and in turn the Meyers depended on the credit facilities of the New Orleans firm to keep their inventory stocked. Unfortunately for the Meyers, they bore all the risks for downturns in the cotton market between the time they purchased the cotton from growers and the time it was sold by Levi at New Orleans.

The Meyers maintained about three hundred accounts with local customers in the years 1869 and 1870; however, no more than half of these were open account relationships that involved the extension of credit for any period of time. Approximately one hundred accounts were of the typical antebellum variety, wherein customers accumulated charges for one year interest-free and settled in January. In 1869 and 1870 the Meyers maintained a total of sixty accounts with black tenants and a few blacks who were cultivating their own land. Most such accounts were for amounts smaller than one hundred dollars and were settled in the space of two months at most, rather than the usual twelve. In 1868 the Meyers had had no open account arrangements with blacks.[41]

Rather than furnishing supplies to black sharecroppers throughout the year on credit, the Meyers as a rule apparently permitted such customers to buy on credit only a few weeks, or even days, before they settled their accounts with cotton or cash. Most such customers were identified in the ledger not only by name and race but also by the name of the white plantation owner on whose land they labored. One notable exception was William Hansberry, identified in the ledger as a free man of color, who charged only merchandise on his account and settled regularly with cash, at least until January 1871.[42] In 1870 Hansberry charged more than thirteen hundred dollars' worth of merchandise and received some cash disbursements from the Meyers as well. The account was promptly settled in January 1871 with payments of cotton and cash. Virtually all the other accounts with black tenants were strictly for purchases of merchandise on short-term credit of one or two months, rather than the customary twelve months.

It is difficult to determine whether the Meyers' arrangement with black tenants was typical of most furnishing merchants in the Clinton area. They appear to have had a somewhat lower default rate than other Clinton furnishing merchants of the period. They accommodated no more than five or six relatively large accounts in 1869 and 1870, and these growers all had direct relationships with A. Levi & Co.[43]

The chief function, then, of the Meyers' store was to serve as an agency for the New Orleans firm. The Meyers had a captive clientele to the extent that they were willing to furnish supplies to blacks on credit, especially those who worked on the plantations of white planters who dealt directly with the Levi firm. These planters, like the Meyers themselves, were looking to A. Levi & Co. for extended credit. They may well have satisfied most of their supply needs through the Meyer store rather than ordering directly from New Orleans; nevertheless, they usually settled their accounts at the Clinton store with drafts on A. Levi & Co.

The Meyers could make money only by charging a significant markup on the merchandise sold to black tenants on credit; they could not do the same with most of their white clientele because such people would buy directly from New Orleans or from other Clinton merchants on more favorable terms. The limited credit facilities afforded black share tenants in 1869 and 1870 has to have been of recent origin. An examination of the records of other planters suggests that in the two or three years after the war, most bore all the risks of supplying their labor force. They bought supplies as needed, either from New Orleans or at the local store, and deducted the price from the agricultural laborer's share when accounts were settled in the winter of each year. The problem with this arrangement was all too obvious. The planter bore all the risks if the proceeds of the crop failed even to meet expenses, and he was obliged to carry his labor force through the next growing season if he could obtain enough credit to furnish them with supplies.

Some planters initially began to limit their exposure by agreeing to furnish their laborers with only a limited amount of supplies during the growing season. It was at this juncture that some of the risks were shifted to the local furnishing merchants to the extent that they were willing to do the same. Their most obvious incentives for doing so were additional business and the prospect of hefty profits if the crop was a good one. Marston, for example, expected a markup of 25 to 50 percent on all merchandise sold through the Ashland store.[44]

However, such arrangements were double-edged swords. By 1874, for example, black tenants had incurred bills receivable with the Meyers for the prior year; nevertheless, the Meyers believed that they could not withdraw their support for fear of losing control of the new year's crop. In the summer of 1874, Emanuel urged Levi to allow him an additional $375 per month to take care of their needs:

We again would beg you to extend our limit about $750 for next two months. Crops are in good condition, and we must feed people, especially as the time approaches when they must be treated a little better than at the beginning of the season. We cannot borrow any money, how else we would not call on you, but it will be to our benefit to feed people, since . . . it is impossible to do without the money. As it is dangerous and they might steal cotton out the fields and get provisions elsewhere.[45]

His reasoning was quite sound.

The Meyers rarely charged interest at the end of the year on unpaid balances for purchases of merchandise, at least in 1869 and 1870. A few black clients, however, were charged interest on their accounts for small unpaid balances for purchases of merchandise. The rate of interest charged was 30 percent on an annualized basis, but because the credit was extended on balances more than twelve months old, the theoretical rate was a more modest 15 percent. However, no more than ten accounts were debited for interest charges in 1869 and 1870.[46] Also, the Meyers made little from the cotton purchased for A. Levi & Co. Their main source of profit was the substantial markup in prices of merchandise retailed through the store. Like their antebellum predecessors, the Meyers discounted prices for cash purchases.[47]

An examination of the Meyer brothers' ledger, their cotton book, and the parish mortgage and suit records for 1869 and 1870 allows for a few generalizations about their operations. At the end of the 1870 growing season, they purchased 501 bales of cotton from no less than sixty growers, two-thirds of whom were blacks whose individual production was one or two bales. Some of the sellers were laborers rather than tenants, and for a few, the Meyers would allow short-term credit facilities of several weeks—usually from the time bales of cotton were consigned to them until the bales were shipped to New Orleans and sold. Most such growers were identified by the name of the owner of the plantation where they had produced the crop. The Meyers purchased one-half of their production from just seventeen growers. Of these, five were black, and they accounted for 10 percent of all the bales purchased by the Meyers in the fall of 1870 and the winter of 1871. Twenty-five bales bought from Hansberry made up the largest number purchased from any grower with the exception of A. J. Gore, from whom they bought forty-five bales. The bulk of their purchases in 1870 and 1871, however, were from white growers, most of whom had numerous bales under their control by virtue of their relationships with black tenants and laborers. Growers such as Hansberry were exceptional, but they were cultivating their own land.[48]

The Meyers recorded no crop privileges in 1869 and 1870. Their ledger for those years shows that few of their accounts contained bills receivable that would have to be liquidated in subsequent years. The average amount of credit extended during each twelve-month period totaled less than five thousand dollars. The total amount of debt carried forward into 1871, in the form of bills receivable, was less than two thousand dollars on more than one hundred credit accounts.

Liquidating unpaid annual balances with bills receivable solved an obvious difficulty: that of collateralizing antecedent debts with the present year's crop. The Meyers were able to solve the problem of the absence of a privilege on the present year's crop for balances owing from prior years by liquidating such balances with bills receivable. In other words, they made a cash advance on the new year's crop, evidenced by a promissory note that liquidated the unpaid balance. The cash advance was charged to the new year's account. This arrangement effectively circumvented the limitation imposed by the 1867 revision, which restricted the privilege to crops grown during the year in which the cash advances or purchases were made. In a letter to one customer, the Meyers wrote that they had enclosed a note the recipient was to sign to close up the previous year's account.[49]

There is evidence that the Meyers transferred some or all of their bills receivable, which were nothing more than promissory notes given to them by their charge customers to settle outstanding balances on open accounts, to their wholesale vendors in pledge as "collateral security" for their own unpaid accounts. On November 5, 1874, for example, Emanuel requested that the Levi firm purchase some of the Meyers' paper held by wholesale merchants in New Orleans. He asked that the redeemed notes be sent to him in Clinton, where he hoped to "compromise them, if [he] . . . could possibly do so."[50] A few days later, he wrote: "Please try and get hold of the Notes we gave to Frank Haas & Co. They are held by Lehman Abraham & Co. one of the notes is passed [*sic*] due. If you can, do bring them, as they are a hard case—This week we will be able to make good Skipwiths. Let us know by Telegram what you can do."[51] Skipwith was one of their regular customers.

The Meyers ran a very conservative business. In the difficult spring and summer of 1874, for example, Emanuel advised the Levi firm:

> We have drawn a little beyond the limit, but not much, and we may here remark that we must feed our customers and bet they make a crop—Everybody does the same thing—farmers and laborers are generally working well, better than they have done any year since the War—and with the help of God, there will be a good crop made and undoubtedly people will pay their last year's debts. We do not wish to brag on ourselves, but we can assure you that up to this date, we have sold less goods in proportion than anyone else here—and we mean to keep it up and get straight once more.[52]

Most account balances were liquidated in the winter when the cotton was sold. No more than sixty accounts ran unpaid balances during the year, and in virtually every instance they were for individuals from whom the Meyers bought cotton. The brothers filed no more than six collection suits in the years from 1867 to 1871. As a general rule, the Meyers permitted those from whom they bought cotton to charge merchandise during the year, and to them alone they made cash advances. They severely limited their exposure to sharecroppers, allowing them no more than thirty, sixty, or ninety days' credit. Such growers were still very dependent on their lessors for whatever credit arrangements they could obtain from the Meyers. Indeed, many such accounts were settled by the lessor at the end of the growing season.[53]

It seems an inescapable conclusion that the crop privilege primarily collateralized antecedent debts (i.e., debts unliquidated by the production of the prior year). The same is also probably true of the crop pledges. If so, the crop privileges and pledges recorded in the mortgage records are not a reliable index of the amount of credit being extended by furnishing merchants and others in aid of production; rather, such instruments may only serve as a means to quantify the amount of accumulated debt from prior years. In 1869 and 1870 the Meyers' accounts showed only small unpaid balances in perhaps a dozen accounts, all settled with bills receivable. They recorded no privileges because they could not collateralize prospectively. It was only when substantial unpaid balances began to accumulate from year to year that credit providers found it necessary to reduce their risks by collateralizing antecedent debts with the next year's crop. Prior to 1874 the recordation of privileges evidences the growing indebtedness of white growers and black tenants. After 1874 furnishers could collateralize prospectively with the crop pledge, and as conditions worsened they increasingly availed themselves of this security device.

The number of privileges and pledges in the parish steadily increased from year to year in the 1870s. In 1870 179 privileges were recorded, with a total dollar value of only $18,329.14. In 1869 and 1870 cotton prices were still relatively high, and the amount of accumulated debt from prior growing seasons was relatively small. By 1876 cotton prices were hitting new lows, and recordations spiraled upward. That year 334 crop pledges were recorded with a dollar value of $59,655.62. The Meyers recorded thirty-four crop pledges that year with a dollar amount totaling twelve thousand dollars. In other words, they recorded 10 percent of all the crop pledges recorded, the dollar amount of which was 20 percent of the total dollar amount. The average dollar amount of each of the Meyer pledges was twice that of all the others recorded that year.

It is difficult to determine what was happening in 1876. Perhaps the Meyers were collateralizing both antecedent and future debts. Unlike other furnishing merchants recording crop pledges that year, the Meyers were combining in the same instrument crop pledges and mortgages on acreage. Mortgages on acreage were clearly intended as additional security; moreover, the

Meyers also executed a mortgage to Levi for sixteen thousand dollars to collateralize their own antecedent debts with the New Orleans firm.[54] Their indebtedness to the Levi firm had grown during the previous five years, and the mortgage encumbered virtually all of their property in the parish. The mortgage to Levi may have also been an attempt to thwart the efforts of wholesale vendors to sue the Meyers and seize whatever property they owned in the parish.

Like Marston, the Meyers were loathe to give Levi a mortgage on their real estate in the parish:

> We have always paid what we owed and we shall continue to do so. You need not to think, that we may do otherwise, as we may flatter ourselves to have acted with you as with everybody else—a straight forward business manner. We have done business with you about 9 years and never have we ever thought of shipping a bale of cotton to anyone but you. If we cannot pay our debts at present it is certainly not our fault. We have worked hard the last season and done all in our power. . . . The only way we can get along this season is to get along with as little as possible. . . . As far as security concerns we cannot mortgage our property for the simple reason that we would ruin ourselves. Our credit would not be worth to be called by our name.[55]

Levi responded by refusing to honor the Meyers' drafts. Eventually, the Meyers relented and gave Levi the mortgage he so much desired.

Levi's other clients in the parish, the planters who transacted much of their business through the Meyer brothers' store, were likewise chagrined when he requested crop pledges from them. Emanuel wrote Levi: "We have this to explain to Mrs. Harrell (as she herself was in town yesterday) why you did not pay her Dft. But we only partially succeeded—Mrs. H. contends that she has trusted you with her money for years and that you had no right to refuse to honor her dft."[56] A few days later, he wrote Levi that he could not "make Mrs. Harrell understand the purpose of your letter to her. . . . she had never pledged her crop before, and it would be too late to begin now."[57]

During the first five years after the war, the Meyers had a low rate of default among their customers. This optimal credit environment deteriorated rapidly in the 1870s. In 1875 and 1876 they filed no less than fourteen suits in the parish court, all for debts in excess of one hundred dollars, and took judgments in all of them. In January 1875 they sued Z. T. Bennett, one of their best sources of cotton, and obtained a judgment against him of $327.77.[58] Most such suits, however, were against black tenants who owed the Meyers less than $150 each.

The Meyers were having problems with a major grower who owed them and the Levi firm. Emanuel advised Levi that he had called upon B. W.

Fauver to discuss his debt to themselves and Levi. Fauver had proved difficult to deal with, and only because of Emanuel's strenuous exertions had he even proposed to make a settlement. Fauver owed the two firms $625; in settlement of their claims, he proposed transferring to them a mortgage note executed by T. L. East for $1,125 that was due in four years with 8 percent interest. Emanuel and his brother were prepared to accept the offer, but they wanted Levi to pay them their share immediately, "pro rata in Cash." They meant for Levi "to take the note" and pay them what they were owed. Emanuel and Henry had concluded that this was as "good a settlement" as they could make, and they had all better accept it. Emanuel was satisfied that nothing would be gained by suing Fauver, probably because he had no assets except his growing crop, which was heavily encumbered with superior claims.[59] It is easy to see why Levi was less than enthusiastic about the proposed settlement. Still, the letter is a valuable indication of the difficulty with many accounts on which suit was never filed. The Meyers obviously needed to liquidate their account with Fauver immediately.

The rate of default experienced by the Meyers on unpaid balances at the end of each planting season in the period from 1873 to 1880 was somewhere between 20 and 30 percent annually. This is not to say that they did not eventually obtain satisfaction on the accounts on which they sued, but they had to resort to legal proceedings, which cost money. Still, the default rate of their customers may have been better than other Clinton firms. Abraham Mayer, for example, recorded thirty-four crop pledges in 1876 with a total dollar value of just five thousand dollars. Mayer filed twenty-two collection proceedings in 1875, twenty-eight in 1876, and twenty-six in 1877. Mayer's clientele showed a much stronger propensity to default than the Meyer brothers', probably because he could not furnish them in successive planting seasons. The need to furnish growers to collect on unpaid balances from prior years was obvious. Emanuel wrote Levi: "When we made our arrangement last February [1874] we calculated that the acct. allowed us by you would carry us and we did not miscalculate . . . in so far as Quantity of Supplies concerned." But the prices of pork and corn meal had risen 25 percent, and supplies that had cost five hundred dollars the previous spring now cost seven hundred. The brothers were so short of supplies that they could not furnish even their best customers. Such customers sent their wagons to town every few days for supplies, and the brothers were forced to send them back empty. If Emanuel and Henry could not furnish them enough "to finish the crop, they . . . [would] find someone else to do it." However, if their customers obtained supplies from other sources, the brothers' bargaining position would be compromised. Emanuel noted that "they will treat us just the same as we have done them, when the Time comes, that we could urge them to gin their cotton & bring it forward, they tell us, that they are in no hurry, we did not seem to be in a hurry when they needed Pork & c." Levi had to see that the need to furnish growers was "almost life and death, [and] to stop now would be ruinous."[60] As for Abraham Mayer, he was sued by the Meyers in 1879 for failing to keep his merchandise account with them current.[61]

In the fall of 1875 and the winter of 1876, the Meyers only purchased 448 bales of cotton at an average price of eleven cents per pound. They bought smaller quantities from twice as many growers. Their largest source of cotton in 1870, A. J. Gore, had moved to Ouachita Parish and was growing cotton there.[62] However, many of the customers who had sold them cotton in prior years were still selling to them and charging merchandise on open accounts. The Meyers had one of the most stable clienteles in the parish. Nevertheless, their collection suits show that all of their judgment debtors had sold cotton to them, charged merchandise, and received cash advances on open accounts. Moreover, the crop pledges recorded in 1876 clearly collateralized most of their open account arrangements. Unlike Mayer, however, they could still furnish a respectable amount of merchandise on short-term credit to their good customers who sold them cotton.

By their own accounting, the Meyers lost between 10 and 20 percent on each bale of cotton purchased by them and shipped to Levi in 1875 and 1876.[63] Their merchandise account appears to have absorbed most of these losses. They were having to pay the local growers higher prices for cotton than they could sell the cotton for at New Orleans. Their arrangement with the Levi firm required that they ship a certain amount of cotton to guarantee their credit facilities. In earlier years, they made a small profit on their cotton purchases or broke even. Although they had had to pay the growers a premium to obtain a sufficient quantity for shipment to Levi, prices were low in those years, and perhaps the premium was more easily absorbed. But in 1875 and 1876 the Meyers were being pressed by the terms of their own credit arrangements with Levi and were still having to pay a premium to attract a sufficient quantity of cotton.

Such losses could only be sustained if they made money elsewhere, namely in sales of merchandise at substantial markups. Whatever credit facilities they could furnish their customers were small ones. About one-third of the total value of crop pledges recorded in 1876 represented antecedent debts from prior years. Their twelve thousand dollars in credit facilities was at least 5 percent of all the credit available in the parish in any given year in the decade of the 1870s.

How much credit was available in consequence of unpaid balances on open accounts at local stores, rolled over from year to year with bills receivable? Recordings of crop pledges peaked in 1879, when there were 633 with an aggregate value of $84,912.94. Arguably, additional sources of credit were the uncollectible judgments taken by local furnishers and New Orleans factors, but debtor defaults did nothing but raise the cost of credit for everyone.

In 1879 the Meyers recorded seventy-five crop pledges with an aggregate value of just $12,620. None of the debts collateralized were as large as those in 1876, and most of the Meyers' debtors were black tenants. It is doubtful that the Meyers were attempting to spread their risks by loaning smaller sums to more growers; rather, like many other furnishing merchants, they had simply inherited by default a clientele whose supply needs were no longer being guaranteed by white employers and lessors. Over the decade they had, in other words, assumed a growing share of the risks for each year's planting. Their recordings declined by 20 percent the following year, and the total dollar amount was almost 25 percent less.

The new state constitution of 1879 eliminated the recordation requirement for privileges. However, pledges, which were preferred by furnishing merchants in their relationships with tenants, still had to be recorded. The 1880 recordings, then, obviously were pledges, and their 20-percent decline in number is an indication, perhaps, that only about 20 percent of the recordings in prior years were intended to evidence privileges. The expanded role of furnishing merchants in supplying the labor force was too conspicuous to be ignored.

1880 and Beyond

Recordings of crop pledges declined steadily in number, and collateralized credit arrangements more similar to antebellum ones began to appear, in the years after 1880. The amount of credit furnished by local merchants such as the Meyers, even for twelve months or less, was very small indeed. At any given time in the twenty years after the Civil War, it was no more than 25 to 50 percent of the anticipated value of the forthcoming cotton crop. As late as 1880, cotton production in the parish was still 55 percent below the level achieved in 1860. Furnishing merchants were not a particularly important source of credit for anyone, including black tenants. For most tenants in the parish, however, they were the only source of even thirty-, sixty-, and ninety-day credit.

The postwar economy of the parish was bereft of most of its prewar capitalization in consequence of emancipation and wartime inflation. The only thing of value was cotton, and cotton alone provided collateral for what credit there was, long-term and short-term. However, production and prices fluctuated drastically from year to year. Cotton was not a suitable commodity for collateralizing long-term loans of capital, and even short-term loans were only relatively free of risk if the underlying security was at least twice the value of the debt collateralized.

Why then did most people in East Feliciana continue to stake their future on growing cotton? Why did Bulow Marston bet the farm year after year on the price of cotton and his own production capabilities? The answer is an obvious one: even at depressed prices, cotton was still far more valuable than any other asset in the parish. The value of all agricultural production in 1860 represented no more than 5 to 8 percent of the gross wealth held by the seven hundred free families in the parish. In 1880 growers in the parish produced only 45 percent as many bales as had been produced in 1860.[64] The value of the 1880 production was less than $500,000; nevertheless, the figure represented between one-third and one-half of all the wealth in the parish.[65] Bulow Marston's gross production in 1875 was at least twice the value of the entire Ashland Plantation. Risk taking was well rewarded with fabulous returns if measured against the amount of capital invested in planting. The value of a single bale of cotton was many times the value of the acreage on which it was grown.

Credit availability, then, was tied directly to cotton production because cotton was the only thing of value in the region. The amount of credit provided to tenant farmers was small indeed, and it was very expensive.

In 1880 the number of crop pledges recorded by local merchants and growers fell to 326, with a total dollar value of $47,152. By 1885 collateralized plantation accounts with New Orleans factors typically provided first for the liquidation of any balance owing from the prior year out of the proceeds of the new year's crop. Such crop pledges collateralized antecedent debts from the prior year and any future advances up to a set limit.

Unlike their antebellum counterparts, New Orleans factors and Clinton furnishing merchants such as the Meyers were in no position to capitalize old debts in the form of bills receivable owing from prior years. Local furnishing merchants actually provided far less credit of the twelve-month variety than had been the case in the antebellum period. Their objective, like that of their New Orleans counterparts, was to keep bills receivable to a minimum. The economy simply lacked the credit resources to discount anything but short-term paper. As the credit resources of the parish and the city contracted in the 1870s, growers who weathered the storm became relatively more liquid. Those who prospered were more likely to hold a substantial portion of their wealth in cash or liquid paper.

One of the most successful of the postwar planters was Joseph M. Young. Young had been a well-to-do small-scale planter before the war. When he died in 1890, he left a gross estate of twenty thousand dollars, 40 percent of it in cash and notes. He had $2,166.48 on deposit at the New Orleans National Bank and $146.98 deposited with his factors, Frankenbush and Borland, the net proceeds of that year's cotton sales. His debts consisted chiefly of succession administration expenses and small sums still owed to black sharecroppers in his employ. The partition among the three heirs contained this recitation: "and whereas there are belonging to said Estate sundry accounts—and notes against Colored persons which are not now estimated to be worth anything, it is considered by the experts, and agreed to by said parties that the same be *left* in the *hands* of John Young and whatever may be realized therefrom. The same John Young to pay one third thereof to McVea Young and one third to Joseph B. Young minor." At the time of his death, Young owned more than thirty-six hundred acres in the parish. All of his land brought a total of $8,565 at probate sale, less than $3.00 per acre. Twenty-four mules, some cows, wagons, and supplies brought $1,464.93. Young was a rich man by the standards of the time, but he was still worth less than what he had been worth in 1860.[66]

At another extreme was the case of Margaret Silliman, whose share of the community property at the death of her husband, William, in 1868, was almost $200,000.[67] What remained of the Silliman fortune after the war was invested in New Orleans real estate, bank stocks, and railroad bonds. By the time of her death in 1879, the fortune had dwindled to slightly more than $100,000.[68] Most of Silliman's losses were due to uncollectible debts, money loaned by her in the 1870s, and to the terms on which she contracted her labor arrangement for her plantations. She continued to absorb all the risks of supplying her sharecroppers and tenants.

Fewer than one hundred crop pledges were being recorded annually in the 1890s, but the transaction value of each was significantly higher. The Newman brothers carried on a thriving business in the parish furnishing well-to-do white planters, some with their own country stores. Over a period of years, they were able to provide more than twenty thousand dollars in long-term loans to local growers. Their clientele, however, was exclusively white. Clinton furnishing merchants continued to collateralize credit arrangements with blacks, but their charge accounts rarely showed bills receivable, and the amounts borrowed, even for a few months, usually were less than two hundred dollars.

Blacks were not barred from purchasing land, and over the space of two decades as many as 10 percent of all black families purchased some acreage. Throughout the twenty years after the war, a few blacks were able to purchase land from white sellers on credit for up to five years. Of the thirty-one credit sales of acreage and town lots in 1880, blacks were purchasers in four transactions. The year before, blacks made seven of twenty-four purchases on credit of acreage and town lots in the parish. As late as 1885, blacks were still purchasing real estate on credit.

Some distressed white landowners in the parish were only too happy to sell land to blacks able to purchase. The extent of the substitution of furnishing merchants for landlords in managing the affairs of some parish tenants can be seen in a communication from Henry Marston to his sister-in-law, dated November 7, 1876. Marston had reached a settlement with the representative of a Clinton furnishing merchant who was now deceased. His sister-in-law owed the merchant money, and the succession representative had planned to sue her to collect the debt. She would be allowed two years to liquidate the debt, but the arrangement was predicated upon selling her land. Marston informed her that he had been applied to by Mr. Weil, a Clinton furnishing merchant, who represented a potential purchaser. Weil wished to know "whether the conveyance . . . to be given to the Negro" would "be perfectly good, and according to law? It seems that Mr. W. transacts all the business of the Negro . . . and expects to pay" the first installment on the sale. Marston believed the buyer had "probably promised Mr. W. a mortgage on the land to secure any advances he [Weil] may make him." Marston told his sister-in-law that she would retain a mortgage on the property to secure the credit portion of the sale.[69] Apparently, she was willing to subordinate her mortgage so Weil could obtain the first ranking as secured creditor.

It is likely, however, that access to credit, rather than affordability of land, was crucial in determining whether blacks achieved economic independence. Land prices declined by at least one-half in the period from 1865 to 1880, and they did not rise again for the rest of the century. Even if blacks could buy land, however, it is unlikely that they could contract viable credit arrangements without the assistance of a white employer, lessor, or furnisher. The amount of credit in the economy available to any borrower, for whatever purpose, was extremely small.

Especially valuable in gauging economic conditions in the parish are the money judgments recorded in the mortgage records. In 1879, for example, 107 such judgments, mostly arising out of suits between furnishing merchants and growers, were recorded. The average amount of each judgment was $300.66. This was about three times the amount of each crop pledge recorded that year. In 1880 the average value of each judgment recorded was $454.40, again three times the value of each crop pledge. In 1875 and 1876 the average value of each judgment recorded exceeded the value of each crop pledge by a relatively modest 25 percent. Almost all the Meyers' primary white growers defaulted and were sued in the period from 1874 to 1878. It appears that at some point after 1875, the Meyers accorded black sharecroppers credit facilities in their own right, or at least no longer expected white lessors and employers to guarantee the payment of supplies in a bad year.

In 1870, however, the dollar ratio of judgments to crop privileges had been four to one. In that year the economy was still digesting antebellum debts, and the average value of each judgment handed down by the district court was almost one thousand dollars. Money judgments for such huge sums would not be seen again for the remainder of the nineteenth century. The extreme ratios of dollar amounts of judgments to crop pledges in the late 1870s suggest that the economy was going through another period of debt liquidation. Moreover, based on the massive recordations of crop pledges, a conclusion that furnishing merchants were collateralizing old bills receivable, not financing a credit expansion, is inevitable.

It seems, then, that characterizations about the postbellum economy, at least in the case of East Feliciana Parish, need to be highly circumspect. The relative amount of credit provided by local furnishing merchants was something less than what they had arranged before the Civil War. Like their New Orleans counterparts, they limited their credit operations to a percentage of the annual cotton crop. Where the antebellum system had supported a debt load of more than $2 million to $3 million, the postbellum one allowed for a maximum of perhaps $200,000 of short-term loans on open accounts that were necessarily liquidated annually.

The persistent decline of cotton prices in the 1870s resulted in the recordation of hundreds of crop pledges to collateralize antecedent debts; these were in the form of bills receivable still owed from the prior year at the beginning of the new planting season. Some portion of this debt also represented anticipated advances of supplies and cash for the forthcoming planting season.

Cotton had not been a significant component of collateralized credit arrangements before the war, but it became central when there was nothing else with which to collateralize debts. The credit arrangements afforded tenants were a relatively insignificant percentage of the furnishing business in the years immediately after the war, but they became relatively more important toward the end of the 1870s.

Responding to postbellum realities, the antebellum systems of production and credit became increasingly attenuated after the war. It is impossible to lay the blame for the postbellum malaise at the doors of the furnishing merchants.[70] Like the growers they serviced, they operated in an environment fraught with risks to an extent never dreamed of before the war. Like the growers, they survived if they were able to maintain their liquidity.

The Meyer firm, along with most other furnishing merchants in the parish, were insolvent during most of the 1870s. The Meyers, for example, took an inventory in June 1880. The value of their inventory was $5,276.68.[71] Their accounts receivable totaled $10,318.94, a figure representing the total charge purchases in 163 accounts. The bills receivable totaled $3,750. They showed $128 in cash. Their liabilities amounted to $14,260.71, $6,500 of which was owed to the Newmans and the balance to twenty wholesale vendors. The Meyers needed very high profit margins to offset the risks inherent in growing cotton. Much of the credit they extended to their customers was only available because their wholesale vendors accepted sixty- and ninety-day paper in settlement of their accounts with the brothers. If the returns and risks in growing cotton were extremely high relative to land costs, it is logical that a very high rate of default and return could be expected in the operations of furnishing merchants.

Most furnishing merchants in the parish were extremely distressed in the

1870s. With the notable exception of the Meyers, they were sued frequently by wholesale vendors. Many were sued by wives for separations of property. Emily Mayer complained that her husband, Abraham Heyman, had "been for years in embarrassed circumstances and insolvent [and] that his pecuniary circumstances, embarrassments and financial blunders and want of thrift constantly endanger[ed] and threaten[ed] to deprive her of a house."[72] Yette Oppenheimer sued her husband, Abraham Levy, for a separation of property in 1875.[73] Levy was the Meyers' uncle and early sponsor in Clinton.

The large number of recordings of crop pledges in the late 1870s suggests little else than the prolongation of the postwar debt distress so evident in the first five years after the war. Cotton growers of every description, as well as New Orleans factors and Clinton furnishing merchants, were increasingly in debt. There was an upper limit to the amount of debt that could be sustained, however, even for growing that most precious commodity—cotton. The dollar amount of judgments recorded in 1879, together with the dollar value of crop pledges that year, suggest that that limit was no more than $150,000, about one-third the value of that year's cotton crop. This amount was between 5 and 10 percent of all the debt in the parish in 1860.

If the antebellum economy had been grounded in credit, the postbellum one certainly emphasized cash. The important distinction, which characterizes the decade of the 1870s, was the extent to which the financial risks of planting would be shifted to the labor force. Henry Marston complained in 1874 that he had not made expenses the year before, scarcely one bale per hand.[74] This seems to indicate that the Marstons were still carrying their labor force and expected to have to provide them with necessities at least until the next year's crop could be sold. True, the sharecroppers at Ashland were entitled to half the crop, but their indebtedness to the Marstons for supplies furnished under their contracts and their debts at the store more than exceeded their share of the cotton. Perhaps, unlike many others in their situation, they could still incur debts at the Marstons' store and provide for their families' needs until the next year's crop was sold.

The primary impetus for the growth of local merchants as furnishers of the credit needs of tenant farmers was the pressure on postbellum planters to relieve themselves of the responsibility of providing for their hands, not only during the growing season but also during years when the planters themselves were going heavily into debt because of low prices or poor crops. Local merchants, by and large, took this share of the market by default.

Furnishing merchants to some extent supplanted planters in supplying tenants. This was true whether the tenant paid his rental to a landlord in pounds of cotton per acre or with a percentage share of the crop he produced. However, such relationships were no more exploitive than those in which the planter was the primary source of supplies. In labor agreements recorded in the early 1870s, the share of the crop received by the landlord for furnishing supplies was one-half, compared with one-third when he provided only implements and livestock. The landlord furnisher's share was an additional 16 percent of the crop. The interest rate was 64 percent if the value of the supplies furnished equaled 25 percent of the total crop or one-half of the tenant's share. That interest rate rose if the value of the provisions was something less than 25 percent.[75]

Furnishing merchants simply accepted the risks that were already conspicuous in such arrangements and charged a correspondingly high rate of interest. They recouped, not with cotton, but by raising the retail price for supplies sold on credit. In the first decade after 1865, planters showed a high propensity to default on credit arrangements with city factors. They, too, had paid a very high rate of interest—20 percent for the best credit risks. In the years after 1873, some city factors and local furnishing merchants settled for twenty-five cents on the dollar rather than opting for protracted litigation. The factorage system would have enjoyed a far more vigorous revival had the risk of default been minimal.

The importance of the shift to fixed-rate tenancies has been exaggerated, at least in the years before 1880. The trend was not necessarily indicative of an expanding population of relatively independent black farmers. Roger Ransom and Richard Sutch argue in *One Kind of Freedom* that blacks withdrew a portion of their labor from production after emancipation in order to enjoy some of the fruits of their freedom. Cotton production in the parish did fall by as much as 55 percent in the decades after the war, but the possibility of long-term unemployment must be considered as a factor in this decline. The anecdotal evidence is full of complaints about the scarcity of labor, but most such accounts are from planters. Unemployment in the 1870s meant being unable to contract for supplies, and recordings in the mortgage records suggest that available credit facilities were stretched exceedingly.[76]

The relative significance of an "agricultural ladder" is another thesis that must be viewed with circumspection when analyzing what was happening in East Feliciana Parish in the two decades after 1865. Certainly, black tenants did acquire farming implements and livestock: such property was frequently seized in collection suits. But how valuable were these assets in collateralizing debt arrangements? The overriding fact is that Louisiana had no chattel mortgage law until 1912. Had such property been a significant factor in debt relationships, it is at least probable that the state legislature would have adopted an institution to effectuate such pledges. The problem was that the landlord already had a privilege on such property for the rent. This property was encumbered by operation of law. The agricultural laborer likewise had a privilege for his wages on the movables of the farm or plantation on which he labored.[77]

The reality was that anyone who loaned on a crop pledge was making an "unsecured" loan. The appraisers of Young's estate estimated that the present value of his claims against workers and tenants was nothing. Everyone expected collections to be made, but until the growing crop was harvested, the debts were worthless.[78] Asset-based lending was no more a feature of post-bellum credit relationships than it had been in the antebellum period.

The "agricultural ladder," from agricultural laborer to share tenancy to fixed-rate tenancy to landowner, is certainly one important way of looking at the relative progress of freedmen in the years immediately after the war. However, the question remains: why is a rental paid in pounds of cotton per acre preferable to one in which the rental is a fixed percentage of the production? In either case, the land rental paid by the tenant was 25 percent of the production. More important is the question of who furnished the supplies, the farming implements, and the livestock necessary for cultivation. In most share tenancies, the landlord was the primary furnisher; in most rental arrangements where rent was paid in pounds of cotton per acre, a third party, usually a furnishing merchant, supplied barrels of pork and flour and other staples. The shift to rentals paid in pounds of cotton per acre reflects the growing importance of furnishing merchants. It also reflects a growing particularization in arrangements that before had been lumped together in one contract (i.e., rentals of mules, farming implements, and rations). A rental paid in pounds of cotton per acre at least marginally reduced the furnishing merchant's risks. Regular inspections of growing crops during the summer months allowed him to gauge his risks and the safety of his previous advances of supplies accurately. He would, however, have attempted to restrict his clientele to the most reliable producers, who had their own mules and farming implements. In this context, the "agricultural ladder" does have particular relevance.

It is ironic that because planters could no longer appropriate all the product of their former slaves' labor, the credit costs for all escalated dramatically. The legacy of plantation production was still pervasive in the agricultural economy; the key credit component, however, was very different. Whether the actual units of production were attenuating is beside the point: credit arrangements were many times more numerous, and the costs per unit had spiraled upward.

Before the war, bad harvests and low prices did not necessarily portend ruin—inconvenience, yes, but not ruin. After the war, there was little except cotton with which to collateralize the debts inherited from years of poor harvests and low prices. The credit system was dependent on cotton to an extent never dreamed of before the war.

7

Tenants, Sharecroppers, and Furnishers

THE EVOLUTION OF postbellum planting arrangements is a complex subject that has received considerable attention. Stephen J. DeCanio and Gerald David Jaynes, as well as Roger Ransom and Richard Sutch and others, have examined the changing relationships between planters and their former slaves in the two decades after 1865. Jaynes's account of the fragmentation of plantations and the eventual shift to share tenancies organized around the nuclear family identifies credit stringencies as agents in shaping the system that eventually emerged. So do accounts by the other aforementioned authors to a greater or lesser extent.[1]

Subtle changes in recorded instruments are valuable tools for identifying crucial divisions in the evolution of planting arrangements. Recorded labor contracts, however, probably account for only 5 percent of planting arrangements in the parish in any given year. Crop privileges and pledges are far more reliable indicators because such recordings evidence as much as one-half of all planting units in the parish. The number of tenancies in the parish by the late 1870s can be estimated with some degree of accuracy.

The evidence for the locality suggests that the rise of furnishing merchants as provisioners of tenant farmers matches a decline in the fortunes of planters in the first postwar decade. The relative importance of this decline in hastening the shift to share tenancies is in the realm of speculation; nevertheless a reordering of relationships among planters, furnishers, and laborers is too obvious to be ignored.

Much of the economic historiography has tended to "deemphasize the impact of the lien laws and the credit system."[2] This study, however, argues that the credit system was a powerful force in the development of tenancies that centered on the family. The legal regimes that formalized credit and planting relationships are not well understood, especially in the case of Louisiana, as discussed in the previous chapter. Changes in the lien laws during and after Reconstruction were not always demonstrative of radical power shifts, whether to radical Republicans or reactionary redeemers.[3]

A much stronger case can be made for viewing such changes as after-the-fact legislative recognition of profound changes in the organization of plantation agriculture. If tenancies come to predominate and labor contracts based on share wages diminish in importance, then not only has the relationship between laborers and employers changed, but relationships between furnishers and planters, factors and planters, and furnishers and laborers have changed as well. Legislative changes in Louisiana coincided with the rise of tenancies and a dramatic expansion in the instances of tenants obtaining supplies from sources independent of their landlords.

What is not clear is whether these changes came about in consequence of the freedmen accumulating property, which enabled them to obtain supplies from a furnishing merchant, the inability or unwillingness of landlords and employers to guarantee supply arrangements, or a complex set of sociological factors that reordered planting arrangements, as Jaynes suggests.[4] The fragmentation of the credit system certainly parallels the breakup of large-scale planting entities.

Far fewer labor arrangements were recorded in the twenty years after the war than supply privileges or crop pledges to secure advances of supplies and cash. Landowners had physical control of growing crops and could collect what was owed them once the crops were harvested. Furnishing merchants, however, had to gamble that processed bales of cotton, consigned to them under the terms of their arrangements with growers of every description, would be placed in their possession. A pledgee who was not a lessor could only guarantee his security interest with a recordation.

In 1866 and 1867 most planting arrangements were on shares in lieu of wages—the employer furnished teams, farming implements, and supplies, and employees reimbursed the employer for supplies advanced during the season. Because cotton prices were declining and production was less than satisfactory, however, many workers found themselves in debt to their employer at the end of the year. By 1869 planters, too, were deeply in debt to local merchants and New Orleans factors for postwar planting activities.

The following letter from J. R. Jackson to Joseph Embree sums up the dilemma faced by planters who absorbed all the risks of planting:

> More than two weeks ago Toby Kelly (cold.) came to my house and engaged to farm with me on my plantation and was to come in a day or two after my wagons to move. He stated to me that he had made *no arrangement for the present year*—He failed to come according to promise and I had given him up until Saturday evening. His brother came and told me that he was still anxious to come and had requested him to move him—had made no contract for the year—If he is in debt to you I will guarantee the payment at the close of the present year—he is also in debt to me—
>
> P.S. If upon settlement with Toby you find him in debt and insist upon it I will pay *it up at once!*[5]

Planters could do little if their hands owed them money at the end of the year for supplies already consumed. The supplier's and lessor's privileges encumbered that year's crop. A planter's relationship with his hands resembled his own with his city factor. Laborers could work elsewhere and obtain supply advances on the next year's crop. The cotton would get planted even if everyone was going broke.

The agricultural laborer had the least risk, but few of the recorded arrangements after 1869 are for anything other than lease.[6] Many of the sharecropping agreements that were recorded were in fact leases on shares, not compensation arrangements for payment of shares in lieu of wages. None of the tenants who were parties to these agreements were entitled to the superior privilege afforded agricultural laborers by Article 3217 of the Civil Code.

Fewer and fewer of the recorded arrangements after 1870 were for leases on shares. It is likely that lessors well understood the risks of such arrangements by then and were attempting to lessen these risks by contracting for a specific amount of cotton and furnishing no mules or supplies. Many continued to furnish mules and horses but for fixed cash rentals that averaged about twenty-five dollars per animal per year.

The 1869 legislation occasioned the first recordings of labor contracts between planters and their former slaves.[7] Employment contracts and leases shared few characteristics. Tenants who leased on shares simply made the best of what was available to them. Lessors and suppliers, however, revealed varying degrees of optimism about the worth of their contributions to plantings and to the capacity of the system to function with very little credit or capital.

S. D. Moody of New Orleans contracted six leases in 1870, all with former slaves; each contract provided for a cash rental payment at the end of one year. The yearly rental of five dollars an acre had more to do with the price of cotton than with the price of land. Moody leased mules to his tenants at a price of twenty-five dollars a mule a year.[8]

Commission merchant Richard Flower contracted with twelve former slaves for the lease of a total of 228 acres. Each tenant contracted for a specific number of acres and agreed to pay Flower 425 pounds of cotton for every ten acres leased. The tenants agreed to consign all their cotton to Flower for sale. Flower obviously wanted cotton, which he no doubt planned to hold for the best possible market. The rentals on both the Moody and Flower leases were essentially the same. Both leases were dated January 1870 but not recorded until September of that year. Flower's tenants, however, did not suffer the risks of market changes in the price of cotton.[9]

G. W. Munday, on the other hand, negotiated long-term leases of up to four years. He wanted to clear and improve land that had lain fallow for most of the previous decade. Tenants furnished their own horses and mules and bore all the expenses of cultivation. Munday's share was one-fourth of the crops. In several cases, no acreage was even specified; Munday simply contracted to furnish the tenant "a sufficient quantity [of land] to afford employment for [him] . . . and his wife."[10] Munday contracted with a squad of workers on shares, and he agreed to furnish them mules and supplies; the supplies were to be paid for out of the workers' portion of the crop. This was an employment contract with shares in lieu of wages. When the lessor or employer furnished the mules, he increased his share of the crop from one-quarter to one-third. Most of the young men making up the squad were minors whose mothers or fathers contracted for them. The contract fixed the value of each man's labor at fifty cents a day. Munday received compensation at that rate for absences during the term of the contract. Like cash rentals, labor costs tracked cotton prices.

Amedie Delambre recorded four labor arrangements with tenants on his plantation in September 1870. In the cases of Solomon King, Henry Rivers, and Adam Cooley, he agreed to furnish them as many acres as they could cultivate and as many mules as they needed at a cost of twenty dollars per mule per year. Two-thirds of the land would be planted in cotton, and the crop would be divided equally between Delambre and the three freedmen. The remaining one-third of the land was to be planted in corn and potatoes solely for the use of the lessees. The annual rental of mules averaged about 15 percent of the gross value of the contract.[11]

One of Delambre's contracts provided that squad members would farm his land four days a week (Monday, Tuesday, Wednesday, and Thursday); in return he would furnish each married man on the squad six acres. He allotted the chief of the squad seven acres; each unmarried man was allotted five acres. The six contracting members of the squad all had different surnames. Perhaps they banded together to form a planting operation to spread some of the risks that fell on a family cultivating by itself. Planting units composed of three or more black families were fairly common in the parish. Delambre furnished them whatever mules and horses they required as well as sixteen pounds of pork per hand.[12] This contract was a hybrid: it partook of both share wages and share rentals. It was not widely adopted and disappeared from use.

Most rentals were on shares, with the lessor receiving either one-half of the crop if he furnished mules and supplies, or one-quarter if the tenant furnished his own. A few rentals were paid in cash, others in pounds of cotton per acre, but most were paid with a percentage of the crop. Share-cropping arrangements predominated. None of the lessors recorded supply privileges, except that leases sometimes included provisioning agreements.

By 1876 recordations indicated a clear shift in direction toward specific parcels of land being farmed by tenant families, not on shares, but with rentals paid either in cash or bales or pounds of cotton. Rentals averaged from twenty to fifty pounds of cotton an acre. Production per acre varied in the parish, so the rentals probably averaged 25 percent of the crop. The percentage remained comparable to share wages and rentals, only a furnishing merchant now provided the supplies. Those who rented for pounds of cotton per acre often leased mules and farm implements from the landlord for stipulated cash payments at the end of the season. Some landlords even furnished supplies up to a set limit.

Rental payments in fixed amounts of cotton shifted more of the production risks to the tenants.[13] If the harvest was a poor one, substantially more than one-quarter of the harvest had to be given over to the lessor for rental payments. However, this was a better arrangement than cash payments, which also shifted the risk of market fluctuations in the price of cotton to the tenant. There were still share leases and employment contracts recorded in 1876 in which a lessor or employer provided mules and supplies, but these were only about 15 percent of the recordings made that year.

By 1879 payments in bales and pounds of cotton predominated over other recorded arrangements ten to one. In one instance, an employer contracted to absorb all the planting and supply risks, and the employee was to receive one-third of the crop produced. It is likely that payments of rentals in a specified amount of cotton had great appeal to tenants generally, even though they bore all of the production risks in such arrangements. The risks may have gone undetected by an overwhelmingly illiterate labor force. Unfortunately, the recorded contracts furnish little empirical data on the degree of control exercised by postbellum planters over their labor force.[14]

However, whether agricultural workers were tenants or agricultural laborers is not especially important. If they were true tenants, they owned the crop outright, subject to the lessor's privilege for rentals and the furnisher's privilege for supplies. Agricultural workers outranked every other claimant, including lessors and furnishers. Even if employees failed to record their privileges, defeating their claims with a recordation would have been difficult. Their employers could not prime them because they were not third parties within the meaning of the Civil Code provisions; neither were the furnishers with whom their employers dealt.[15] Only a third-party claimant of the employer who had a recorded security interest might defeat this unrecorded privilege. It was certainly arguable that a New Orleans factor or local furnisher who had an arrangement to furnish the employer and his employees was not a third party within the meaning of the statute. The cases where such problems arose appear to have been relatively rare.[16]

It is not especially important, either, who had legal or physical control over the crop.[17] If the tenant was indeed a tenant, the lessor could not dispose of the crop to anyone, and he who bought the cotton from the lessor did so at his peril. If the sharecropper was indeed an agricultural laborer, in many instances his privilege on the crop survived a subsequent fraudulent transfer of the crop by the employer. Moreover, there are indications in the Meyer brothers' correspondence that tenants and laborers settled in cotton. A division was made after the cotton was picked, and each sharecropper or tenant took his share to town to settle with the local furnishing merchant and dispose of the balance of the crop, either for cash or credit at the furnishing merchant's store. On January 18, 1876, Emanuel Meyer wrote Abraham Levi that he did not know how John Dutart, a customer of the Meyers as well as Levi, had disposed of his cotton: "We have seen several times cotton brought to town, but his hands at all times claimed the same. As it happens we did not get any of it, nor did we desire to purchase it . . . [because of its poor quality]."[18] Some tenants and sharecroppers enjoyed a substantial measure of control over their cotton.

In the early years after the war, planters essentially controlled all of the crop they consigned to their factors in New Orleans for sale.[19] During these years, however, it is likely that most agricultural workers became indebted to their employers.[20] There was little that an employer could do if an indebted worker left him and went to work for another planter. Many planters probably worsened their financial condition by absorbing all the risks of production and marketing.

Contracting with tenants for a specified amount of cotton shifted most of the financial risks to the labor force. Planters who continued to furnish their tenants often did so at their peril. For example, all of the collection suits filed by Joseph M. Young in the 1870s involved arrangements in which he had furnished supplies, land, utensils, and mules. In every case, he claimed the lessor's and furnisher's privilege, or a pledge, and he claimed them on the current year's crop. He also asked for, and got, writs of sequestration, a clear indication that he expected the tenant to dispose of the crop to his prejudice.[21] In every instance where a writ of fieri facias was issued against a black tenant, substantially more property was seized than the amount of the claim. In one instance, Young claimed a vendor's privilege on a mare, and he had the sheriff seize the mare, cows, corn, and one bale of cotton.[22]

The Meyer brothers' operations throughout the first half of the 1870s suggest a highly differentiated clientele: a few relatively large-scale white growers, some of whom went broke midway throughout the decade owing the Meyers and Levi money, and more than one hundred black tenants to whom they furnished supplies, most on very short credit of three to six months. Most of the bills receivable were generated by white growers, not blacks. There is also a strong correlation, at least in the first half of the decade, between the black charge customers and the white growers for whom they labored.[23]

By the end of the decade, the Meyers had enlarged their credit facilities for their black customers, not by increasing the charge limits on open accounts but by allocating a significantly larger percentage of their credit resources in general to blacks at the expense of white customers. Customers in general were charging the same total amount in 1880 that they had charged in 1876, but blacks rather than whites now accounted for two-thirds of the dollar amount charged. Whites had accounted for 80 percent of the dollar amount charged in 1876. The fact that blacks could charge at all leads to the inescapable conclusion that they had control over some portion of the crop they produced and were free to dispose of it.[24]

Although the Meyers probably served all their customers professionally, one especially revealing letter to Levi in 1876 suggests their own ambivalence toward their black clientele:

> We have carefully read the proposition of your letter about a new guarantee, and come to the conclusion that you take us for a sett [*sic*] of *Negroes*; that's just about the way they have to do; sign their names whenever it is told them to do so. It matters very little for what purpose. But please remember that we pride ourselves enough to be gentlemen. We have never had any idea of doing any thing of the kind as you insinuate, and we always intend to pay the open account [with you] first. But we don't need Mr. Kilbourne [Levi's lawyer] to accept the paper. We know him to write letters up and we are very glad that we need not call on your Friend every time our business requires a letter written.[25]

This letter accurately summarizes the stresses imposed on postbellum credit relations. By 1876 the Meyers were practically bankrupt, and they were having to address humiliating supplications to the arrogant Levi to extend them long enough to reap the fruits of the next harvest.[26] They believed that they were paying Levi a usurious interest rate on their open account, and they probably were. However, an interest rate of 20 percent may have been fairly usual in the 1870s. When the Meyers' arrangement with Levi broke down altogether in 1876, leaving them without the credit resources of a New Orleans commission merchant, they attempted to discount paper from their customers at New Orleans to raise money to service their own accounts payable with wholesale vendors. Eight-percent notes had to be discounted at 12 percent, which made the effective rate on short-term paper 25 percent. They needed cash with which to buy supplies.[27]

Unfortunately, the Meyers communicated verbally with their customers, so there is hardly any record of the stresses placed on relationships as a result of their own difficulties. They did, however, serve at least one customer who was operating outside the vicinity of Clinton; hence, there is some evidence of their own credit constraints and how they affected their clientele. In April

1876 they wrote to A. T. McKneely, who was planting in Pointe Coupee
Parish, that they could not fill his order because doing so would cause him
to exceed their prearranged limit for that year's planting. Emanuel noted that

> we are not about to do the kind of business we have been doing, to sell our
> Friends and Customers goods without any limit. . . . [It is all we can do] to
> keep our head above water. . . . If you think you can do better, elsewhere,
> we are willing to raise our lien upon condition that you pay us the amount
> already purchased or give us good security for the stock you took from
> here.[28]

McKneely clearly did not like the Meyers' reply because the following month
they felt compelled to chastise him for having failed to sign and return the
bill receivable that was intended to "close up last years account."[29] It was
understood, they continued, that the unpaid balance would be closed with a
note as soon as the crop could be sold.

By July the Meyers were attempting to mollify McKneely's hurt feelings:
"We hope you have planted some 25 acres [in cotton] so you will make
enough for your supplies a/c for this year and have enough left to go one
again another year in which case we shall do all in our power for you."[30]
Whatever difficulties McKneely may have been experiencing finding supplies
for the next year's planting, there can be little doubt that the Meyers themselves were surviving from year to year.

The Meyers, however, had little luck in collecting on their overdue account with McKneely. In April 1877 they were pleading with him to make
some kind of settlement of the prior year's account. Emanuel reminded him
that he had promised to ship them at least one bale of cotton to cover the
unpaid balance on the previous year's account. McKneely had not only left
the account unsatisfied, but had also refused to ship even one bale. He had
persisted in ignoring their numerous entreaties.[31] A few weeks later, the
Meyers were writing to an attorney in the parish where McKneely resided
to commence collection proceedings and seize some portion of the new
year's crop.

Far less information is available on the relationships between black sharecroppers and tenants, furnishing merchants, lessors, and employers. As mentioned earlier, some of the lease arrangements seem to indicate that blacks
sometimes organized themselves into an extended family planting unit, an
arrangement that would have lessened some of the risks for all in the event
of sickness or death of the head of a household. There is evidence, too, in
such recorded arrangements, that several black families banded together and,
through a designated intermediary or spokesman, negotiated a labor arrangement with a white landowner. Such spokesmen may well have supervised the
planting activities of all and substituted as de facto overseers. It is not clear

whether such black leaders were in the employ of white landowners who obliged them to find black sharecroppers and tenants or whether they were elected in a poll of all the squad members, men and women.

Increasingly in the 1870s, women were parties to labor arrangements, receiving an average of three quarters of the share accorded to a man.[32] The petition of Eliza Silliman contained an accurate description of what could go wrong in pool arrangements. In 1874 she and Samuel Carter, a black man, had worked on the plantation of D. W. Pipes. The two constituted a squad and worked for Pipes on halves. The division of the squad's half of the crop was in the proportion of four to three, with "said Carter getting a full share and petitioner [Silliman] three-quarters of a hand's share." They had made a total of six bales, "three of which went to the Squad." The sale of the three bales had realized $165, and Silliman's share of the proceeds was $70.75. "After deducting the price of a barrel of meat and meal, say thirty-two Dollars, the balance was received by said Carter," who had "failed to account to petitioner [Silliman] for any portion thereof."[33] The squad clearly had had to reimburse Pipes from its share of the crop for supplies consumed during the planting season.

In another case, Mary Davis alleged that she had been induced through fraud and misrepresentations of the Meyer brothers to give them "a pledge or lien" upon her horse to secure the purchase price of a mule bought by one Spencer Jackson. She averred that she was unmarried, but the Meyers contended that she was married to Jackson and that the horse was community property; consequently, the horse was subject to seizure for Jackson's debts. Davis's attorney correctly argued that the privilege confected by the Meyers was "illegal and unwarranted by Law . . . and [was] null and void for error"; moreover, the mule had been returned to the Meyers. The Meyers finally prevailed because they were able to prove that they had sold the horse to Davis and had a vendor's privilege on the animal for the unpaid balance of seventy dollars. It is likely, however, that the sale from the Meyers to Davis had in fact been a simulated one, a means of obtaining a vendor's privilege on Davis's horse as additional security for Jackson's credit purchase of the mule.[34]

However, a subtle transition was under way beginning in the early 1870s. Emanuel and Henry Meyer's correspondence, for example, is full of references to the planters of the parish in the years 1870 to 1875. After 1875 their correspondence contains frequent references to obtaining pledges and collaterals from their customers. On May 10, 1871, Emanuel advised Levi that they were "compelled to see Planters through [who they had] . . . consented to furnish, else they [would] . . . pledge their crops to someone else."[35] In 1874 the Meyers wrote that "planters in general ha[d] made the crop on half or less, charged . . . [the previous year], and with a good crop they [would] . . . be able to pay their debts."[36] However, in the fall of 1875, Levi was advised that the Meyers were "convinced that . . . [their] customers [would] . . . make more cotton than the [previous] . . . year. . . . [They themselves] had been very cautious in selling goods and [had] . . . hopes that [they would] be very close in collections."[37] Plainly, "customers" had supplanted "planters" in the brothers' thinking.

Even as late as 1890, 95 percent of the acreage in the parish was in the hands of white owners.[38] There were perhaps twenty or twenty-five large-scale planting units on which planters still conducted comprehensive planting operations under a variety of arrangements with their black employees, sharecroppers, and tenants. These units embraced considerably more acreage than their antebellum counterparts. Much of the acreage in the parish, however, was simply leased to tenants for a specific number of bales of processed cotton.

Many of the Meyers' best planter customers in the early years had gone broke by 1875, and the Meyers themselves were the proprietors of three tracts of land in East Feliciana Parish and one tract in St. Landry Parish on which they were conducting planting operations. They acquired all of this land by conveyance, in satisfaction of unpaid balances owed to them, rather than with foreclosure suits.[39] By 1875 their position vis-à-vis their planter clientele was analogous to that of their commission merchant, Levi, who was owed money by the same individuals who were in debt to the Meyers.

Whether the arrangement was on shares or involved the payment of a rental in bales or pounds of cotton or cash was less important for risk allocation purposes, however, than who furnished the supplies and livestock to the planting unit. The suit records make it abundantly clear that tenants and sharecroppers of every description often still looked to their lessors for supplies, rather than to a furnishing merchant. In such suits, plaintiffs not only claimed a lessor's privilege on the crop but a supply privilege as well.

If the lessor contracted for a payment only in pounds or bales of cotton and furnished no supplies, the furnishing merchant had to be extremely careful in determining what supplies he could furnish to the tenant. One of the Meyer brothers, for example, was always in the countryside visiting the farms and estimating how the crops were faring. At least in the 1870s, credit facilities for black tenants were highly constrained by prospective estimates on the forthcoming crops. Black tenants were not permitted charge facilities on a twelve-month basis but rather were permitted to purchase supplies on credit during the summer commensurate with the condition of the crops.

This relative circumspection regarding black tenants during the 1870s probably explains why the dollar value of judgments in some years was four times the amount of the average crop pledge. In the case of the Meyers, their large debtors were white planters to whom they had extended rather generous credit facilities. Even as late as 1880, it is improbable that rural furnishing merchants were extending credit facilities to tenants for more than a few months. The price of cotton and the prospects for that year's crop must have influenced their decisions in this regard.

The transition from planters supplying their tenants to furnishing merchants providing that service was lengthy, complex, and subtle. A composite picture of the progressions and regressions in the process may never emerge, but it is obvious that no analysis of postbellum planting arrangements is complete without a quantification of credit and supply facilities. In the early years, supply facilities were integral to most growing arrangements. By the mid-1870s the furnishing merchant occupied a conspicuous place in the local credit picture. It is not enough simply to determine the relative incidence of tenancy and sharecropping; determining how the risks involved in furnishing supplies were allocated among lessors, furnishers, tenants, and agricultural workers is far more critical to understanding what was going on in the postbellum economy. The supplies component ran a close second to the labor component in the hierarchy of components necessary for growing a crop. How supplies figured in labor relations in general is not well understood.

It is clear, however, that the credit system was functioning very poorly at every level. The pressure for liquidity is an obvious symptom of an economy in the throes of asset deflation. To blame furnishing merchants for the heavy concentration on cotton in agriculture and the perennial indebtedness of most growers places too much emphasis on one component of a system that overall was functioning poorly.[40]

Nor were interest rates necessarily usurious just because they ranged in excess of 50 percent. The risk premium in every kind of credit relationship, especially in the growing of a cotton crop, has to have been very high in the 1870s. Most credit relationships anticipated an eventual default of some kind, even if it was only a temporary one.

Appendix

Pledge Agreement

Know all men by these presents that Whereas the German Society of New Orleans has this day discounted Fellowes & Co.,'s Note for the Sum of Seventy, Seven hundred & Eighty three 94 Dollars, say $ 7,783.94—favor of the Society dated 15 October 1861 and payable on the 12th Day of April 1862.

NOW

in order to Secure the punctual payment of said Note at Maturity or any Renewal thereof the Said Fellowes & Co. do by these presents pledge, pawn and deliver unto the Said German Society

Certificate No. 298 for 25 Shares Stock in the Crescent City Bank

Certificate No. 2041 for 50 Shares Stock in the Bank of New Orleans

Note of A. J. Joyce dated 21 June 1861 payable to order Fellowes Co. (and by them endorsed) on the 17 April 1862 for the sum of thirteen hundred Dollars say $1,300—

and it is hereby agreed that in the event of the nonpayment of Said Note at its Maturity or of any renewal thereof, the said German Society shall have the right to sell the securities herein pledged for Cash at Public or private Sale at their Option and the proceeds of Said Sale or enough thereof, shall be appropriated to the payment of Said Note with interest and Costs and Charges attending the Sale.

New Orleans, October 1, 1861
(Signed) Fellowes & Co.

Witness

Jno. P. Vairin

Notes

Introduction

1. Gavin Wright, *Old South, New South: Revolutions in the Southern Economy Since the Civil War* (New York: Basic Books, 1986), p. 87.

2. Roger L. Ransom, *Conflict and Compromise: the Political Economy of Slavery, Emancipation, and the American Civil War* (Cambridge: Cambridge University Press, 1989), pp. 245, 247.

3. Gerald David Jaynes, *Branches Without Roots: Genesis of the Black Working Class in the American South, 1862–1882* (Oxford: Oxford University Press, 1986), pp. 39–41.

4. Harold D. Woodman, *King Cotton and His Retainers: Financing and Marketing the Cotton Crop of the South, 1800–1925* (Reprint, Columbia: University of South Carolina Press, 1990).

5. Robert William Fogel and Stanley L. Engerman, *Time on the Cross: The Economics of American Negro Slavery* (New York: W. W. Norton, 1989). Robert William Fogel, *Without Consent or Contract: The Rise and Fall of American Slavery* (New York: W. W. Norton, 1985). George D. Green, *Finance and Economic Development in the Old South: Louisiana Banking 1804–1861* (Stanford: Stanford University Press, 1972). Larry Schweikart, *Banking in the American South, from the Age of Jackson to Reconstruction* (Baton Rouge: Louisiana State University Press, 1987).

6. Wright, *Old South, New South*, p. 78.

7. Gavin Wright, *The Political Economy of the Cotton South: Households, Markets, and Wealth in the Nineteenth Century* (New York: W. W. Norton, 1978), pp. 128–39.

8. Michael Tadman, *Speculators and Slaves: Masters, Traders, and Slaves in the Old South* (Madison: University of Wisconsin Press, 1989), pp. 52–55.

9. This conclusion is based on an examination of New Orleans factorage firms both before and after the war. Prewar firms, which were interested primarily in financial services, numbered upwards of 150.

10. Woodman, *King Cotton*, pp. 139–53.

11. Ibid., pp. 36–39.

12. Wright underscores the difficulty of applying a modern concept of "savings" in a historical context. See *Old South, New South*, p. 20.

13. Woodman, *King Cotton*, p. 148, note 26.

14. Wright, *Old South, New South*, pp. 18, 49.

15. Roger Ransom and Richard Sutch, *One Kind of Freedom: The Economic Consequences of Emancipation* (Cambridge: Cambridge University Press, 1977), pp. 40–51. Wright, *Old South, New South*, p. 87. Jaynes, *Branches Without Roots*, pp. 29–30.

16. Jaynes, *Branches Without Roots*, p. 35.

17. Wright, *Old South, New South*, p. 49.

18. Ibid., pp. 99–115.

19. Jaynes, *Branches Without Roots*, p. 38.

20. Ibid.

21. Ransom and Sutch, *One Kind of Freedom*, pp. 126–71.

22. Roger Ransom and Richard Sutch, "Capitalists Without Capital: The Burden of Slavery and the Impact of Emancipation," *Agricultural History* 62 (1988): 133–60.

23. Wright, *Political Economy*, p. 84.

24. Act no. 195, To Amend and Re-enact Article Three Thousand One Hundred and Eighty-four of the Civil Code (1825), March 28, 1867, *Acts Passed by the General Assembly of the State of Louisiana*, Second Legislature, Second Session, pp. 351–53.

25. United States Department of Commerce, Bureau of the Census, Eighth Census of the United States, 1860.

1. The Origins of the Antebellum Credit System

1. Green, *Finance and Economic Development*.

2. Schweikart, *Banking in the American South*. Fritz Redlich, "The Role of Private Banks in the Early Economy of the United States," *Business History Review* 41 (1977): 90–93.

3. Green, *Finance and Economic Development*, p. 76.

4. Ibid., pp. 146–47.

5. Union Bank v. Alex E. Brady, 2315, Third District Court, East Feliciana Parish, April 2, 1840. All references to district courts in the state of Louisiana are hereinafter referred to as DC followed by an abbreviation for the parish: 3 DC (EF) (for East Feliciana Parish) or 3 DC (O) (for Orleans Parish).

6. Succession of William Silliman, Conveyance Office Book T, East Feliciana Parish. All references to Conveyance Office Books in Louisiana are hereinafter referred to as COB followed by an abbreviation for the parish: COB T (EF). COB T (EF), pp. 439–43. COB V (EF), pp. 229–90. Probate records, Book F, 5 DC (EF), pp. 79–183, 258, 343–49, 493–94, 579–83. Parish Court, East Feliciana Parish, docket no. 1. All references to parish courts in Louisiana are hereinafter referred to as PC followed by an abbreviation for the parish: PC (EF).

7. Mortgage Office Book E, East Feliciana Parish, pp. 57, 67, 73, 75, 100–101, 127, 133–34, 136, 147–49, 238, 254, 308, 370. All references to parish Mortgage Office Books in Louisiana are hereinafter referred to as MOB followed by an abbreviation for the parish: MOB E (EF). MOB E (EF), pp. 71–72.

8. Ibid.

9. Union Bank v. Malachiah H. Bradford, 909, 3 DC (EF), December 15, 1836; v. John and Ann Bell, 1976, 3 DC (EF), October 16, 1839; v. Sarah Rhodes, 1988, 3 DC (EF), October 17, 1839; v. Ruhannah Whitaker, 1989, 3 DC (EF), October 17, 1839; v. William and Temperance Brian, 1995, 3 DC (EF), October 17, 1839; v. James and Margaret Morgan, 2001, 3 DC (EF), October 17, 1839; v. James H. Shropshire, 2323, 3 DC (EF), April 14, 1840; v. John Moffit, 2623, 3 DC (EF), November 1841; v. William H. and L. L. Fairchild, 2724, 3 DC (EF), May 20, 1842.

10. "An Act to Incorporate the Subscribers to the Union Bank of Louisiana," April 2, 1832, *Acts of the Louisiana Legislature*, Tenth Legislature, Third Session, pp. 42–72.

11. Union Bank v. Darius L. Green, 893, 3 DC (EF), October 26, 1836.

12. Union Bank v. Elias Boatner, 1417, 3 DC (EF), October 18, 1838; 1418, 3 DC (EF), October 18, 1838.

13. Union Bank v. Frederick Taylor, 1508, 3 DC (EF), January 30, 1839.

14. Richard H. Kilbourne, Jr., *Louisiana Commercial Law: The Antebellum Period* (Baton Rouge: Paul M. Hebert Law Center Publications Institute, 1980), pp. 200–202.

15. Union Bank v. Dudley Babcock, 841, 3 DC (EF), October 1835.

16. MOB E and F (EF).

17. Marston to J. B. Perault, February 29, 1839, Letter Copy Book I, hereinafter referred to as LCB, Henry W. Marston and Family Papers, Louisiana and Lower Mississippi Valley Collections, hereinafter referred to as MP, LLMVC, Louisiana State University Libraries, Louisiana State University.

18. Marston to Samuel J. Peters, April 12, 1839, LCB I, MP, LLMVC.

19. Marston to L. Sturgis, August 22, 1839, LCB I, MP, LLMVC.

20. Marston to Charles Black, September 3, 1839, LCB I, MP, LLMVC.

21. Marston to Horace Bean & Co., May 8, 1841, LCB I, MP, LLMVC.

22. Marston to Horace Bean & Co., May 21, 1841, LCB I, MP, LLMVC.

23. Green, *Finance and Economic Development*, pp. 146–47.

24. Marston to Grant & Barton, June 8, 1841, LCB I, MP, LLMVC.

25. Marston to Grant & Barton, March 9, 1842, LCB I, MP, LLMVC.

26. Peter Temin, *The Jacksonian Economy* (New York: W. W. Norton, 1969), pp. 31–35.

27. Marston to DeForest & Co., September 22, 1842, LCB I, MP, LLMVC.

28. Marston to L. & V. Kirby, October 6, 1842, LCB I, MP, LLMVC.

29. Marston to DeForest & Co., April 8, 1843, LCB I, MP, LLMVC.

30. Marston to Smith, Henderson & Co., October 22, 1842, LCB I, MP, LLMVC.

31. Marston to L. & V. Kirby, April 8, 1843, LCB I, MP, LLMVC.

32. Marston to Smith, Henderson & Co., June 15, 1843, LCB I, MP, LLMVC.

33. Marston to Gasquet & Co., June 22, 1843, LCB I, MP, LLMVC.

34. Marston to Smith, Henderson & Co., November 4, 1843, LCB I, MP, LLMVC.

35. Richard H. Kilbourne, Jr., "Securing Commercial Transactions in the Antebellum Legal System of Louisiana," *Kentucky Law Journal* 70, no. 3 (1981): 609–41.

2. The Emergence of Factors as Investment Bankers

1. Woodman, *King Cotton*, p. 155.

2. Louisiana Civil Code (1825), Articles 2823, 2841, 2843–2846. All references to the Civil Code are hereinafter referred to as CC (1825), followed by the numbers of the Articles. Kilbourne, *Louisiana Commercial Law*, pp. 62–65, 108, 115, 120.

3. Cutrer, Harrison v. Their Creditors, 16,777, 4 DC, (O), March 5, 1866; Thomas Henderson v. His Creditors, 15,989, 4 DC, (O), December 9, 1865. Elliott Ashkenazi, *The Business of Jews in Louisiana, 1840–1875* (Tuscaloosa: University of Alabama Press, 1988), pp. 69–70, 79–91, 98–102.

4. Census, 1860, St. Landry Parish, Louisiana. Succession of Jacob Upshur Payne, 64,306, Civil District Court (O). All references to civil district courts in Louisiana are hereinafter referred to as CDC followed by an abbreviation for the parish.

5. Succession of Richard Flower, 38,670, 2 DC (O). Ashkenazi, *The Business of Jews*, p. 83.

6. Pickersgill & Co. v. Brown, 7 *Louisiana Annual Reports* 297 (May 1852).

7. Walker & Vaught v. G. W. Kimbrough, Administrator, 23 *Louisiana Annual Reports* 637 (July 1871).

8. Kilbourne, *Louisiana Commercial Law*, pp. 121–56.

9. Woodman's examination concentrates primarily on short-term credit transactions, most of which were connected with annual planting expenses and the credit mechanisms for transferring cotton from producers to consumers. Woodman, *King Cotton*, pp. 60–71. Ralph W. Hiddy's study of the Baring firm is especially good in providing a full picture of the international exchange operations that eased the flow of cotton and sugar to Europe. Ralph W. Hiddy, *The House of Baring in American Trade and Finance, English Merchant Bankers at Work, 1763–1861* (New York: Russell & Russell, 1949).

10. Act no. 92, "An Act to Facilitate the Liquidation of the Property Banks Chartered by the State," April 5, 1843, *Acts Passed at the First Session of the Sixteenth Legislature of the State of Louisiana*, pp. 56–63.

11. COB N (EF), pp. 107–12, December 23, 1851.

12. This estimate is based on a summary of the total value of judgments taken on antebellum debts in the postbellum years, the cumulative total of collateralized mortgage debt in the last twelve years of the antebellum period, and one-half the average value of the staples shipped from the parish annually in the 1850s. Obviously, this is a rough estimate. Ten percent of the aggregate wealth in the parish is a reasonable estimate of long-term debt. Short-term debt probably aggregated to no more than half the gross value of staples shipped from the parish annually.

13. The annual value of staples produced in and shipped from the parish in the 1850s was between $1,100,000 and $1,500,000 annually. However, at least one-quarter of the three hundred planters resident in the parish had income from plantations outside the parish, and there is no way to determine what income free households received from stocks, bonds, and debt instruments in general remitted from outside the parish.

14. William Silliman to Henry Marston, March 13, 1851, MP, LLMVC.

15. Marston to Robert G. Beele, Esq., June 28, 1855, LCB II, p. 386, MP, LLMVC.

16. Marston to George F. Webb, April 14, 1855, LCB II, p. 361, MP, LLMVC.

17. Marston to Dr. C. G. Trask, February 22, 1854, LCB II, p. 169, MP, LLMVC.

18. Marston to W. Marbury, February 9, 1854, LCB II, p. 162, MP, LLMVC.

19. Marston to James W. Schenck, April 11, 1855, LCB II, p. 359, MP, LLMVC.

20. Marston to J. A. Maryman, October 17, 1855, LCB II, p. 417, MP, LLMVC.

21. Marston to Payne, Harrison, March 11, 1854, LCB II, p. 175, MP, LLMVC.

22. Marston to Payne, Harrison, December 9, 1854, LCB II, p. 293, MP, LLMVC.

23. Marston to George A. Freret, December 30, 1854, LCB II, p. 293, MP, LLMVC.

24. Marston to Payne, Harrison, November 9, 1854, LCB II, p. 249, MP, LLMVC.

25. Marston to Alfred Penn, September 21, 1854, LCB II, p. 229, MP, LLMVC.

26. Marston to P. N. Wood, December 3, 1854, LCB II, p. 272, MP, LLMVC.

27. Louisiana Bank Act of 1842. Green, *Finance and Economic Development*, pp. 118–29.

28. Citizens Bank v. William Fellows, Jr., 19,973, 4 DC (O), January 6, 1868.

29. Census, 1860, East Feliciana Parish. MOB M (EF), p. 11, January 29, 1861. Ashkenazi, *The Business of Jews*, pp. 81–82.

30. Marston to Payne, Harrison, February 22, 1853, LCB II, p. 51, MP, LLMVC.

31. Marston to Richard Pritchard, June 15, 1853, LCB II, p. 91, MP, LLMVC.

32. Marston to Matthias G. Mills, March 28, 1854, LCB II, p. 181, MP, LLMVC.

33. Ibid.

34. Marston to Payne, Harrison, March 8, 1853, LCB II, p. 52, MP, LLMVC.

35. Marston to Thomas Lombard, February 18, 1853, LCB II, p. 42, MP, LLMVC.

36. Marston to James W. Schenck, February 4, 1854, LCB II, p. 159, MP, LLMVC.

37. Marston to W. S. Pike, March 3, 1855, LCB II, p. 331, MP, LLMVC.

38. Marston to George A. Freret, February 26, 1855, LCB II, p. 328, MP, LLMVC.

39. Marston to Payne, Harrison, March 11, 1853, LCB II, p. 54, MP, LLMVC.

40. Marston to Payne, Harrison, March 29, 1853, LCB II, p. 64, MP, LLMVC.

41. Marston to Payne, Harrison, March 18, 1853, LCB II, p. 58, MP, LLMVC.

42. Marston to Payne, Harrison, April 4, 1854, LCB II, p. 185, MP, LLMVC.

43. Marston to Payne, Harrison, April 11, 1854, LCB II, p. 188, MP, LLMVC.

44. Marston to Payne, Harrison, December 1, 1852, LCB II, p. 15, MP, LLMVC.

45. Marston to Payne, Harrison, February 20, 1855, LCB II, p. 326, MP, LLMVC.

46. Marston to Eugene Rousseau, February 15, 1855, LCB II, p. 324, MP, LLMVC.

47. Succession of Samuel Oakey, 10,732, 2 DC (O), transferred to 90,528 CDC (O).

48. Ibid.

49. Citizens Bank v. William Fellows, Jr., 19,973, 4 DC (O), January 6, 1868.

50. Marston to Payne, Harrison, March 8, 1853, LCB II, p. 52, MP, LLMVC.

51. Payne, Harrison v. Joanna McManus, 690, 5 DC (EF), September 6, 1866.

52. Succession of Samuel Oakey, 10,732, 2 DC (O).

53. Marston to George A. Freret, December 30, 1854, LCB II, p. 293, MP, LLMVC.

54. Accounts current filed in evidence in various court proceedings show as much (see Chapter 4).

55. Kilbourne, "Securing Commercial Transactions," pp. 619–20.

56. Schweikart, *Banking in the American South*, pp. 225–66.

57. Succession of Gilbert S. Hawkins, 21,270, 2 DC (O).

58. Ibid.

59. See Chapter 4.

60. Succession of Gilbert S. Hawkins, 21,270, 2 DC (O).

61. Ibid.

62. Citizens Bank v. William Fellows, Jr., 19,973, 4 DC (O), January 6, 1868.

63. Ibid.

64. Ibid.

65. Ibid.

66. Woodman, *King Cotton*, pp. 117–18.

67. MOB L (EF), p. 11, January 7, 1857.

68. Ibid.

69. MOB L (EF), p. 24, January 28, 1857.

70. MOB L (EF), p. 226, May 31, 1858; MOB L (EF), p. 183, February 17, 1858.

71. MOB L (EF), p. 423, September 1, 1859.

72. Ibid.

73. Ibid.

74. The consensus among many historians is that the South depended on northern and European capital to finance economic development. Although there was a large volume of short-term debt instruments that financed movements of goods and services between Europe and the United States and between regions within the United States, the evidence of foreign or northern capital in the development of East Feliciana is practically nonexistent. Whatever the total volume of debt instruments for trading purposes was during the span of one year, it must have been a tiny percentage of the total capitalization and debt of the southern economy. But see Woodman, *King Cotton*, pp. 139–53.

75. Lee v. Cummings and Pickett, 27 *Louisiana Annual Reports* 529 (July 1875). Urquharts v. Their Creditors, 17,624, 6 DC (O), November 6, 1865.

76. LCB II, MP, LLMVC.

3. Securing Antebellum Credit Transactions with Slaves

1. Act no. 195 (1867).

2. Gavin Wright, "What Was Slavery?" *Social Concept* 6, no. 1 (1991): 29, 34–35, 48.

3. Tadman, *Speculators and Slaves*, pp. 104–5. Laurence J. Kotlikoff, "The Structure of Slave Prices in New Orleans, 1804 to 1862," *Economic Inquiry* 17 (1979): 504.

4. The importance of out-of-state traders in particular localities of the lower Mississippi Valley is well documented by Tadman, *Speculators and Slaves*, pp. 94–97.

5. This estimate comports with Tadman's findings. Tadman, *Speculators and Slaves*, pp. 11–46.

6. Conveyance Office Books, East Feliciana Parish.

7. Henry Skipwith, *East Feliciana, Louisiana, Past and Present: Sketches of the Pioneers*, 1892 (Reprint, Baton Rouge: East Feliciana Pilgrimage and Garden Club, 1957), p. 50.

8. See Table 1.

9. COB P (EF), p. 285, January 5, 1856.

10. Ibid.

11. COB P (EF), pp. 505–6, November 8, 1856.

12. Tadman, *Speculators and Slaves*, pp. 25–31, 42–43, 233–35.

13. Marston to A. Foreman, January 25, 1856, LCB II, p. 457, MP, LLMVC.

14. Ransom and Sutch, *One Kind of Freedom*, pp. 80–84. Ransom, *Conflict and Compromise*, pp. 248–49.

15. CC (1825), 3256.

16. CC (1825), 3101, 3102, 3143–3148.

17. MOB K (EF), p. 145, April 17, 1854.

18. MOB K (EF), p. 27, June 16, 1853.

19. MOB A (EF), p. 368, July 14, 1828.

20. MOB A (EF), pp. 172–73, September 14, 1825.

21. MOB A (EF), p. 253, April 9, 1827.

22. MOB E (EF), p. 208, February 20, 1838.

23. MOB F (EF), p. 15, August 20, 1838.

24. MOB D (EF), p. 348, June 6, 1836.

25. MOB E (EF), p. 152, November 18, 1837.

26. MOB D (EF), p. 17, January 31, 1835.

27. Tadman, *Speculators and Slaves*, pp. 52–55.
28. MOB D (EF), p. 101, August 6, 1835.
29. See generally MP, LLMVC.
30. MOB D (EF), p. 325, May 12, 1836.
31. MOB D (EF), p. 336, May 23, 1836.
32. MOB E (EF), p. 126, July 31, 1837.
33. MOB E (EF), pp. 88–90, 92–97.
34. Tadman documents a similar pattern among other traders. Tadman, *Speculators and Slaves*, pp. 179–210.
35. MOB G (EF), p. 119, September 30, 1841.
36. COB N (EF), pp. 107–12, December 23, 1851.
37. MOB G (EF), p. 477, March 29, 1845.
38. MOB G (EF), p. 491, May 12, 1845, p. 499, June 28, 1845.
39. MOB H (EF), p. 19, May 4, 1846.
40. MOB H (EF), p. 21, May 12, 1846, p. 45, December 26, 1846.
41. MOB G (EF), p. 289, May 11, 1843.
42. Wright, *Political Economy*, pp. 139–40.
43. Woodman, *King Cotton*, pp. 60–71.
44. MOB K (EF), p. 498, February 20, 1856.
45. MOB K (EF), p. 171, May 29, 1854.
46. MOB K (EF), p. 185, July 14, 1854.
47. MOB K (EF), p. 322, May 17, 1855.
48. MOB K (EF), p. 309, April 24, 1855.
49. MOB K (EF), p. 349, June 4, 1855.
50. MOB K (EF), p. 371, August 1, 1855.
51. MOB K (EF), p. 480, February 8, 1856.
52. Green, *Finance and Economic Development*, pp. 163–82.
53. Gavin Wright, "Cotton Competition and the Post-bellum Recovery of the American South," *Journal of Economic History* 34 (September 1974): 610–35.
54. *Feliciana Democrat*, Clinton, Louisiana, April 12, 1856.
55. See *Correspondence With My Son, Henry Kirk White Muse. Embracing Some Brief Memorials of His Character, and Essays From His Pen, While a Student at Princeton College, New Jersey* (New York: J. A. Gray, 1858). Copies in possession of the author and LLMVC.

4. The Nemesis of Prewar Debt

1. Marston to Henry Green, December 7, 1871, LCB III, p. 358, MP, LLMVC.
2. Roger Ransom and Richard Sutch, "The Impact of the Civil War and of the Emancipation on Southern Agriculture," *Explorations in Economic History* 12 (1975): 13. But see Wright, *Old South New South*, p. 87, and Jaynes, *Branches Without Roots*, p. 33.
3. Samuel Silliman to McVea and Kilbourne, February 12, 1869. Letter in the possession of the author.
4. Marston to Jacob U. Payne, March 4, 1871, LCB III, p. 268, MP, LLMVC.
5. Green, *Finance and Economic Development*, pp. 118–29. Schweikart, *Banking in the American South*, pp. 140–41.

6. This estimate is based on the aggregate banking capital in the state in 1860 and the total wealth in the state, real and personal, according to the 1860 census.

7. Union Bank of Louisiana v. Isaac Jackson, 813, 5 DC (EF), February 9, 1867.

8. See generally George W. Helm v. Wright, Allen, 14,673, 5 DC (O); George M. Bagly v. Wright, Allen, 15,210, 5 DC (O); Meyers, Hoffman v. Wright, Allen, 16,230, 4 DC (O); Henry Frellsen v. Wright, Allen, 16,274, 4 DC (O); C. E. Picardey v. Wright, Allen, 16,288, 4 DC (O); Benjamin Sanford v. Wright, Allen, 16,289, 4 DC (O); J. P. O'Leary v. Wright, Allen, 17,272, 4 DC (O); Sarah J. Tillerton v. Wright, Allen, 17,809, 4 DC (O); William Collord v. Wright, Allen, 18,702, 4 DC (O); Samuel Smith & Co. v. Wright, Allen, 20,334, 4 DC (O); and Crescent City Bank v. Wright, Allen, 18,592, 5 DC (O).

9. Union Bank of Louisiana v. Isaac Jackson, 813, 5 DC (EF), February 9, 1867.

10. Schweikart, *Banking in the American South*, pp. 286–93.

11. Federal authorities attempted to liquidate the New Orleans banks forcibly in 1863, especially those with strong Confederate sympathies. In the case of E. H. Wilson v. Ambrose Lanfear et al., 19,839, 4 DC (O), January 9, 1868, the Bank of Louisiana's president had removed "upwards of $2,000,000." of coin before the commencement of the federal occupation and shipped it to Georgia. Wilson had purchased $78,581.62 of the coin for $86,439.88 in bank notes. Wilson then had more than eight hundred bales of cotton belonging to the bank in Alabama attached.

12. Joseph W. Dougherty v. John F. McKneely, 706, 5 DC (EF), April 19, 1866. Census, 1860.

13. Thomas Wainwright, Administrator v. Mrs. Alice Bridges et al., 19 *Louisiana Annual Reports* 234 (May 1867). Louisiana Constitution of 1868, Articles 127–130.

14. R. H. Draughon, Adm. v. Mrs. Jane White, 776, 5 DC (EF), Supreme Court of Louisiana, docket no. 2109.

15. A. Miltenberger & Co. v. Mary E. Purnell, Adm., 1226, 5 DC (EF), February 11, 1867. New Orleans Insurance Co. v. K. P. Muse, Deceased, 2521, 5 DC (EF), October 13, 1879.

16. Richard Pritchard v. H. S. Perkins and Alex Smith, Jr., 793, 5 DC (EF), May 2, 1866.

17. Sarah Dupree v. Alex Smith, Jr., 1259, 5 DC (EF), February 2, 1867.

18. Payne, Harrison v. Joanna McManus, 609, 5 DC (EF), September 6, 1866.

19. Edward Nalle & Co. v. Mrs. R. B. Dunn, 815, 5 DC (EF), May 2, 1866.

20. Payne, Harrison v. J. L. Singletary, 561, 5 DC (EF), February 2, 1866.

21. Marston to Payne, March 4, 1871, LCB III, p. 268, MP, LLMVC.

22. Citizens Bank v. J. M. Sessions, 1458, 5 DC (EF), September 11, 1867; Citizens Bank v. Lafayette Brown, 761, 5 DC (EF), May 1, 1866; Citizens Bank v. Mary S. Steadman and George Steadman, 757, 5 DC (EF), April 30, 1866.

23. See generally Abel John Norwood Papers, LLMVC.

24. COB Y (EF), pp. 191–93, June 27, 1878.

25. Succession of Gilbert S. Hawkins, 21,270, 2 DC (O).

26. Union Bank of Tennessee v. J. B. Smith and Abel J. Norwood, 858, 5 DC (EF), May 2, 1866.

27. Catherine Norwood v. A. J. Norwood, 878, 5 DC (EF), May 17, 1866; Mrs. Catherine Norwood v. A. J. Norwood, 863, 5 DC (EF), May 14, 1866.

28. L. G. Perkins v. A. J. Norwood, 876, 5 DC (EF), May 16, 1866.

29. See generally J. G. Kilbourne and Family Papers, LLMVC.

30. Mechanics and Traders Bank v. J. B. Smith and A. J. Norwood, 890, 5 DC (EF), May 24, 1866. But see note 48.

31. Mechanics and Traders Bank v. Abel J. Norwood, 1022, 5 DC (EF), September 24, 1866.

32. Citizens Bank v. A. J. Norwood, 1159, 5 DC (EF), January 7, 1867.

33. See German Society of New Orleans v. Fellows & Co., 19,064, 4 DC (O), March 16, 1867, and copy of pledge agreement (Appendix 1).

34. Citizens Bank v. A. J. Norwood, 1159, 5 DC (EF), January 7, 1867.

35. See generally 782, 789, 794, 1010, 1012, 1016, 1269, and 1657, 5 DC (EF).

36. Payne, Harrison v. J. L. Singletary, 561, 5 DC (EF), February 2, 1866.

37. Byrne, Vance & Co. v. W. W. Dunn, 1242, 5 DC (EF), February 29, 1867.

38. David Pipes v. Wright, Allen, 18,342, 6 DC (O); Judgment Book C, p. 189, East Feliciana Parish Courthouse records.

39. Emily Hatcher v. S. E. Hunter, 997, 5 DC (EF), September 19, 1866.

40. Ruth Johnson v. Henry Marston, 1714, 5 DC (EF) (original judgment filed February 14, 1867).

41. Henry Marston v. J. D. Worthy, 1390, 5 DC (EF), May 30, 1867.

42. Payne, Huntington v. John Marston, 1730, 5 DC (EF), February 20, 1868.

43. Succession of A. D. Palmer v. Marston, 81 *United States Reports*, 10–12, United States Supreme Court (1871).

44. Marston to Michael Boyce, June 30, 1871, LCB III, p. 303, MP, LLMVC.

45. Thomas Wainwright, Administrator, v. Mrs. Alice Bridges et al., 19 *Louisiana Annual Reports* 234 (May 1867). See John P. Dawson and Frank E. Cooper, "The Effects of Inflation on Private Contracts: United States, 1861–1879: The Confederate Inflation," *Michigan Law Review* 33 (1935): 712–13, notes 22 and 23; and Robert J. Haws and Michael V. Namarato, "Race, Property Rights, and the Economic Consequences of Reconstruction: A Case Study," *Vanderbilt Law Review* 32 (1979): 305–29.

46. New Orleans Canal and Banking Co. v. Samuel Templeton, 20 *Louisiana Annual Reports* 141 (February 1868).

47. Edward Groves v. K. M. Clark and R. H. Carnal, 21 *Louisiana Annual Reports* 567 (August 1869).

48. Alexander T. Stewart et al. v. S. Bloom, S. Kahn, A. Levi, and A. Adler, 78 *United States Reports*, 493–507, United States Supreme Court (April 10, 1871).

49. William White v. John R. Hart, 80 *United States Reports*, 646–53, United States Supreme Court (April 22, 1872).

50. Henry T. Osborn v. Young A. G. Nicholson, 80 *United States Reports*, 654–64, United States Supreme Court (April 22, 1872).

51. Henry A. Boyce, Exr. of Henry Boyce, Plff. in Error v. Thomas S. Tabb, 85 *United States Reports*, 546–48, United States Supreme Court (October 27, 1873).

52. Marston to Michael Boyce, January 16, 1869, LCB III, p. 73, MP, LLMVC.

53. John D. Worthy, Exr. of Archibald D. Palmer, Deceased, Plff. in Err. v. Henry Marston, 81 *United States Reports*, 10–12, United States Supreme Court (April 1, 1872); Marston to Bulow W. Marston, February 11, 1872, LCB III, p. 381, MP, LLMVC.

54. Marston to J. U. Payne, February 13, 1872, LCB III, p. 384, MP, LLMVC.

55. Marston to J. U. Payne, March 5, 1872, LCB III, p. 392, MP, LLMVC.

56. Marston to James H. Muse, December 9, 1871, LCB III, p. 359, MP; Marston to Muse, December 23, 1871, LCB III, p. 362, MP; Marston to S. J. Randall, December 23, 1871, LCB III, p. 366, MP; Marston to Randall, January 28, 1872, LCB III, p. 373,

MP; Marston to Randall, February 6, 1872, LCB III, p. 379, MP; Marston to Randall, February 23, 1872, LCB III, p. 385, MP; Marston to Randall, May 22, 1872, LCB III, p. 417, MP, LLMVC.

57. Marston to Randall, February 23, 1872, LCB III, p. 385, MP, LLMVC.

58. Worthy v. Marston.

59. Boyce v. Tabb.

60. Henderson v. Merchants' Mutual Insurance Co., 23 *Louisiana Annual Reports* 651 (July 1871); 25 *Louisiana Annual Reports* 343 (April 1873).

61. CC (1825), 2360–2368.

62. CC (1825), 2371.

63. CC (1825), 2402, 2367.

64. CC (1825), 2412; R. H. Draughon v. Octave A. Ryan, 16 *Louisiana Annual Reports* 309 (May 1861).

65. CC (1825), 2399.

66. CC (1825), 2402.

67. CC (1825), 2408.

68. CC (1825), 2409.

69. CC (1825), 2411.

70. Emily Stanley, Wife, v. James B. Smith, Husband, 665, 5 DC (EF), February 9, 1866.

71. Mary W. Steadman v. George W. Steadman, 1191, 5 DC (EF). CC (1825), 2411. Walsh, Smith & Co. v. G. W. A. Steadman, 1191, 5 DC (EF), January 11, 1867.

72. Bank of Kentucky v. M. C. Kirkland, 1284, 5 DC (EF), March 21, 1867.

73. Sarah Dupree, Wife, v. Alex Smith, Husband, 1259, 5 DC (EF), February 2, 1867.

74. Dixon, Wife, v. Dixon, Husband, 713, 5 DC (EF), June 6, 1866.

75. Eliza J. Winter v. A. F. Currie, 615, 5 DC (EF), January 22, 1866.

76. Letchford & Co. v. John Shelton, 1136, 5 DC (EF), December 21, 1866; R. E. Carr v. John Shelton, 1129, 5 DC (EF), December 21, 1866.

77. R. C. Shelton, Wife, v. John Shelton, Husband, 1247, 5 DC (EF), February 4, 1867.

78. Confederate States v. Lewis Nauman, 59, 5 DC (EF).

79. Mrs. Bythella Haynes, Wife, v. Lewis Nauman, Husband, 409, 5 DC (EF), September 30, 1865.

80. Catherine Gore v. Clement Gore, 617, 5 DC (EF), January 22, 1866.

81. Ann Elfrith v. Josiah Elfrith, 660, 5 DC (EF), February 12, 1866.

82. MOB 1 (EF), 1868; CC (1825), 263 et seq.

83. MOB 1 (EF), pp. 421, 455, 1868.

84. Ibid., p. 453.

5. The Truncation of the Factorage System

1. My thesis in this part departs significantly from Woodman's explanation of the decline of the factorage system in the postbellum agricultural economy. See Woodman, *King Cotton*, Chapter 23, "The Decline of Cotton Factorage." Michael Wayne's study of the Natchez District from 1860 to 1880 suggests that planters were slow to abandon their traditional relationships with factorage firms. Michael Wayne,

The Reshaping of Plantation Society: the Natchez District, 1860–1880 (Baton Rouge: Louisiana State University Press, 1983), p. 180.

2. Wayne, *Reshaping of Plantation Society*, p. 97.

3. Open account statements showing such balances in favor of planter clients are to be found in numerous postbellum law suits against factors, both in East Feliciana Parish and at New Orleans.

4. LCB II of the Henry Marston Papers is full of references to the large dividends paid by the Citizens and Union banks and to the desirability of owning stock in those institutions. See MP, LLMVC.

5. For an explanation, see Note 12 for Chapter 2 of this study.

6. An examination of numerous accounts current in suit records shows that while factors purchased many items for their clients, those same clients purchased directly from wholesalers in St. Louis and Cincinnati and settled their accounts with sight drafts on their factors.

7. Act no. 22, "An Act to Revive the Charters of the Several Banks Located in the City of New Orleans, and for Other Purposes," *Acts Passed at the Second Session of the Fifteenth Legislature of the State of Louisiana*, 1842, pp. 34–62.

8. Some of these firms were Byrne, Vance & Co.; A. Miltenberger & Co.; J. W. Burbridge & Co.; Wright, Allen & Co.; Oakey, Hawkins; Payne, Harrison; A. Levi & Co.; Carroll, Pritchard & Co.; Pritchard & Flower; Hawkins and Norwood; Hull, Rodd & Co.; W. A. Andrew & Co.; and Edward Nalle & Co.

9. Marston to B. W. Marston, December 24, 1870, LCB III, p. 247, MP, LLMVC.

10. Daniel Brown to Payne, Huntington & Co., October 14, 1865. Lucy Harnnett, Widow v. Payne, Huntington & Co., 23,730, 5 DC (O), February 3, 1867.

11. Marston to B. W. Marston, February 20, 1871, LCB III, p. 263, MP, LLMVC.

12. Marston to J. U. Payne, March 4, 1871, LCB III, p. 268, MP, LLMVC.

13. Marston to B. W. Marston, April 22, 1871, LCB III, p. 285; also p. 277, MP, LLMVC.

14. Census, 1860.

15. Marston to Michael Boyce, February 13, 1872, LCB III, p. 383, MP, LLMVC.

16. Marston to Michael Boyce, June 20, 1871, LCB III, p. 303, MP, LLMVC.

17. Marston to B. W. Marston, December 7, 1870, LCB III, p. 239, MP, LLMVC.

18. Marston to B. W. Marston, May 20, 1871, LCB III, p. 292, MP, LLMVC.

19. Marston to J. U. Payne, March 4, 1871, LCB III, p. 268, MP, LLMVC.

20. Marston to B. W. Marston, May 20, 1871, LCB III, p. 292, MP, LLMVC.

21. Marston to J. U. Payne, June 10, 1871, LCB III, p. 300, MP, LLMVC.

22. Marston to Michael Boyce, June 20, 1871, LCB III, p. 303, MP, LLMVC.

23. Marston to B. W. Marston, August 10, 1871, LCB III, p. 310, MP, LLMVC.

24. Marston to B. W. Marston, September 3, 1871, LCB III, p. 323, MP, LLMVC.

25. Marston to B. W. Marston, December 26, 1871, LCB III, p. 367, MP, LLMVC.

26. Marston to Payne, Dameron & Co., February 6, 1872, LCB III, p. 380, MP, LLMVC.

27. Marston to B. W. Marston, February 11, 1872, LCB III, p. 381, MP, LLMVC.

28. Marston to Michael Boyce, February 13, 1872, LCB III, p. 383, MP, LLMVC.

29. Marston to B. W. Marston, August 10, 1870, LCB III, p. 204, MP, LLMVC.

30. Marston to Michael Boyce, January 16, 1869, LCB III, p. 73, MP, LLMVC.

31. Marston to B. W. Marston, January 17, 1869, LCB III, p. 74, MP, LLMVC.
32. See Chapter 2 of this study.
33. Marston to Payne, Huntington, November 8, 1869, LCB III, p. 45, MP, LLMVC.
34. Marston to Payne, Huntington, October 27, 1868, LCB III, p. 37, MP, LLMVC.
35. William Fellows v. Mrs. I. Ann Fluker, 1897, 5 DC (EF), July 17, 1869.
36. Byrne, Vance & Co. v. John Collins, 1023, 5 DC (EF), September 25, 1866.
37. Marston to Alfred Penn, September 21, 1854, LCB III, p. 229, MP, LLMVC.
38. Richard Pritchard v. James M. Doyle, 232, 5 DC (EF), January 25, 1867.
39. Woodman, *King Cotton*, p. 370.
40. James R. Chambers, agent for Ann Chambers, to Frankenbush and Borland, MOB 11 (EF), p. 410, May 5, 1879.
41. Joseph M. Young to Nalle, Cammack, MOB 11 (EF), p. 162, March 21, 1879; MOB 12 (EF), p. 155, January 31, 1880.
42. Amedie Delambre to Jacob M. Frankenbush, MOB 11 (EF), p. 86, March 8, 1879.
43. Charles Gayarre, *History of Louisiana*, Vol. IV (Reprint, New Orleans: Pelican Publishing, 1965), pp. 165, 345.
44. Chambers to Bank of Louisiana, MOB L (EF), p. 226, May 31, 1858.
45. Chambers to Chambers, MOB 1 (EF), p. 455, December 30, 1869.
46. Chambers to Chambers, MOB 1 (EF), p. 478, January 19, 1870.
47. Chambers to Jurey & Gillis, MOB 6 (EF), p. 55.
48. James R. Chambers to John R. Gaines, February 8, 1875, J. G. Kilbourne and Family Papers, LLMVC.
49. Chambers to Chambers, MOB 8 (EF), p. 63, September 2, 1875.
50. Chambers to Wilmer, MOB 8 (EF), p. 41, December 16, 1875.
51. Chambers to Wilmer, MOB 8 (EF), p. 73, January 17, 1876.
52. CC (1825), 3216–3218.
53. MOB 8 (EF), p. 286, April 19, 1876; MOB 9 (EF), p. 291; MOB 14 (EF), p. 114, July 18, 1885.
54. John Chaffe & Sons v. James R. Chambers, 2161, 5 DC (EF); MOB 11 (EF), p. 233, March 31, 1879.
55. MOB 11 (EF), p. 410, May 5, 1879.
56. MOB 11 (EF), pp. 414, 453, May 6, June 11, 1879.
57. C. L. Walmsley v. James R. Chambers, 2506, 5 DC (EF); MOB 12 (EF), p. 69, November 5, 1879.
58. John Chaffe & Sons v. J. R. Chambers, 2444, 5 DC (EF); MOB 12 (EF), p. 70, November 5, 1879.
59. Mrs. I. McWillie v. J. R. Chambers, 2524, 5 DC (EF); MOB 12 (EF), p. 71, October 22, 1879.
60. MOB 12 (EF), p. 69, November 5, 1879.
61. James R. Chambers, Declaration of Homestead Exemption, MOB 12 (EF), p. 387, June 8, 1880. James R. Chambers v. Sheriff, 2530, 5 DC (EF); MOB 12 (EF), p. 403, July 8, 1880.
62. Marston to J. U. Payne, July 6, 1872, LCB III, p. 433, MP, LLMVC.
63. Marston to B. W. Marston, August 30, 1872, LCB III, p. 447, MP, LLMVC.

64. Anna R. DeLee to Frankenbush and Borland, MOB 14 (EF), p. 3, February 16, 1885.

65. G. W. Munday to J. L. Harris & Co., MOB 14 (EF), p. 6, February 18, 1885.

66. A. Delambre to Lehman, Abraham & Co., MOB 14 (EF), p. 62, April 13, 1885.

67. Ashkenazi, *The Business of Jews*, p. 90.

68. H. A. Lea to H. & C. Newman, MOB 14 (EF), p. 10, February 19, 1885.

69. Ada S. Beauchamp to H. & C. Newman, MOB 14 (EF), p. 65, April 16, 1885.

70. Marston to J. U. Payne, July 1873, LCB IV, p. 2, MP, LLMVC.

71. Marston to J. U. Payne, July 23, 1873, LCB IV, p. 12, MP, LLMVC.

72. Marston to B. W. Marston, June 14, 1874, LCB IV, p. 94, MP, LLMVC.

73. See LCB IV generally: June 14, 1874, July 2, 1874, August 2, 1874, October 18, 1874, December 15, 1874, January 7, 1875, November 10, 1875, November 20, 1875, December 5, 1875, December 31, 1875, and January 14, 1876, MP, LLMVC.

6. Decline and Default

1. *Official Journal of the Proceedings of the Senate [1874] of the State of Louisiana*, p. 17.

2. Woodman, *King Cotton*, Chapter 24, "The Furnishing Merchant." Wayne, *Reshaping of Plantation Society*, p. 168. Woodman, "Post–Civil War Southern Agriculture and the Law," *Agricultural History* 53, no. 1 (1979): 328–29. Woodman, "Postbellum Social Change and Its Effects on Marketing the South's Cotton Crop," *Agricultural History* 56, no. 1 (1982): 218–21.

3. C. Vann Woodward, *Origins of the New South, 1877–1913* (Reprint, Baton Rouge: Louisiana State University Press, 1971), p. 180.

4. CC (1825), 3184, 3214. (Article 3184 of the 1825 code became Article 3217 in the 1870 Civil Code.)

5. S. D. Moore v. Mayo Gray, 22 *Louisiana Annual Reports* 289 (May 1870).

6. CC (1870), 3217. General Quitman v. John D. Packard, 22 *Louisiana Annual Reports* 70 (February 1870).

7. Louisiana Constitution, 1868, Article 123.

8. Act No. 95, "To Carry into Effect Article 123 of the Constitution, and to Provide for Recording All Mortgages and Privileges," March 8, 1869, *Acts Passed by the General Assembly of the State of Louisiana*, First Legislature, Second Session, pp. 114–17.

9. CC (1870), 3290–3310.

10. My explanation of the shift from sharecropping arrangements to tenancies differs substantially from Joseph D. Reid, Jr., "Sharecropping in History and Theory," *Agricultural History* 49, no. 2 (1975): 430–35. I have emphasized risk allocation between landowners and tenants in the formation of such arrangements, but with the inclusion of the credit component in such relationships. See also Donald L. Winters, "The Agricultural Ladder in Southern Agriculture: Tennessee, 1850–1870," *Agricultural History* 61, no. 3 (1987): 53. Jaynes, *Branches Without Roots*, p. 148, note 17.

11. Marston to B. W. Marston, January 17, 1869, LCB III, p. 74, MP, LLMVC.

12. Marston to B. W. Marston, March 16, 1869, LCB III, p. 96, MP, LLMVC.

13. Marston to B. W. Marston, February 5, 1871, LCB III, p. 260, MP, LLMVC.

14. Marston to B. W. Marston, May 20, 1871, LCB III, p. 292, MP, LLMVC.

15. Marston to B. W. Marston, December 20, 1871, LCB III, p. 367, MP, LLMVC.

16. Marston to B. W. Marston, January 27, 1872, LCB III, p. 376, MP, LLMVC.
17. Marston to B. W. Marston, September 25, 1870, LCB III, p. 219, MP, LLMVC.
18. Marston to B. W. Marston, October 6, 1870, LCB III, p. 222, MP, LLMVC.
19. It is important to the understanding of the evolution of postbellum credit arrangements that relationships be carefully described: employer and employee (laborer), landlord and tenant, merchant and customer. Innovations in legal institutions were responsive to changes in such relationships; they did not reorder them. But see Woodman, "Post–Civil War Southern Agriculture," p. 528; Jonathan M. Weiner, *Social Origins of the New South: Alabama, 1860–1885* (Baton Rouge: Louisiana State University Press, 1978), p. 91; Wayne, *Reshaping of Plantation Society*, p. 185; and Jaynes, *Branches Without Roots*, p. 145.
20. Act no. 66, "To Enable Planters, Farmers, Merchants, Traders and Others to Pledge and Pawn Cotton, Sugar, and Other Agricultural Products to Merchants, Factors, and Others," March 21, 1874, *Acts Passed by the General Assembly of the State of Louisiana*, Third Legislature, Second Session, pp. 114–15.
21. Jaynes, *Branches Without Roots*, pp. 166–68, 173–90. Wayne, *Reshaping of Plantation Society*, p. 187.
22. Act No. 66 (March 21, 1874).
23. But see Wayne, *Reshaping of Plantation Society*, p. 185; Woodman, "Post–Civil War Southern Agriculture," p. 329.
24. *House and Senate Journals*, 1874.
25. Marston to A. Foster Elliot, October 19, 1875, p. 251; October 17, 1875, p. 253; to William B. Hamilton, October 19, 1875, p. 254; to B. W. Marston, November 19, 1875, p. 262; LCB IV, MP, LLMVC. *House Journal*, 1874, pp. 110–11.
26. Kilbourne, "Securing Commercial Transactions," p. 609.
27. Succession of Richard Flower, 38,670, 2 DC (O). Transferred to Civil District Court, Orleans Parish, hereinafter cited as 4675, CDC (O).
28. Flower and Maes to Joseph Embree, May 24, 1867, Joseph Embree Papers, hereinafter cited as JEP, LLMVC.
29. Flower and Maes to J. Embree, September 12, 1867, JEP, LLMVC.
30. Flower and Maes v. Joseph Embree, 1618, 5 DC (EF), December 13, 1867.
31. Embree, Wife v. Embree, Husband, 1629, 5 DC (EF), February 1, 1868.
32. Richard Flower to Joseph Embree, November 25, 1868, JEP, LLMVC.
33. There was no way to recognize and record a privilege on a standing crop for a prior year's planting debt that would have priority over claims arising in consequence of the present year's planting.
34. A. Levi to Wall & Embree, May 14, 1871, JEP, LLMVC.
35. Meyer Brothers Store Records, hereinafter cited as MBP, LLMVC.
36. Marston to B. W. Marston, November 13, 1870, LCB III, p. 234, MP, LLMVC.
37. April 20, 1862, Box 3, Folder 27, Item 2, MP, LLMVC.
38. Box 3, Folder 30, Item 6, MP, LLMVC. For an excellent account of Clinton's large Jewish commercial community see Ashkenazi, *The Business of Jews*, Chapter 3.
39. Ledger books, 1868–1870, MBP, LLMVC.
40. Letter book, vol. 29, to G. King & Co., May 30, 1867, p. 23; to Meyer & Levy, June 25, 1867, p. 27; to Levi & Nauman, August 5, 1867, p. 34; to Levy, Miller & Co., September 19, 1867, p. 50, MBP, LLMVC.

41. Ledger books, 1868–1870, MBP, LLMVC.

42. Ledger books, 1868–1870, p. III, MBP, LLMVC.

43. Ledger books, 1868–1870, account of A. J. Gore, pp. 65, 188, 246, 275–76, 386–88, 480; account of A. Depue, pp. 43–44, 174, 257, 334, 373, 427, 467, MBP, LLMVC.

44. Marston to B. W. Marston, August 2, 1874, LCB IV, p. 112, MP, LLMVC.

45. Meyer to Levi, July 4, 1874, vol. 32, p. 146, MBP, LLMVC.

46. Ledger books, 1868–1870, MBP, LLMVC.

47. See generally annual statements of accounts, MP, LLMVC.

48. Cotton book, 1870–1876, MBP, LLMVC.

49. Meyer to A. T. McKneely, May 25, 1876, vol. 33, p. 105, MBP, LLMVC.

50. Meyer to Levi, November 5, 1874, vol. 32, p. 237, MBP, LLMVC.

51. Meyer to Levi, November 9, 1874, vol. 32, p. 243, MBP, LLMVC.

52. Meyer to Levi, April 6, 1874, vol. 32, p. 108, MBP, LLMVC.

53. Ledger books, 1868–1870, MBP, LLMVC.

54. E. Meyer & Bro. to A. Levi, MOB 8 (EF), p. 314, May 5, 1876.

55. Meyer to Levi, March 29, 1876, vol. 33, p. 65, MBP, LLMVC.

56. Meyer to Levi, June 6, 1876, vol. 33, p. 115, MBP, LLMVC.

57. Meyer to Levi, June 17, 1876, vol. 33, p. 120, MBP, LLMVC.

58. E. Meyer & Bro. v. Z. T. Bennett, 1387, PC (EF).

59. Meyer to Levi, April 6, 1874, vol. 32, p. 110, MBP, LLMVC.

60. Meyer to Levi, July 10, 1874, vol. 32, p. 152, MBP, LLMVC.

61. E. Meyer and Bro. v. A. Mayer & Bro., 2049, 2050, PC (EF).

62. Meyer to A. J. Gore, August 20, 1874, vol. 32, p. 173, MBP, LLMVC.

63. Cotton book, MBP, LLMVC.

64. Eugene W. Hilgard, *Report on the Cotton Production of the State of Louisiana* (Washington, D.C.: Department of the Interior, Census Office, 1884), p. 57.

65. East Feliciana Parish Assessment Roll, 1889; also see assessment roll, 1890.

66. Succession of J. M. Young, COB D-2 (EF), pp. 456–60, December 26, 1890.

67. Succession of William Silliman, COB T (EF), pp. 439–43; COB V (EF), pp. 229–90; probate records, book F, 5 DC (EF), pp. 179–83, 343–49, 258, 493–94, 579–83; 1, PC (EF).

68. Succession of Margaret Silliman, COB Z (EF), pp. 392–419; probate records, book D, 472, PC (EF), pp. 10–17, 32.

69. Marston to Ruth Caulfield, November 7, 1876, LCB IV, MP, LLMVC.

70. Ransom, *Conflict and Compromise*, pp. 244–46. Ransom and Sutch, *One Kind of Freedom*, pp. 126–70.

71. Inventory, 1880, MBP, LLMVC.

72. Emily Mayer v. Abraham Heyman, 1454, PC (EF), March 17, 1875. See also Mrs. Alice Delery, wife v. J. D. Delery, husband, 2188, 5 DC (EF); Hannah Goodman v. Bernard Goodman, 2109, 5 DC (EF), June 9, 1873; Emily Flonacher v. J. Flonacher, 2280, 5 DC (EF), June 4, 1875; and Dora Hiller v. Julius Reinberg, 2200, 5 DC (EF), August 5, 1874.

73. Yette Oppenheimer v. Abraham Levy, 2233, 5 DC (EF), December 11, 1874.

74. Marston to Brown, Hoffman, May 9, 1874, LCB IV, p. 87, MP, LLMVC.

75. For a different perspective on the subject of interest rates, see Ransom and Sutch, *One Kind of Freedom*, pp. 128–31.

76. Ibid., pp. 44–55. Jaynes, *Branches Without Roots*, pp. 143–47.

77. Wright, *Old South, New South*, pp. 99–104. Winters, "The Agricultural Ladder," pp. 36–52.

78. COB D-2 (EF), pp. 456–60, December 26, 1890.

7. Tenants, Sharecroppers, and Furnishers

1. Stephen J. DeCanio, *Agriculture in the Postbellum South: The Economics of Production and Supply* (Cambridge: Massachusetts Institute of Technology Press, 1974). Jaynes, *Branches Without Roots*, pp. 158–90. Ransom and Sutch, *One Kind of Freedom*, pp. 65–80. DeCanio, "Productivity and Income Distribution in the Postbellum South," *Journal of Economic History* 34 (June 1974): 422–46. Robert Higgs, "Patterns of Farm Rental in the Georgia Cotton Belt, 1880–1900," *Journal of Economic History* 34 (June 1974): 468–82.

2. Jaynes, *Branches Without Roots*, p. 148.

3. But see Woodman, "Post–Civil War Southern Agriculture," p. 329, and Weiner, *Social Origins of the New South*, pp. 77–108.

4. Jaynes, *Branches Without Roots*, p. 190.

5. J. R. Jackson to Joseph Embree, January 24, 1870, JEP, LLMVC.

6. But see Ransom, *Conflict and Compromise*, p. 238; Joseph D. Reid, Jr., "The Evaluation and Implications of Southern Tenancy," *Agricultural History* 53, no. 1 (1979): 154–58; and "Sharecropping in History," p. 432.

7. MOB 2 (EF), pp. 146–202, 221, 225, 247–249, 264, 273, 289–295, 319, 380, 1870.

8. MOB 2 (EF), pp. 147–51, December 21, 1869.

9. MOB 2 (EF), p. 154, September 8, 1870.

10. MOB 2 (EF), p. 178, September 14, 1870.

11. MOB 2 (EF), pp. 201–2, September 17, 1870.

12. Ibid.

13. But see Reid, "Sharecropping in History."

14. The prevailing view among economic historians is that production units became progressively smaller with less and less supervision being provided by landlords. See Wright, *Old South, New South*, pp. 90–98.

15. Act No. 95 (March 8, 1869).

16. Only rarely in postbellum collection proceedings were there contests between landlords and furnishing merchants.

17. But see Woodman, "Postbellum Social Change and Its Effects on Marketing the South's Cotton Crop," *Agricultural History* 56, no. 1 (1982): 217–20; and "Post–Civil War Southern Agriculture," pp. 326–30.

18. Meyer to Levi, January 18, 1876, vol. 33, p. 18, MBP, LLMVC.

19. Joseph Embree shipped all of his cotton, and that of his sharecroppers, under his name to his New Orleans factors. The same arrangement prevailed on the Marstons' Ashland Plantation.

20. See Jackson to Embree, January 24, 1870, JEP, LLMVC.

21. J. M. Young v. Nos. 1263, 1252, 1281, 1283, PC (EF).

22. J. M. Young v. Henry Washington, 846, PC (EF), October 19, 1873.

23. Ledger books, 1868–1870, MBP, LLMVC.

24. Inventory, 1880, MBP, LLMVC. C. Vann Woodward and others have described such arrangements as lacking fixed terms (i.e., tenants could never be sure of

what they owed until balances were struck at the end of the year). In Louisiana at least all recorded privileges and pledges had stated limits, usually from seventy-five to one hundred dollars. Furnishers who exceeded limits were unsecured for any excess. The "problem" therein described, however, is not a problem and hardly evidences overreaching by furnishers. Stated contractual terms are far more onerous in contracts between factors and planters, but I contend that this is merely evidence of a stringent credit environment, not overreaching by factors. Woodward, *Origins of the New South*, p. 180.

25. Meyer to Levi, September 12, 1876, vol. 33, p. 175, MBP, LLMVC.
26. Meyer to Levi, September 15, 1876, vol. 33, p. 177, MBP, LLMVC.
27. Meyer to Leon Levy, March 12, 1876, vol. 33, p. 57, MBP, LLMVC.
28. Meyer to A. T. McKneely, April 1876, vol. 33, p. 69, MBP, LLMVC.
29. Meyer to McKneely, May 25, 1876, vol. 33, p. 105, MBP, LLMVC.
30. Meyer to McKneely, July 23, 1876, vol. 33, p. 138, MBP, LLMVC.
31. Meyer to McKneely, April 12, 1877, vol. 34, p. 10, MBP, LLMVC.
32. MOB 8 (EF), pp. 93–94, 270, 276, 335, 446, 1876.
33. Eliza Silliman v. Samuel Carter, 1416, PC (EF), March 12, 1875.
34. Mary Davis v. the Sheriff, et al., 1745, PC (EF), February 24, 1876.
35. Meyer to Levi, May 10, 1871, vol. 30, p. 349, MBP, LLMVC.
36. Meyer to Levi, July 22, 1874, vol. 32, p. 159, MBP, LLMVC.
37. Meyer to Levi, October 11, 1875, vol. 32, p. 455, MBP, LLMVC.
38. East Feliciana Parish Assessment Rolls, 1890.
39. Meyer to A. J. Gore, December 9, 1877, vol. 34, p. 346, MBP, LLMVC.
40. Ransom, *Conflict and Compromise*, pp. 257–58. Ransom and Sutch, *One Kind of Freedom*, pp. 126–36.

Bibliography

Published Works

Ashkenazi, Elliott. *The Business of Jews in Louisiana, 1840–1875.* Tuscaloosa: University of Alabama Press, 1988.

Dawson, John P., and Frank E. Cooper. "The Effects of Inflation on Private Contracts: United States, 1861–1879: The Confederate Inflation." *Michigan Law Review* 33 (1935): 706–57.

DeCanio, Stephen J. *Agriculture in the Postbellum South: The Economics of Production and Supply.* Cambridge: Massachusetts Institute of Technology Press, 1974.

———. "Productivity and Income Distribution in the Postbellum South." *Journal of Economic History* 34 (June 1974): 422–46.

Fogel, Robert William. *Without Consent or Contract, the Rise and Fall of American Slavery.* New York: W. W. Norton, 1985.

Fogel, Robert William, and Stanley L. Engerman. *Time on the Cross: The Economics of American Negro Slavery.* New York: W. W. Norton, 1989.

Gayarre, Charles. *History of Louisiana.* Vol. IV. Reprint. New Orleans: Pelican Publishing, 1965.

Green, George D. *Finance and Economic Development in the Old South: Louisiana Banking, 1804–1861.* Stanford, Calif.: Stanford University Press, 1972.

Haws, Robert J., and Michael V. Namarato. "Race, Property Rights, and the Economic Consequences of Reconstruction: A Case Study." *Vanderbilt Law Review* 32 (1979): 305–29.

Hiddy, Ralph W. *The House of Baring in American Trade and Finance: English Merchant Bankers at Work, 1763–1861.* New York: Russell & Russell, 1949.

Higgs, Robert. "Patterns of Farm Rental in the Georgia Cotton Belt, 1880–1900." *Journal of Economic History* 34 (1974): 468–82.

Hilgard, Eugene W. *Report on the Cotton Production of the State of Louisiana.* Washington, D.C.: Department of the Interior, Census Office, 1884.

Jaynes, Gerald David. *Branches Without Roots: Genesis of the Black Working Class in the American South, 1862–1882.* Oxford: Oxford University Press, 1986.

Kilbourne, Richard H., Jr. *Louisiana Commercial Law, the Antebellum Period.* Baton Rouge: Paul M. Hebert Law Center Publications Institute, 1980.

———. "Securing Commercial Transactions in the Antebellum Legal System of Louisiana." *Kentucky Law Journal* 70 (1981): 609–41.

Kotlikoff, Laurence J. "The Structure of Slave Prices in New Orleans, 1804 to 1862." *Economic Inquiry* 17 (1979): 496–517.

Muse, James H. *Correspondence with My Son, Henry Kirk White Muse. Embracing Some Brief Memorials of His Character, and Essays from His Pen, While a Student at Princeton College, New Jersey.* New York: J. A. Gray, 1858.

Ransom, Roger L. *Conflict and Compromise: The Political Economy of Slavery, Emancipation, and the American Civil War.* Cambridge: Cambridge University Press, 1989.

Ransom, Roger L., and Richard Sutch. *One Kind of Freedom: The Economic Consequences of Emancipation*. Cambridge: Cambridge University Press, 1977.

————. "The Impact of the Civil War and of the Emancipation on Southern Agriculture." *Explorations in Economic History* 12 (1975): 1–28.

————. "Capitalists Without Capital: The Burden of Slavery and the Impact of Emancipation." *Agricultural History* 62 (1988): 133–60.

Redlich, Fritz. "The Role of Private Banks in the Early Economy of the United States." *Business History Review* 41 (1977): 90–93.

Reid, Joseph D., Jr. "Sharecropping in History and Theory." *Agricultural History* 49 (1975): 426–40.

————. "The Evaluation and Implications of Southern Tenancy." *Agricultural History* 53 (1979): 153–69.

Schweikart, Larry. *Banking in the American South, from the Age of Jackson to Reconstruction*. Baton Rouge: Louisiana State University Press, 1987.

Skipwith, Henry. *East Feliciana, Louisiana, Past and Present. Sketches of the Pioneers.* 1892. Reprint. Baton Rouge: East Feliciana Pilgrimage and Garden Club, 1957.

Tadman, Michael. *Speculators and Slaves: Masters, Traders, and Slaves in the Old South*. Madison: University of Wisconsin Press, 1989.

Temin, Peter. *The Jacksonian Economy*. New York: W. W. Norton, 1969.

Wayne, Michael. *The Reshaping of Plantation Society, the Natchez District, 1860–1880*. Baton Rouge: Louisiana State University Press, 1983.

Weiner, Jonathan M. *Social Origins of the New South: Alabama, 1860–1885*. Baton Rouge: Louisiana State University Press, 1978.

Winters, Donald L. "The Agricultural Ladder in Southern Agriculture: Tennessee, 1850–1870." *Agricultural History* 61 (1987): 36–52.

Woodman, Harold D. *King Cotton and His Retainers: Financing and Marketing the Cotton Crop of the South, 1800–1925*. Reprint. Columbia: University of South Carolina Press, 1990.

————. "Post–Civil War Southern Agriculture and the Law." *Agricultural History* 53 (1979): 319–37.

————. "Postbellum Social Change and Its Effects on Marketing the South's Cotton Crop." *Agricultural History* 56 (1982): 215–30.

Woodward, C. Vann. *Origins of the New South, 1877–1913*. Reprint. Baton Rouge: Louisiana State University Press, 1971.

Wright, Gavin. "Cotton Competition and the Post-Bellum Recovery of the American South." *Journal of Economic History* 34 (September 1974): 610–35.

————. *The Political Economy of the Cotton South: Households, Markets, and Wealth in the Nineteenth Century*. New York: W. W. Norton, 1978.

————. *Old South, New South, Revolutions in the Southern Economy Since the Civil War*. New York: Basic Books, 1986.

————. "What Was Slavery?" *Social Concept* 6 (1991): 29–50.

Manuscripts and Manuscript Collections

Joseph Embree Papers, J. G. Kilbourne and Family Papers, Henry W. Marston and Family Papers, Abel John Norwood Papers, and Meyer Brothers Store Records. Louisiana and Lower Mississippi Valley Collections. Louisiana State University Libraries, Louisiana State University. Baton Rouge.

Orleans Parish, Civil District Court Records. New Orleans Public Library, Louisiana Division. New Orleans.

Silliman, William file. In possession of Richard H. Kilbourne, Jr. Clinton, La.

Public Records, Louisiana

Conveyance Office Books; Mortgage Office Books; suit records for Third District Court, Fifth District Court, parish courts, and probate courts. Clinton, La.

Notarial Archives. New Orleans.

Public Records (Printed), Louisiana

Acts Passed by the General Assembly of the State of Louisiana.

Dainow, Joseph, ed. *Civil Code of Louisiana. Revision of 1870 with Amendments to 1947.* St. Paul, Minn.: West Publishing Co., 1947.

Louisiana Annual Reports.

Louisiana Constitutions, 1868 and 1879.

Morgan, Thomas Gibbes, ed. *Civil Code of the State of Louisiana: With the Statutory Amendments, from 1825 to 1853, Inclusive; and References to the Decisions of the Supreme Court of Louisiana to the Sixth Volume of Annual Reports.* New Orleans: J. B. Steel, 1855.

Official Journal of the Proceedings of the House of Representatives of the State of Louisiana, Official Journal of the Proceedings of the Senate of the State of Louisiana.

Public Records, United States.

United States Department of Commerce, Bureau of the Census. Fifth Census of the United States, 1830; Sixth Census of the United States, 1840; Seventh Census of the United States, 1850; and Eighth Census of the United States, 1860.

Wallace, John William. *United States Reports.*

Index

ABOUT THE AUTHOR

Richard Holcombe Kilbourne, Jr., is a partner, Kilbourne Law Offices, Clinton, Louisiana. He received his B.A. in history and English and his M.A. in history from Louisiana State University and his J.D. from the Paul M. Hebert Law Center, Baton Rouge. He is author of *Louisiana Commercial Law, the Antebellum Period* (1980) and *A History of the Louisiana Civil Code, the Formative Years, 1803–1839* (1988).